World History

This edition published by Barnes & Noble Inc.,
by arrangement with Parragon

2003 Barnes & Noble Books
Copyright © Parragon 1999

M 10 9 8 7 6 5 4 3 2 1

Cover design by Blackjacks

ISBN 0-7607-4512-9

Printed in Indonesia

World History

GENERAL EDITOR:
Professor Jeremy Black

BARNES
&NOBLE
BOOKS
NEW YORK

Contents

Introduction

THIS IS AN ACCESSIBLE HISTORY for the close of one millennium and the start of another. In looking back we understand better not only the fascination of the past, but also ourselves, our world and our possibilities for the future. This, then, is an exciting tale of bold coverage. The key thematic perspectives through which each century is seen offer both a comprehensive account of world history and provide a coherent coverage of crucial dynamics of the human past. Individually they offer important perspectives and collectively they build towards a compelling whole, in which aspects of all cultures, regions and periods are covered.

Overarching issues in human history covered here – all as important for our future as for our past – include human relations with the environment; the demographic history of the species; relations between the generations and the sexes – the crucial issues in social structure; the structures of productive society, such as class; the world belief, particularly religion; the ways in which people identify themselves, their families and their worlds: place, ethnic group, language, religion, each of which is often in a dynamic but also unsteady relation with the others; the organisation of political society: units of authority and the objectives, relations within and between states; and the march of scientific knowledge, technological capability and economic development.

These issues are all approached through the themes and entries of this book. The issues link. Greater technological strength requires more resources and thus puts more pressure on the environment. Indeed, in this century, man has altered his environment more than in any other. Yet, this process of change is not new, and an understanding of the ongoing nature of change is important when looking at our own age. Thus, deforestation – the clearing of natural woodland to provide agriculture and settlement – has been going on for centuries.

Change is the issue in history. The past is not a series of static shots, frozen in time, for example, Paris in 1650 or the life of the factory

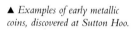

▲ *Examples of early metallic coins, discovered at Sutton Hoo.*

▼ *Tea being thrown into the sea by disguised Bostonians, in retaliation against British trade restrictions.*

▲ *Chain mail armour, in common usage in the eleventh century.*

worker in 1850. Such an approach can yield interesting images, but it is essentially rigid. Instead it is necessary to understand how the past is part of a living process of change, and was and is given energy and meaning, importance and explanation by this change. Without an understanding of change, we cannot appreciate the 'whys' of the past and thus of the present: why did they do this in 1700, 1900, 2000? Change also provides the dynamic of history. The effects of, for example, rising or falling populations, economies, governments and religions were the fabric of the past and the cause of altering experiences for its people.

The reality is with us today. Take anyone of 80. In their life they have seen what would have been regarded as inconceivable or unlikely when they were born: space rockets and micro-chips, antibiotics and artificial hips. We take all this for granted, but also know how important it is to understand these changes. History is not just a record of change; it also helps us understand it.

At the cusp of the millennium there is both hope and uncertainty; a sense of particular balance between past and future. That is a useful image, but much of the thrust of this book rests on the notion that past and future are not rival worlds. Instead we see them as part of a continuous process, bound together by the energy of change. The people of the past knew there would be a future and were affected by this knowledge. If in the sixteenth cen-

▲ *Chinese Communist Leader Mao Zedong.*

tury Europeans explored the – to them – New World, they did so knowing there were other worlds to explore.

This is part of the excitement of history: purposeful exploration and understanding of others and ourselves. Take, for example, an obvious feature of life, the darkness of night. The modern world can overcome this with electric lighting, but earlier the dark was a world of danger and menace. This was especially true for the traveller literally unable to see his route, as in Shakespeare's *Macbeth:*

> *The west yet glimmers with some streaks of day;*
> *Now spurs the lated traveller apace,*
> *To gain the timely inn.*

To see how we have overcome the abrupt shift from light to darkness one has to see the fearful world of dark in the past. Look at the

▲ *Mahatma Gandhi.*

pictures from the period. In twilight and at night, space shrank to the shadowy spots lit by flickering lights.

Different readers will draw varied conclusions from history. Some see it as a cause for celebration or optimism; others are more pessimistic. Both interpretations can find support. What is clear, however, is that in assessing how far and why we have done better or worse it is necessary to look back and around us, to consider history as a source of our world, not as something that is past and gone. History is interesting and fun, stimulating and thought-provoking. It is also valuable, an important source of knowledge, reflection and understanding.

PROFESSOR JEREMY BLACK

CHAPTER 1

The Ancient World

Power and Politics

509 BC   THE REPUBLIC

THE ROMAN Republic was set up in 509 BC. Because their kings had been dictators, the Romans were determined that no one should gain complete power in the city, so they created a complex system of controls on all officers of state. Power was exercised by two officials, called consuls, who were elected every year. One stayed in Rome and one took command of the army. There were also elected officials in charge of the treasury, the police and the city itself. The Romans hoped that the rapid change of personnel would stop anyone seizing total power, but they also realised that in an emergency it might be necessary to allow one man to take charge, so the Republic allowed the appointment of a 'Dictator' for a period of up to six months.

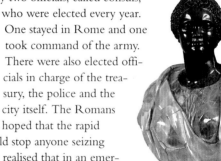

▲ *A Roman official and his wife.*

508 BC   DEMOCRACY

DEMOCRACY was first developed in Athens, where there was an Assembly that all citizens were entitled to attend and address. After the Reforms of Solon in 594 BC, the Assembly had the right simply to reject or approve legislation. Laws were introduced by the Council which, after 508 BC was chosen by lot.

Real power, however, was exercised by the nobles through their council, the 'Areopagus'. They elected the Archons, who ran the city. But from 488 BC, the Archons were also chosen by lot. This meant that the nobles lost much of their power. There were other important aspects of democracy even so. Magistrates were elected by all freemen; jurors in trials were paid fees, which meant that any citizen could sit, not just the rich. Athenian democracy did not involve equality, but it did accept the right of all citizens to be involved in some form or another in the governing of their city.

400 BC PHILOSOPHERS AND KINGS

THE Greeks were the first people in Europe to develop a cursive script. Although Egyptian hieroglyphics and Babylonian cuneiform were efficient for making lists, writing records and publishing laws, they did not allow sophisticated analysis or discussion. Socrates founded a school of philosophy, which was continued by his pupil Plato. Plato's *Republic* was the first treatise on political ideals written in Europe. The Greeks were, therefore, the first Europeans, capable of analysing and explaining political institutions and considering alternatives. Socrates, Plato and Aristotle provided an analysis of human behaviour, which was not to be equalled until the seventeenth century.

▲ *The Greek philosopher Plato, one of the earliest exponents of political ideals.*

336 BC   ALEXANDER THE GREAT

ALEXANDER the Great was the son of Philip of Macedon and succeeded his father in 336 BC at the age of 20. Philip had crushed the army of the Greek city states at the Battle of Chaeronea in 338 BC and had forced the states to join the Hellenic League. Only Sparta refused. He then planned to invade Asia, but was murdered before he was able to put his plans into action. After the death of Philip, the Greek states revolted, but Alexander crushed the rebellion and appointed a governor in Greece before he left for his invasion of Persia. When Alexander died in

▲ *Illuminated manuscript depicting Alexander the Great on horseback in battle against the Persians.*

322 BC Athens rebelled again and formed a new Hellenic League. The revolt was once again crushed and the Athenian navy completely destroyed. The Macedonians had changed the face of Greece for good.

44 BC   THE TRIUMVIRATES AND THE
DEATH OF CAESAR

IN THE middle years of the first century BC two groups of men fought for control of the Roman Republic. Between 60 and 48 BC, Julius Caesar and Pompey fought a civil war, that became even more violent after the death of Crassus, the third member of the First Triumvirate, in 53 BC. After the Battle of Pharsalus in 48 BC and Pompey's murder in Egypt in the same year, Julius Caesar was the undisputed master of Rome. Increasingly he acted like a king, and it was this behaviour that brought about his murder at the hands of a group of Republicans in 44 BC. This act led to the formation of the Second Triumvirate in 43 BC. The members, Mark Antony, Lepidus and Octavian, hunted down Caesar's murderers, but then fell out amongst themselves. Finally, Octavian defeated Mark Antony at Actium in 31 BC, after which Mark Antony and his wife Cleopatra committed suicide.

AD 306   CONSTANTINE

BY THE early third century, it was becoming increasingly obvious that the empire could not be governed by one man. Constantine (306–337) took the extreme step of dividing the empire in half and building a new capital for the eastern half at Constantinople. For all the strength of its army, the Roman Empire never developed real political stability. Success depended upon the character of the emperor and on the support of the army. When the empire became increasingly attacked from the outside in the fourth century, the chaos that ensued only encouraged attempts to seize control. These attempts were a major factor in the collapse of the Roman

▲ *Emperor Constantine.*

Empire in the West by the end of the fifth century. But Constantine's creation, the empire in the East, survived, in one form or another, for over a thousand years.

War and Peace

1027 BC   THE WARRING STATES

THE EARLIEST reliable period in Chinese history, the Chou Dynasty, dates
from 1027 BC. China was a feudal land and champions and their retinues fighting
a small pitched battle dealt with many of the conflicts. As the strength of the
Chou declined in the sixth century BC, warfare became a more serious game;
chariots remained the important factor, but foot soldiers were fast becoming
the dominant force on the battlefield. When the Chou Dynasty fell in 249,
the Chin took control and it had become essential to present a united front
against incursions from outside the empire. As the Chin had fought for years
against the nomads in the north, it was natural that they should adopt the
horse as their main means of warfare.

669 BC   THE HOPLITES

THE FIRST true hoplite force was
created by the Argives and used at the
Battle of Hysiae in 669 BC. These
close-order formations of heavy
infantry consisted of men armed with
a long thrusting spear, sword, helmet,
breastplate, greaves and a 3-ft round
shield. They confronted the enemy
with a solid line of alternating shields
and spears, the continuity of the line

▶ *Alexander the Great, in battle against the
Persians under the leadership of Darius.*

was all-important and each man depended on his neighbour. At Plataea (479 BC), the Spartans fought eight deep, the rear ranks filling in at the front as men fell. Steadiness and weight of numbers in the right place were the key to victories on the field. Tactics were still rather limited and sieges rare.

431 BC THE PELOPONNESIAN WAR

THE DELIAN League (478 BC) was formed by the Greeks with the aim of driving the Persians out of the Aegean Sea. The Athenians took control and absorbed 150 states into their empire. The Spartans reacted violently and in 431 BC, the Peloponnesian War broke out. For the next 27 years, the Greek states would be at war. The Athenians ruled the seas, whilst the Spartans were dominant on land. The Spartans won the Battle of Mantinea (418 BC), forcing the Athenians to risk all. They invaded Sicily in 415 BC in the hope of cutting off Spartan trade and supplies, but in 413 BC, the fleet was lost at Syracuse. Athens hung on until 405 BC, losing another fleet at Aegospotami; they surrendered the following year.

▲ *Greek urn dating from the fourth century BC, showing the figure of Citharode.*

322 BC HELLENISTIC WARFARE

ALEXANDER the Great died in 322 BC without naming a successor and, deprived of his personality, the empire fell apart. Despite his warlike life, he had hoped that the lands would be melded together, but all his governors claimed territories. Chief among them were Antigonus I, Antipater, Demetrius I, Poliorcetes, Lysimachus, Perdiccas, Ptolemy I and Seleucus I. This period is known as Diadochi ('successors') and was marked by the extensive use of the phalanx (pike blocks of infantry), Persian cavalry, siege equipment, elephants and camels. This generation is taken to end with Seleucus's death in 281 BC. Pyrrhus, the King of Epirus, continued the Hellenistic style of warfare, beating the Romans in 280 BC using elephants, but was decisively defeated by their infantry at Beneventum in 275 BC.

59 BC   JULIUS CAESAR

AT 41, Julius Caesar was thrust into prominence when, in 59 BC, he became Governor of Illyricum, Cisalpine and Transalpine Gaul. He checked the threat of the Helvetii in 58 BC and advanced north of the old Roman frontier

▼ *Classical painting showing Roman Emperor Julius Caesar.*

to clear Alsace of the German tribes. In the spring of 57 BC, he defeated a massive 300,000-strong Belgae army on the Aisne and by 56 BC had added nearly all of Gaul to the empire. He landed in Britain in 55 BC, but had to turn his attention elsewhere. The Gauls, under Vercingetorix, rebelled in 52 BC, and at the siege of Alesia they were crushed for many years. He faced Pompey in a civil war that lasted until 45 BC, but Brutus and Cassius murdered him the following year.

AD 476   THE FALL OF ROME

AFTER AD 410, there was a lull in warfare. The Vandals had settled in North Africa, the Burgundians and Franks in France and the Visigoths had moved on to Spain and Gaul. A graver danger for all lay ahead. By the middle of the fifth century, under Attila, the Huns descended on the western world. The Chinese had repelled them between 207 BC–AD 39, so they had turned west. Attila came to power in 433 and after invading the Balkans in 440–447, he crossed the

▲ *Attila, the king of the Huns, whose attacks in Italy contributed to the fall of Rome.*

Rhine and faced the Visigoths and Romans at Champagne. Attila was defeated, but in 451, he invaded northern Italy. They were turned back, but Rome was not saved. Odovacar, commander of the Roman army, was a barbarian and he seized the capital (AD 476).

Society and Culture

PREHISTORY HUMANS EVOLVE

ABOUT 20 million years ago, somewhere in Africa, ape-like creatures whom anthropologists call proconsul came down out of the trees and began to live on the ground, searching for their food on the broad savannahs. In time, they adapted to this new life, began to walk upright, used tools, made fire and

eventually began to reason and talk. Now markedly different from their ape-like ancestors, they had become hominids, the first creatures to be noticeably human-like. There was a long way to go, of course, before the hominids evolved into *Homo sapiens*, our own species. However, the way was now open for gradual development towards organised bands of hunter-gatherers and cave-dwelling families little different in basic essentials from families today.

▲ *Man began to forge a hunter-gatherer lifestyle in prehistoric times.*

PREHISTORY EARLY TECHNOLOGY

THE PRACTICAL demands of prehistoric life led to a range of technological discoveries. Chipping or flaking flints to produce sharp edges was succeeded by a cleverer method – using stones to grind them. Levers and wedges were developed for lifting heavy objects, as was rope, made from the plaited fur or hair of animals. Making fire by striking flint on stone was a much more convenient method than waiting for lightning to set the forests ablaze, and the supply of long-distance weapons for hunting was extended to bows and arrows, boomerangs and slings for throwing large stones. The greatest pre-historic discovery of all was made when the rolling qualities of large round stones inspired the making of the first wheel.

900 BC   THE FIRST MILITARY STATE

THE ASSYRIANS, who came on the scene around 900 BC, were the first people to form a military state. In conquering their extensive empire, the Assyrian armies used mighty siege machines, some made of iron, to batter down walls and shower opponents with missiles. The Assyrians were not all warlike though. They took care to preserve the libraries they found in cities they captured. Assyrian astronomers made observations of the Moon and recorded them on circular clay discs. The knowledge the Assyrians amassed was considerable. In 1929, the library of Ashurbanipal, who became king in about 626 BC, was discovered at his capital of Nineveh. It contained over 20,000 clay tablets, inscribed with information on mathematics, botany, chemistry, medicine and history.

776 BC   THE FIRST OLYMPIC GAMES

EVERY FOUR years, the Greek city states, so often at loggerheads, set aside their differences to take part in the Olympic Games. Held on Mount Olympus, in east-central Greece, the Games attracted athletes from all over Greece and wars were suspended while they continued. Contestants competed naked in javelin-throwing,

▲ *Mount Olympus in Greece – home of the original Olympic Games.*

boxing, wrestling and chariot racing. The winners received branches of wild olive. Inaugurated some time before 776 BC, when records began, the Games were held until, in AD 394, they were abolished by the Romans – by then the masters of Greece. It was not surprising that these foreign conquerors should take this step, since the basic idea behind the Games was to unify the Greeks, even if only for a short time.

214 BC   THE GREAT WALL OF CHINA

▲ *The Great Wall of China, built to defend the empire against invading Mongols and Turks.*

IN 214 BC, after the Qin dynasty ended nearly two centuries of violent conflict to create the first strong, centralised empire in China, Emperor Shi Huangdi ordered that a great wall, eventually some 2,350 km (1,450 miles) long, be built in the north to keep out aggressive Mongol and Turkish nomads. The 7.6-m (25 ft-high) wall, later extended by the Han dynasty (202 BC–AD 220), was made of earth and stone faced with brick and featured a series of watchtowers. Today, it is Earth's only artificial construction visible from space. Though internal Chinese politics remained perennially in flux, this mighty defence line stood for over 1,400 years before the nomads – the much more powerful Mongols – managed to break through.

149 BC   THE ROMAN EMPIRE

THE EARLY Romans hated kings and ejected their last, tyrannical, monarch, Tarquinius Superbus in 509 BC. Some five centuries later, however, the Romans accepted their first Emperor, Augustus, because a strong individual was needed to cure the Roman Republic, then blighted by anarchy. The Roman Empire itself began much earlier, after 149 BC when the Romans smashed the Carthaginians of North Africa and took over their territories. In time, the empire stretched from Britannia in the north to the deserts of Saudi Arabia in the south. Within its strongly guarded borders, Pax Romana (the Roman Peace) prevailed, allowing Roman subjects the security to travel and trade, a life of comparative luxury for the rich and comforts unique in the ancient world.

100 BC   THE SEVEN WONDERS OF THE ANCIENT WORLD

TOURISM IS not a modern phenomenon. Tourists, armed with guidebooks, travelled the ancient world to visit great cities and impressive monuments, buy souvenirs and return home to enthuse about the wonders they had seen. The most comprehensive 'package' tour took in the Seven Wonders of the Ancient World – the pyramids of Egypt, the 'hanging' gardens of Semiramis at Babylon, the statue of Zeus at Olympia, the temple of Artemis and the mausoleum at Halicarnassus, all three in Greece, the Colossus of Rhodes, and the pharos or lighthouse at Alexandria in Egypt. It is doubtful if large numbers of people could afford the time and expense of visiting all seven, but it seems that tourist guides did a lively trade nevertheless.

▲ *The Egyptian pyramids count amongst the ancient world's greatest feats of engineering.*

Exploration and Empires

▲ *Excavations have revealed much about seafaring techniques from some of the earliest civilisations, particularly Egypt.*

2600 BC   THE EARLIEST EXPLORATIONS

ONCE ONE early urban society became aware of the existence of other lands producing valuable products, it was also possible to trade for them. In 2600 BC the Egyptian pharaoh sent a fleet of at least 40 ships north along the Mediterranean coast to the town of Byblos, in modern Lebanon. This expedition brought back shiploads of timber, a commodity in comparatively short supply in the parched lands of the Nile valley. The Egyptians also explored south, along the Nile and the Red Sea. Somewhere here was a land they called Punt, where a supply of incense was available. During the third millennium BC, two major expeditions are known to have taken place. One during the reign of the pharaoh Sahure, and the other led by an Egyptian named Hennu.

2371 BC   IMPERIALISM IN THE ANCIENT NEAR EAST

IN MESOPOTAMIA the most dramatic change occurred during the time of Sargon the Great (2371 BC). Where previous victors had allowed the governments of defeated cities to continue to rule, only demanding payment of tribute, Sargon did away with enemy ruling dynasties and placed his conquests under the control of governors appointed by him. This ensured a loyal subordinate who could administer the internal affairs of a city state with a free hand, while still sup-plying the dominant ruler with the means to support an army capable of enforcing his authority. The effect of the Mesopotamian practice of ruling conquered territories through governors meant that if an empire fell, the bulk of it simply transferred its allegiance to the victor.

▲ *Mask depicting the head of Mesapotamian ruler Sargon the Great.*

610 BC   THE CIRCUMNAVIGATION OF AFRICA

ONE OF the earliest expeditions ever ordered by a government expressly to achieve greater geographical knowledge was made dur-ing the reign of the Pharaoh Necho (*c.* 610–594 BC). Necho instructed a group of Phoenician sailors to voyage around Libya. During the third year, they sailed through the Strait of Gibraltar and back into the Mediterranean. Herodotus did not believe this account because, when the Phoenicians took a westward heading, the sun was unexpectedly on their right, in the northern quadrant of the sky – which is exactly where it would be if one was sailing west around the Cape of Good Hope!

AD 50s   VOYAGES TO INDIA

THE EMPERORS of Rome occasionally commissioned expeditions, but they were generally uninterested in exploration. During the first century AD, however, a Greek merchant named Hippalus discovered a secret that Arab traders with India had jealously guarded for centuries – that the monsoon winds of the Indian Ocean reversed themselves. He was the first European to sail across the Indian Ocean instead of the slow process of following the coast. Mediterranean merchants and geographers knew of a land beyond India, and a geographer writing in the second century described several places in Southeast Asia, including Malaya and possibly Hanoi, but the details of distance and location are very vague.

AD 97   EXPLORATION IN THE FAR EAST

CHINA ITSELF, in the second century AD, was the location of another great empire on earth. While it had knowledge of Southeast Asia and India as well, its information about the lands beyond the Central Asian desert were as sketchy as that of the Ancient Romans of East Asia. In AD 97 a Chinese general named Ban Chao reached the shores of the Caspian Sea. He sent a subordinate of his, named Gan Ying, further west, and he reached the Black Sea. Here he came into contact with the Roman Empire, which he called Da Qin. This was described as a land of great wealth, but the length of the journey further westwards was too daunting for Gan Ying, and both he and Ban Chao returned to China.

AD 600s   THE GREAT CONQUESTS BEGIN

BETWEEN AD 634 and 638 Arab armies defeated both the Byzantine heirs of Rome and the Persian Empire. They had gained domination over the whole of the Middle East when, in 639, they invaded Egypt. By the end of 645, all the land in Egypt had become part of the Islamic world. The pace of conquest now slowed, but its movement nevertheless seemed inexorable. In 672 a Muslim fleet began a five-year blockade of the great city of Constantinople,

◄ *Bas-relief showing Constantine the Great defeating Emperor Maxentius.*

▼ *The fall of Carthage at the hands of the Arabs.*

but they lacked sufficiently advanced siege-warfare technology to tackle the mighty walls of the Byzantine capital. Arab-led armies marched west across North Africa. Carthage fell to them in 698.

AD 600s THE RISE OF SCANDINAVIA

THE COLLAPSE of the Roman Empire paradoxically allowed the foundations of the European supremacy of the eighteenth and nineteenth centuries to be laid. The lack of a central bureaucratic authority permitted individual initiatives on the part of different societies. The Scandinavian region of Denmark, Norway and Sweden, at the end of the eighth century AD, suddenly produced an aggressive seafaring culture that is collectively known as the Vikings. The technological basis for this lay in the excellent ocean-going craft that the Vikings built. The best example that has survived is the Gokstad ship, now in a museum in Oslo.

Trade and Industry

4000 BC THE FIRST TOOLMAKERS

SOME OF the first people to make implements were the flint- and axe-makers of the neolithic period (or New Stone Age, *c.* 4000–1000 BC). Flint is a hard stone found in chalk in layers. It can be broken, or 'knapped', into sharp-edged flakes, that make good cutting tools. An example of a flint mine

is Grimes Graves in Norfolk, UK. Here people used antlers as picks to chip out the flint. In the mine shafts they worked by the light of candles made with grease and a wick. When the flint was brought to the surface it was broken up and shaped into axe-heads, arrowheads, knives and scrapers. Around 3500 BC flint was used for barter against animal skins, pottery and food.

▲ *Early flint tools and weapons.*

2590 BC TRIUMPHS OF THE ANCIENT EGYPTIANS

BETWEEN 2630 and 1640 BC the pharaohs, or kings, of Egypt had gigantic stone pyramids made to serve as their tombs. The largest remaining pyramid, at Giza (*c.* 2590 BC), took 84,000 workers 20 years to build. Although the enormous blocks of stone used in construction were placed and measured with amazing accuracy, the simplest tools were used – levers, pulleys, rollers and human muscle. Pictures and models found in the tombs show what Egyptian life was like. One picture shows a simple boat made of bundles of reeds bound together and covered with pitch. Later, rowing or sailing ships were used for trading in the Mediterranean region. The Egyptians developed an accurate calendar of 365 days. To measure time, they used sundials and water clocks.

1700 BC   EARLIEST ROAD-BUILDING

THE ASSYRIANS and Persians (*c.* 1700–500 BC) controlled great political and military empires; their success largely attributable to economic and technological advances. Systematic road-building, for example, permitted goods to be concentrated in sufficient supply to keep large numbers of men in the field under arms all year round. Wheeled vehicles using these roads could not only provision the troops but could also keep them moving quickly, cheaply and over long distances. Traders received legal protection and merchants were exempt from military service. Key cities inhabited by merchants and artisans paid a money tribute in return for extensive rights of self-government. The imperial government and field armies both policed the roads to allow passengers unhampered, safe passage. Thus inter-regional traders and the armies entered into an alliance of mutual support.

600 BC   MODERN MONEY

THE WORLD'S first metallic money appeared around 2000 BC. Before that time, cattle had been used for currency, and indeed in some parts of the world they still are. The word 'pecuniary' comes from the Latin word for 'cattle', *pecus*. The first money was made of bronze ingots shaped to resemble cattle. Unlike later coins, which had a fixed value, the value of these coins was determined by weight. Around 800 BC bean-shaped ingots were introduced. The first coins of the modern type – round and flat, with a value and images or inscriptions

marked on the surface –
appeared in Lydia, Asia Minor
(now Turkey) *c.* 600 BC. They were
made in copper and silver. From then on,
commodities, land, taxes and services could be
valued in terms of money.

*Examples of early metallic coins,
discovered at Sutton Hoo.*

AD 23   TRIUMPH OF THE RED EYEBROWS

UNDER THE emperor Wudi (141–87 BC) the Han dynasty in China (206
BC–AD 220) expanded south of the Yangtze River (now the Chang), absorbing
land as far afield as the borders of modern China. To recoup the costs of their
campaigns, the rulers imposed tax increases and state monopolies over key
production items such as iron and salt, and the currency became debased.
The population soon outgrew the supply of land. In the first century AD,
great provincial families were exempt from taxes while the peasants had to
pay more. The reforming ruler Wang Man nationalised the tax-exempt
estates, redistributed them among the peasantry, expanded state monopolies
and abolished slavery. Maintenance of the water systems was neglected, however. In a peasant uprising in AD 23, led by the 'Red Eyebrows', Wang Mang
was killed.

AD 300 THE MAYAN EMPIRE FLOURISHES

THE MAYA arrived in the Yucatán peninsula, Mexico, from Central America about 1500 BC. The early Maya were slash-and-burn farmers, working plots called *milpa*. At the height of its greatness, *c.* AD 300–900, the Mayan Empire included more than 40 cities. Many of these had stone pyramids, plazas, temples and palaces, together with an enormous stairway and an observatory from which astronomers and mathematicians could take sightings and measurements. Mayan irrigation and terracing methods were advanced. Their principal food crop was maize. They also grew cotton and had highly perfected the techniques of spinning, dyeing and weaving cotton. The Maya domesticated the dog and the turkey but had no draught animals. They were the only ancient American people to develop an accurate calendar.

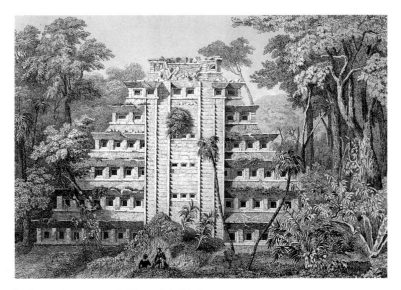

▲ *The magnificent pyramid of Papantla in Mexico.*

Science and Technology

1000 BC MATHS AND GEOMETRY

WHILE THE Greeks were pondering philosophically over science and technology, the Romans were far more concerned with putting theory into practice. Their technology, particularly related to engineering and architecture, benefited greatly from the application of geometrical and mathematical formulae, which optimised the use of materials and processes available to them. Mathematics was important for making accurate calculations of criteria such as angles, areas, quantities, dimensions and proportions. Geometry played an equally vital role in determining appropriate structural shapes for maximising strength against economy of materials, as well as imposing a general aesthetic discipline, including symmetry. Strict mathematical principles also governed the design of engines and machines used by the Romans for warfare and construction, to be sure that they performed their tasks properly and safely.

1000 BC ROADS AND BRIDGES

TO BUILD and maintain an empire it was essential to be able to maintain communications between different regions and the central government. The Romans, realising this, went to enormous lengths to construct an infrastructure of roads and bridges that could be relied upon to send troops and supplies to trouble spots as quickly as possible and quell any uprising against the state. Roman roads consisted of closely fitting stone slabs set on a foundation of hard core made from sand, gravel and masonry rubble, and lined with stone kerbing. The land was surveyed to keep the road as level as possible and to find the straightest route from one location to the next. Some sections of Roman road even had a cambered surface with drainage ditches to deal with heavy rainfall. When it came to spanning rivers and valleys, Roman

◀ *The Old Appian Way, one of the finest surviving examples of Roman roads.*

engineers solved the problem with expertly constructed bridges, viaducts and aqueducts, which featured use of the arch. This was an invention of the Romans and enabled them to build strong yet relatively lightweight structures, requiring less effort and materials.

1000 BC THE RISE OF THE WHEEL AND AXLE

AS HUMANS began building settlements and early civilisations started to appear, aided by Bronze Age technology, there came an increased need for an efficient way to transport bulky goods from one place to another. Pressures of trade, industry and warfare provided the necessity that mothered the invention of the wheel and axle. Various wheeled vehicles, such as carts, wagons and chariots, pulled by oxen or horses, were adopted rapidly, such were the advantages they offered. The wheel and axle proved to be of vital importance because it effectively opened the door for more effective communications between human populations and provided a far more efficient means for transporting people, equipment and goods; the net result was an infra-structure within, and between, early civilisations.

550 BC   UNIVERSAL CURRENCY

SCHIST IS a flint-like black stone that can be used to indicate the purity of gold when rubbed on its surface, by displaying marks in a range of possible colours. Following this discovery, Croesus, ruler of

▶ *Croesus introduced standardised gold coinage.*

▲ *The introduction of universal currency improved trading and exploration in the ancient world.*

Lydia, was prompted to introduce the first standardised imperial gold coinage, which was called the stater, in 550 BC. The idea was immediately popular and other civilisations around the Mediterranean followed suit. Coinage had the effect of unifying and defining the parameters of the European civilised world, which had previously comprised fairly disparate populations. The reason was that people from different cultures were able to place their collective trust in the quality of the metal being minted. This resulted in more diverse and flexible trade, which eventually extended to Asia and encouraged a flow of ideas and information as well as goods.

250 BC   MAPPING THE ANCIENT WORLD

A GREEK geographer and mathematician called Eratosthenes (c. 276–194 BC) was the first map-maker to apply a mechanism to maps that made them practicable for navigation. He included lines of longitude and latitude so that a grid was created, which meant that different locations were referenced in relation to one another according to real space. It was also possible to determine a position at sea or on land on the map according to the predictable movements of the stars throughout the year.

▲ *Eratosthenes, one of the earliest geographers.*

Based on his astronomical observations, Eratosthenes was even able to make a surprisingly accurate calculation of the world's circumference, and at a time when the world was generally considered to be flat. Maps were useful tools for understanding the overall layout of the known world in the context of empires and enemies during the Iron Age, rather than being navigational aids.

AD 100s GALEN AND MEDICINE

ANATOMY and physiology became areas of detailed study for the Greeks, because they had a curiosity about how things work and the components of the body seemed to have clearly defined roles. Of course, this was essentially true when it came to muscles and bones and so on, but they had no appreciation of the scientific complexity with which life was maintained, so they came up with other, less scientific explanations. The

▲ *Greek physician Claudius Galen, whose theory of 'humours' formed the basis of medicine for centuries.*

most noted physician and anatomist of the era, Galen (*c*. AD 129–200) asserted that there must be mysterious energies called humours, which gave and maintained life in the body in the form of natural, vital and animal spirits. His idea dominated European medicine for some 1,500 years, until science eventually proved him wrong.

Religions, Belief and Thought

1500 BC   THE VEDAS AND THE VEDIC AGE

THE EARLIEST Hindu scriptures are the four Vedas and the earliest of these is the *Rig Veda* ('song of wisdom'), 1500–1000 BC, consisting of 1,000 hymns that were mainly for the Aryan priests (Brahmins) to use during rituals. The hymns are directed towards nature gods such as Agni, god of fire, and Indra, the sky god, and some of these may have been used by Brahmins before their arrival in India. This was followed by the other three Vedas ('books of wisdom'), the *Sama Veda*, *Yajur Veda* and *Atharva Veda* and, around 800 BC, by the Brahmana-scriptures.

▲ *David, King of Israel.*

995 BC   KING DAVID BUILDS JERUSALEM

DAVID, ISRAEL'S greatest king, was originally a shepherd and musician from Bethlehem and is best known for his allegorical defeat of the Philistine giant Goliath – he probably became the leader of a small Hebrew army that defeated a larger Philistine one. He was elected King of the Hebrews, united the various Jewish tribes and in 995 BC captured the small town of Jerusalem, which he rebuilt as his capital. Thereafter it has been known as the City of David. The Ark of the Covenant was moved to the new city, making it the religious centre of the nation. He was also responsible, according to tradition, for the creation of many of the Psalms – although many appear to have been written at a later date.

850 BC   HOMER, THE GREEK GODS AND TROJAN WARS

THE *ILIAD* and the *Odyssey*, attributed to the blind poet Homer (*c.* 850 BC), are the earliest and greatest Greek epic poems and provide a detailed picture of early Greek religion. This could be described as an anthropomorphic polytheism derived from earlier nature gods. The many gods, both male and female, who live on Mount Olympus, are ruled over by Zeus, the powerful thunder god. Other gods include Apollo, the sun god, Demeter, the goddess of harvests and Neptune, god of the sea. All have different human person-alities – they can plot against one another and be influenced through prayers and sacrifices. There was no central dogma, theology or revelation, although later philosophies made use of the ancient myths.

551 BC   CONFUCIUS

CHINA'S great sage, K'ung Fu-Tze ('Master K'ung') is generally known in the West by his latinised name 'Confucius'. Born in 551 BC, he came from an aristo-cratic but poor family in the state of Chou and was orphaned at an early age. At this time China was in a state of chaos and had divided into many warring states. Much of Confucius's teachings, which could be more accur-ately described as moral and political than religious, were directed towards restoring the kind of social order that was believed to have existed in ancient times. To Confucius this was a matter of restoring to Earth the perfect Order of Heaven, *T'ien ming*. This could be done through virtuous living and the correct practice of the ancient rituals.

▲ *Chinese philosopher Confucius.*

399 BC   PLATO AND THE DEATH OF SOCRATES

PLATO'S TEACHER, Socrates, was put to death for his teachings in 399 BC. This event is recorded in Plato's *Dialogues*, which are a form of memorial to

Socrates and which contain many discussions ascribed to him. He argues that knowledge can only exist if there are eternal things to which knowledge can refer, and as material things change, they must therefore be only expressions of unchanging 'Forms'. He believed in Forms such as the Good, the True and the Beautiful, which all things expressed to greater or lesser degree. In his *Republic* he depicts a State based on his ideals and ruled by philosophers. This was the inspiration for many other visions such as the Utopia of Thomas More.

367 BC   ARISTOTLE'S STUDIES

ARISTOTLE studied at Plato's Academy from 367 BC and became a teacher to Alexander the Great. Although he believed in and developed many of Plato's ideas, he rejected the theory of Forms, arguing that material things were the primary reality and that any properties that they had, such as colour or taste, were just aspects or properties of that matter. His rigorous use of logic and rejection of all unnecessary hypotheses resulted in him being seen as the founder of logical theory. His thought covered almost every subject from politics to literature, logic to psychology and ethics to science.

▲ *Scenes from the life of Christ.*

7 BC   THE LIFE OF CHRIST

BORN TO a poor family in Galilee around 7 BC, the son of a carpenter, Jesus showed interest in religious matters from an early age. His cousin, John the Baptist, was at that time a radical and ascetic preacher who was highly critical of the Jewish establishment. Jesus underwent the ritual of baptism, which symbolised the cleansing of the spirit. After a retreat into the wilderness, he became a wandering preacher and attracted a large following. He rejected the pursuit of wealth and the use of violence, proclaiming that these would prevent us from entering the kingdom of heaven. This message is most explicit in his Sermon on the Mount. His message that we can all, like him, become sons of God, led to his persecution by the priesthood. The traditional teaching of the church is that, after his crucifixion, Jesus rose from the dead, but many early Christians and the Jews and Muslims (for whom he is a great prophet) did not share this belief.

AD 50   DECLINE OF TAOIST THOUGHT

FROM AROUND the first century there was a marked decline in philosophical and contemplative Taoism. What had previously been the pursuit of a natural and spontaneous way of life became the pursuit of eternal life – or *Hsien*. This saw the use of magic potions and forms of sexual yoga. Contemplation of the ineffable 'order of nature' was gradually replaced by the worship of countless household gods and the practices of divination, alchemy, astrology and magic. This 'Hsien' Taoism flourished under the influences of Chan Tao Ling and Chang Lu.

AD 300s   THE DESERT FATHERS

THE MONASTIC life and the practice of contemplative prayer originated with the lives of the 'desert fathers', saints and hermits who lived alone and in small communities in the deserts of Syria and North Africa, especially around Alexandria. St Antony of Egypt (AD 251–356), a pupil of St Paul of Thebes, is referred to as the father of Christian monasticism. He created a loose community of hermits whose lives were based upon work and prayer (*laborare et orare*). Other important saints include Athanasius (AD 298–373) and the colourful St Simeon Stylites (AD 390–459) of Syria, who lived for 36 years on top of a tall pillar to escape from his many followers.

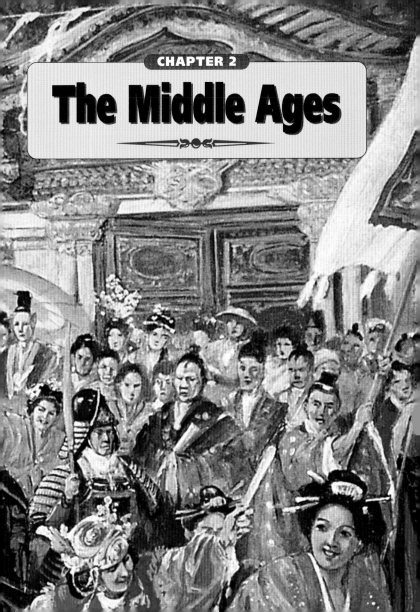

CHAPTER 2
The Middle Ages

Power and Politics

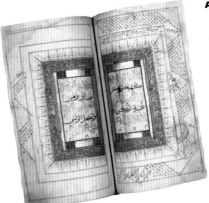

▲ *The Qu'ran, the Holy Book of the Islamic faith.*

AD 622   THE HEGIRA ('FLIGHT')

ARABIA at the beginning of the seventh century was wild, pagan and unsafe when in AD 612 the Prophet Muhammad began to preach in Mecca. He gained few followers and in 622 was forced to flee from Mecca to Medina. Here the impact of the teachings of the Prophet Muhammad was immediate. After the Hegira, he organised an alliance of the tribes in Medina and attacked and captured Mecca in 630. By the time of the Prophet Muhammad's death in 632 most of Arabia was Muslim. The Prophet Muhammad's teachings were based on the 'Five Pillars of Islam and it was the belief and hope that they offered which attracted so many followers and made Islam such a powerful force.

AD 750   THE RISE OF BAGHDAD

BAGHDAD became the centre of the Islamic Empire in the years after AD 750. The Ummayads were replaced after civil wars by the Abbasids who built Baghdad. It was a round city surrounded by a wall with four gates. Each gate was defended by 1,000 men. This shows the power and importance of the Caliph, who lived in the centre of the city in an enormous palace. The most famous of the Abbasid Caliphs was Haroun al-Rashid. He had an inventory of all the objects in the palace drawn up and it included 4,000 different sets of clothing. The Abbasids also encouraged learning and medicine. Libraries were set up throughout the empire and there were hospitals in every city.

1066 WILLIAM OF NORMANDY

WHEN William Duke of Normandy became King of England in 1066 he took control of all land. Faced with the problem of ruling and controlling a large country, William imposed feudalism upon England. His main aim was to ensure that he had military forces at his disposal and that the dangerous areas of the country were under control. His most important barons were given estates throughout the country. His own half-brother Odo, Bishop of Bayeux, held many areas of Kent, the site of a likely invasion. When the kingdom of France emerged, a similar process was followed. In origin, kings were only the most powerful and successful barons. Their position depended upon their ability to handle and control their own subjects.

1100s BARON KNIGHTS

WHEN barons came to perform military service, they had to be accompanied by the correct number of knights, and each knight had to be properly equipped. Different kings set different standards of equipment, but horse, spear, sword, helmet and hauberk (armour) were common. Barons solved the problem of providing knights by passing on their land to tenants, who had to perform knight service when required. Knights were professional soldiers, they did little else but prepare and practise for war. The

▲ *Illuminated manuscript depicting Baron knights.*

vast number of knights, with little to do, was one factor in the development of crusades from the late twelfth century onwards. To try to ensure that knights performed military service when needed, barons forced them to go through the same ritual of homage and swearing allegiance.

1215   MAGNA CARTA

KING JOHN (1199–1216) was faced by enormous debts as a result of his brother's, Richard I, continual campaigns on the Third Crusade and in

France. This forced him to raise higher taxes. John's attempts to recapture the English possessions in France failed when he was defeated at the Battle of Bouvines by Philip II of France. Finally, John's barons forced him to accept the Magna Carta at Runnymede in 1215. In theory this guaranteed the rights of freemen, but in fact the most important clauses were attempts to limit the king's power and protect the rights of the barons. John probably intended to disregard the Magna Carta as soon as he felt strong enough, but he died the following year and left the throne to his young son, who became Henry III.

◀ *King John signing the Magna Carta.*

1264   SIMON DE MONTFORT

MEDIEVAL kings were expected to lead their barons into battle and win victories. Henry III, the son of John was only nine when he became king in 1216. When he took control of the kingdom he proved to be a poor military leader. In 1264 there was a revolt against him led by Simon de Montfort, who captured Henry III. Simon de Montfort then summoned a 'Parliament' to which he invited both the barons, or 'Lords' as they came to be called, and also, for the first time, representatives of the Commons. Two knights were summoned from every shire, or county, and two burgesses from every town. This is regarded as the first real evidence of the existence of Parliament, although the name had been used since the 1240s. In 1965 Parliament celebrated its 900th anniversary as a result.

1300s   PEASANTS

PEASANTS were the lowest level in medieval society. There were villeins, who owned some land, cottars, who owned a cottage and borders, who owned virtually nothing. What they all had in common was the obligation to work for, and pay taxes to, their lord, whether he was a knight, a baron or even the king. Work meant tilling their lord's fields for several days every week. Taxes meant handing over a proportion of their produce to their lord or to the church and also paying to use their lord's mill to grind their wheat. In addition they could neither leave the village nor marry without his permission.

1340s   EDWARD III AND PARLIAMENT

IN THE 1340s Parliament began to grant money to the king. This became more and more important as Edward III (1327–77) embarked on his campaigns against France, which became known as the Hundred Years' War. In the 1350s the Commons and Lords began to meet as distinct bodies at the same time and the post of Speaker, someone who would put forward the views of the Commons after their debates, was created. Royal officials also stopped attending meetings of the Lords, which meant that the house was now made up exclusively of bishops and barons. By the end of Edward's reign the two houses had developed into something like their modern form.

▲ *King Edward III with Guy, Earl of Flanders.*

War and Peace

AD 717 THE SIEGE OF CONSTANTINOPLE

IN AUGUST AD 717, the Arab general Maslama attacked the city of
Constantinople. Having been repulsed by the city's catapults, he organised a
blockade. The Arab fleet, under Suleiman, was ordered to intercept any
Byzantine shipping and to block the Bosphorus and entry into the Black Sea.
As an Arab fleet passed the harbour, the Byzantines struck with their war-
ships sinking over 20. In the spring, the Arabs were reinforced, but again the
Byzantines struck and sunk many vessels. By August 718, believing that the
Franks were *en route* to raise the siege, the Caliph gave up, very few of his
troops making it home. Leo, the Byzantine emperor, pursued the Arabs, but
his victory in 739 at Acroninon in Phrygia finally forced the Arabs out of
Asia Minor.

AD 768 CHARLEMAGNE

CHARLEMAGNE was Charles the Hammer's
grandson and became king in AD 768. Between
768–814, Charlemagne fought against the Saxons,
Lombards, Spanish Muslims, Avars, Frisians,
Bretons and Byzantines. His empire covered the
major part of western Europe and the Pope
crowned him Emperor in Rome in 800. It
was his wars against the Muslims in Spain for
which he will be most remembered, but his
introduction of the feudal system allowed him

▶ *Holy Roman Emperor Charlemagne.*

to maintain a strong cavalry force, so vital in defending the enormous borders and striking out at his enemies. After his death in 814, the empire fragmented under the pressure of the combined raids from the Arabs, Magyars and Vikings in the ninth–tenth centuries, the last proving the most dangerous.

AD 866   CHARLES THE BALD AND ALFRED THE GREAT

BY THE end of the ninth century, both the Franks and the English had learned to cope with the Vikings. The Franks could now raise a large force of cavalry, vital for being able to catch and fight the fast-moving Vikings. In AD 866, Charles the Bald completed a series of fortifications along the Seine and the Loire. In England, Alfred the Great had built up a strong force of heavy infantry and an impressive fleet to counter the Vikings. When Canute became king of England (1016–35) after the death of Aethelred's son, Edmund Ironside (1016), he won acceptance from the English nobility, to whom he promised, and gave, strong government. He forged strong links with the Viking successors, the Normans and other Scandinavian civilisations.

1066   NORMANS AND SAXONS

HAROLD II was the last Anglo-Saxon king of England. Harold succeeded his father Godwine (d. 1053) to the powerful earldom of Wessex and was named heir to the English throne by Edward the Confessor when Edward was on his deathbed in January 1066. However, his claim to the throne was immediately challenged by William of Normandy and by the Norwegian king, Harold III. Harold III allied himself with Tostig, the

▲ *Edward the Confessor.*

brother of the English Harold, and invaded northern England. Harold II stopped this attack at Stamford Bridge in Yorkshire on 25 September 1066, but had to make a forced march south to confront the Norman invaders who landed in England on 28 September. He was ill prepared for the decisive encounter at Hastings.

1071 THE RISE OF THE OTTOMANS

THE SELJUK Turk victory over the Byzantines at Manzikert in 1071 opened the way for a Turkish invasion of Asia Minor. The Turks had been interested in settling in Arabia, but the attractive land of Anatolia was too good an option to ignore. Inspired by their faith as Ghazis (warriors of the Muslim faith) they attacked the ruins of the Byzantine Empire. Osman (1281–1326) fearlessly led the Ottomans in the early days followed by Orkhan (1326–62); Europe was no in condition to repel them. When the crusaders sacked Constantinople in 1204, the Ottomans quickly annexed Anatolia. The Europeans failed to support Byzantium as they knew that a superior military force faced them. The poor performance of the crusaders was confirmed by a string of defeats against the Turks.

1250 THE DEVELOPMENT OF ARMOUR

ARMOUR developed rapidly during the twelfth to thirteenth centuries; conical helmets gave way to pot-helms, with visors added around 1300. Long mail tunics became lighter, more supple and better fitting, with a quilted surcoat adding to the protection of the rider. By 1250, metal caps were being added to elbows and knees for greater protection, soon to be replaced with a cuirass, which covered the whole of the upper body. Light cavalry

▶ *Thirteenth-century knight in armour.*

re-emerged for skirmishing and scouting. The main fighting was still the task of the man-at-arms, flung at the enemy in a series of mass charges. Simon de Montfort used this tactic at Lewes against Henry III in 1264 and Charles of Anjou used the same methods at Benevento against Manfred in 1266.

1274   THE MONGOL INVASIONS

YORIMOTO emerged as a strong leader of the Japanese in 1185, establishing a strong central government, whilst maintaining the feudalism and fighting character of the nation. Japan was well prepared for the first Mongol invasion in 1274. For a whole day the Japanese held the Mongols at their landing point on Kyushu until a storm forced the Mongols to retire to Korea. Since the Japanese had underestimated the fighting skills and numbers of Mongols, it was inevitable that they would be back. The Japanese did not waste the seven years' respite – they built a stone wall along the shore of Hakozaki Bay from which they would defend their country. The Mongols reappeared off the coast in 1281, but were unable to breach the defences. They never returned.

▲ *Edward III and his army, showing how armour had developed by the fourteenth century.*

1300s   GUNPOWDER AND FIREARMS

ROGER Bacon, an English monk, was the first to record the process and composition of gunpowder in 1260. It would be 50 years before anyone took the concept seriously. A gun was fired at Metz in 1324 and Edward III probably used cannons against the Scots at Berwick in 1327. The French also used cannons against the English at Quesnoi in 1340 and Edward repaid the compliment at Calais in 1346. Another new firearm was being developed, the ribauldequin, which consisted of several tubes mounted on a wagon that could be fired at the same time. It was a primitive rocket battery. Edward ordered 100 of these to be made in 1345. By the mid-fourteenth century, firearms were coming into regular use, but they had not yet made an impact on warfare.

1327   THE HUNDRED YEARS' WAR

▲ *Edward III at court.*

THE Hundred Years' War began as a result of Edward III's claim to the French throne in 1327 and a series of territorial and trade disputes between the two nations. England won a comprehensive naval victory off Sluys in 1340, but it was not until 1346 that Edward felt strong enough to face the French in a decisive battle. Edward landed in France and headed for Calais with 15,000 men. He was immediately pursued by Philip VI with at least 40,000 troops including 29,000 mounted knights. Taking up a position overlooking a valley, Edward turned to face them. The French advanced to within 150 yds and the skies were filled with English arrows. Wave after wave were slaughtered. The French lost 10,000 to England's 200.

Society and Culture

AD 618 TRAVELLERS AND TRADERS IN CHINA

SINCE the earliest times, the Chinese had shown little interest in exploration. Uncharacteristically, however, the T'ang emperors of China (AD 618–907) were very receptive to foreign ideas and imports. Subsequently, Arabian, Persian, Korean and Japanese merchants brought spices to the country, which soon found their way into Chinese food. Persian cakes and sweetmeats also beacme a special delicacy. Before long, tales of the gold, jewels and other luxuries in China whetted the appetites of European merchants, for whom spices, vital for preserving meat, were of as much interest as the luxuries. The trade became rich, although Islamic powers blocked the route at times. After the Europeans entered the Indian Ocean, sea links from Europe to China developed in the sixteenth century.

AD 700s CITIES OF ISLAM

EARLY ON in the Muslims' campaign of conversion, they attacked and captured towns such as Damascus (AD 635) and Aleppo (AD 638) and in time turned them into magnificent cities, with elegant mosques, minarets, gardens, fountains and houses decorated with elaborate mosaics. Such beautiful structures became, and still remain, particular features of many Muslim cities, and the lives of culture and luxury enjoyed by their rulers in the Middle Ages became legendary. One of the most prominent od Islam's cities was Baghdad, now the capital of Iraq, which was founded in AD 762 by the Muslim caliph (civil and religious leader), Al-Mansur. Baghdad later became a centre of culture and learning. The most famous of all caliphs in Baghdad, Harun al-Raschid (AD 766–809) was himself a great scholar and possessed a library of some 600,000 books.

▲ *Peasants – the lowest order of the feudal system which continued for centuries in the British Isles.*

AD 800s HOW THE FEUDAL SYSTEM WORKED

THE FEUDAL system in England was a pyramid. At its apex was the king, whose vassals, the nobility, owed him fealty and the duty of providing forces for his wars. These were recruited from the mass of ordinary people who, in their turn, were the nobles' vassals. Oaths of fealty were solemn, binding contracts, sworn before God. Breaking them was therefore blasphemy, an awesome crime in an age of superstition. However, in return for fealty, and the labour of their humble vassals, the nobles owed them protection, if necessary physical protection within the walls of their castles. Most feudal estates consisted of these castles, together with a church and tracts of land. Outside, any land was common land, there for the use of all.

AD 800 AN INTERVAL OF PEACE

WHEN Charlemagne was crowned Holy Roman Emperor on Christmas Day, AD 800, Europe was able to contemplate a return of law and order and protection from attack it had not known since the end of the western Roman Empire. The respite, however, was brief. Charlemagne died in 814, and with that, Europe was once more vulnerable to assaults by Vikings from Scandinavia, Magyars from Hungary and those fiercest of Christendom's foes, the Arabs. The areas most at risk were in France, Germany, Italy and northern Spain, where feudalism was imposed as a system of mutual self-defence. Tsarist Russia, too, adopted the system and it persisted there for a thousand years, until the feudal serfs were freed in 1861.

AD 930 THE TOLTECS, WARRIORS AND CONQUERORS

THE TOLTECS seem to have lived for war and conquest. They seized power in Yucatan in about AD 930 and occupied Chichen Itza, doubtless with all the ferocity for which they were notorious. Not long afterwards, they founded their own capital city of Tollan (Tula). At Tollan, known as the 'city of reeds', the Toltecs built temples with roofs supported by giant statues. They created massive sculptures of warriors and decorated their pyramids with carvings of Quetzalcoatl. Quetzalcoatl it appears was

▲ *The Toltec God Quetzalcoatl.*

the real-life Ce Acatl Topiltzin, who founded Tollan. In 999, however, he was forced into exile and fled east across the Atlantic. A legend soon arose that one day, Quetzalcoatl would return, punish his enemies and reclaim his kingdom.

1095 MUSLIMS AND CRUSADERS: A CLASH OF CULTURES

IN 1095, Pope Urban II appealed for an army to 'take the Cross' and rescue the Holy Land from the Muslims, who had been looting and destroying churches and killing Christians. However, the Crusades, which lasted from 1096 until the last crusader presence was expunged in 1303, gave Christians a rather different picture from the one they had expected. Many were impressed by Muslim culture, the dedication and sense of honour of the Muslim knights whom they fought and the practicality of many Muslim ideas, in castle-building, clothing for the desert heat and hygiene. They took much of what they had learned back with them when they returned home.

1324   RICHES IN AFRICA

IN AFRICA great fortunes were being made in trading kingdoms like Ghana, known as the Land of Gold. Ostrich feathers, leather, kola, more ivory and solid-gold weapons were traded across the Sahara. In 1324, one Muslim king, Mansa Musa of Mali, made a pilgrimage to Mecca accompanied by 500 attendants carrying golden staffs and 80 camels laden with 10 tons of gold dust, which he distributed amongst the poor as his journey progressed. Much later, in the nineteenth century, rich kingdoms in Africa like Benin, ruined by the slave trade, and Oyo, destroyed by civil war, were to fall. However, as long as it lasted, the prosperity of medieval Africa was, both literally and metaphorically, a 'golden age'.

1348   THE BLACK DEATH

IN 1348 three ships arrived at Genoa, Italy, infected with a deadly disease, bubonic plague. The Genoese drove the ships away, but it was already too late. The Black Death, as the plague was later called, spread throughout Europe and by 1350 had killed one-quarter of its population. Another of its casualties was the feudal system. With the workforce drastically reduced, those villeins who survived were able to demand higher wages and greater independence, so undercutting the power that the lords had once held over them. The Black Death was not the only cause, though. Wealthy merchants in the towns, who had never been included in the feudal system, also contributed to its break-up. So did the development of guns and gunpowder, which made the nobles' castles more impregnable.

▼ *Rats were commonly believed to have carried the plague to Europe.*

Exploration and Empires

1095 THE CRUSADES

IN 1095 a council of the Catholic Church met in Clermont. Pope Urban II then called on Christians throughout Europe to fight a holy war to recover Jerusalem. The Christian kings of Spain had begun to use religion as an excuse for waging war against their Muslim neighbours. In northern France, the younger sons of the landed gentry wanted land. The idea of a pilgrimage to the sites of relics in order to gain the remission of

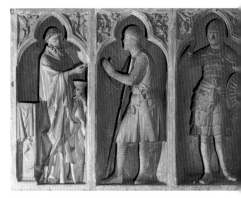

▲ *Carvings depicting crusader knights, who began their holy wars in the eleventh century.*

sins had become popular. The First Crusade was a great success. In the spring of 1097 a huge army drawn from western Europe had assembled outside Constantinople. It marched across Asia Minor and into Syria. The great city of Antioch was captured in 1098, and Jerusalem in the following year.

1187 JERUSALEM CONQUERED

THE Christian states of the Middle East became known as Outre-mer (French for 'overseas'). Because the bulk of the crusaders came from France or from parts of Italy and Germany strongly influenced by the kingdom of France, Outre-mer was effectively a French colony in the Middle East. It maintained a precarious existence for some two hundred years. Its survival depended on the ability to receive periodic reinforcements from Europe, in the shape of new crusades, and Muslim disunity. But when the Muslim world was united, the kingdom suffered. In 1187, a combined Syrian-Egyptian army conquered Jerusalem, and confined the Christian kingdom to the cities of the coast. The final blow came in 1291, when the stronghold of Acre was captured in a bloody assault.

▲ *An early picture of the holy city of Jerusalem.*

1206   THE MONGOLS UNITE

TO THE north of China, in Mongolia and eastern Siberia, an anarchic world of nomadic and semi-nomadic clans was in a perpetual state of intrigue and warfare. This was partly stimulated by gold that was shipped north by the Chinese emperors. Towards the end of the twelfth century, however, things began to change as a young man named Temujin rose to become 'khan', or 'ruler', of one of these groups – the Mongols. He skilfully manipulated the political situation so that in 1206 all of the nomadic groups – the Naiman Turks, the Keraits and the Tartars – acknowledged his supremacy. He took the name Ghengis Khan, and went on to become one of the most infamous warrior leaders in history.

1251   PAPAL EMISSARIES

THE FACT that the Mongols attacked the Muslim world as well was of great interest to European

▲ *The Mongol conqueror Genghis Khan.*

rulers. Pope Innocent IV sent a Franciscan friar, Giovanni de Plano Carpine offering an alliance. Giovanni's account of his travel has survived. His report warned the Pope that the Mongols were just after conquest, and would prove unreliable allies. A second emissary, the friar William de Rubuquis, travelled to the court of the Great Khan in 1251. He describes how there were embassies from the Byzantine emperor, the caliph of Damascus, the king of Delhi in India, the sultan of the Seljuk Turks and Russian princes. In between these European visits, the Mongols sent their own embassy to King St Louis IX of France, who was on Crusade in Cyprus.

1271   THE POLO FAMILY

THE MONGOL Empire had made the caravan routes across Central Asia as safe as they had been in the first and second centuries. Merchants began moving east, for the products of the Far East – silks and spices – were luxury items in Europe. A pair of Venetian brothers, Niccolo and Maffeo Polo, reached Bokhara in Central Asia and then travelled on to Peking before returning briefly to Venice. They then set out once more for the empire of the Great Khan, taking with them their nephew Marco, in 1271. The journey lasted three-and-a-half years, and the Great Khan, Kublai, allowed Marco to remain at his court until 1292, when all three Polos began the three-year journey back to Venice.

1300s   EARLY MISSIONARIES TO CHINA

WHILE the names of the merchants who ventured east from Italy are largely unknown to history, several missionaries who carried the Christian Gospel to India and China have left more detailed records. One of the best-known is Giovanni of Monte Corvino who became the first Christian archbishop of Peking, and who sent two letters back to Italy in 1305 and 1306. He built a church in Peking and converted some 150 boys to Christianity, teaching them both Greek and Latin. The second letter led to three Franciscan friars being sent to China. One of them, Andrew of Perugia, became bishop in

Ts'uenchow on the south-east coast. Giovanni de Monte Corvino died in 1328, and the Khan's own court asked for a successor to be sent to China.

1334   IBN BATTUTAH

THE MAIN Muslim travel narrative from the fourteenth century was written by Ibn Battutah, a Moroccan. He left Tangier and crossed the Islamic world to Aden, whence he took a ship down the east coast of Africa. He then went north to visit Russia and the great city of Constantinople, before turning east along the Silk Road. In 1334 he went to Delhi in India, and stayed there for eight years before joining an embassy from the Sultan to the emperor of China. Ibn Battutah's ship was wrecked on the Malabar coast of southern India, however, and his trip to China was delayed. Instead he went to the Maldives, and then claims to have made a voyage via Sri Lanka and the Malay archipelago to China.

1368   BREAKING THE BONDS

THE GOLDEN Age of medieval exploration came to an end in the second half of the fourteenth century. One cause was the Great Plague in Europe, which significantly reduced the population of many of the richest parts of the Continent. The plague itself was a product of the contact between the different societies of Eurasia, spread along the Silk Road by flea-infested rats. Another cause was the rise of new, militantly Islamic societies in Central Asia and Asia Minor. Timur the Lame, a new conqueror worthy of comparison with Genghis Khan, swept across the Middle East and into India. His savage empire was strictly Islamic and inhospitable to Christian travellers. Finally, in China itself, the cosmopolitan Yuen dynasty founded by Genghis Khan was overthrown by the Ming family, in 1368.

▶ *Timur the Lame with a captive.*

Trade and Industry

AD 600s CHINA IN THE MIDDLE AGES

THE T'ANG dynasty (AD 618–907) marked the beginnings of significant economic development. Rice paddies were extended to yield enough rice to maintain an expanded, urban population of craftsmen, landlords and officials. Trade was often in foreign hands, especially those of Uighurs and Arabs. According to Confucian doctrine, merchants were social parasites. Nevertheless, external and internal trade grew. The land-owning gentry remained the dominant class, served by others, leaving them free to pursue such gentlemanly activities

▲ *Modern rice paddies in China.*

as painting and poetry. In the eleventh and twelfth centuries China built up a massive iron industry using coal for fuel. Regional specialisation permitted the expansion of trade, and seagoing ships developed overseas commerce on an unprecedented scale. But trade was not entirely respectable, and once a merchant had made his fortune he generally bought land and took up a more civilised occupation. Tradition and state control triumphed, preventing a thoroughgoing industrial and social revolution.

AD 750   THE KINGDOM OF GHANA

THE kingdom of Ghana was the first of several West African empires to grow rich on trade. The kingdom, founded before AD 750, was favourably

positioned on river plains and its alluvial gold was carried north on the trans-Saharan routes in exchange for salt, textiles, weaponry, copper goods and horses. Imports came from as far afield as Egypt, Germany and Italy. The Ghanaian state included slaves among its exports, and charged taxes at relay stations along the trade routes. West Africa was a key source of gold until the metal was discovered in the Americas in the fifteenth century.

▲ *Asante people figures, from the kingdom of Ghana.*

The kingdom reached the height of its prosperity about the tenth century, when it extended from Timbuktu (now in Mali) to the Atlantic Ocean, and its capital had a population of 30,000.

1000   DEVELOPMENTS IN EUROPE

AROUND the year 1000 German cultivators invented a new type of heavy mould-board plough, capable of draining wet, low-lying lands and strong enough to work the heavy, clay soils that covered much of northern Europe, where the light scratch ploughs known in the Mediterranean and the Middle East proved useless. Most of the villages of western Europe were under the control of a professional fighting man equipped with a horse, a lance and armour. Other developments were the construction of windmills and water-mills (not new inventions but of much improved design) and the horse collar and horseshoes, which allowed horses to be used as work animals instead of oxen. Trading settlements also grew up at this time. The eleventh century in Europe was in fact a very productive time.

1086 WATERMILLS

LONG before windmills were built in Britain, watermills were used to drive machinery. At the time of the Domesday survey in 1086 there were more than 5,600 watermills. At first they were used for grinding corn but later waterwheels drove various kinds of machinery. They could move a hammer up and down to scour and tighten the weave in cloth to make it thicker: this process was called 'fulling' the cloth. Hammers were also used in early iron foundries to shape the iron and to grind dyes.

▲ *Watermills were used in early industries for driving machinery and grinding corn.*

There were three types of wheel, called undershot, overshot and breast. They differed in the point at which water struck them – from underneath, on top or half way up.

1100s THE FEUDAL MANOR SYSTEM

THE FEUDAL period in Europe began soon after the fall of the Roman Empire and reached its height around 1100. The feudal society (from 'fief', an inherited estate) was a self-contained community, often comprising the home of the fief holder (sometimes called 'lord'), a parish church and one or more villages. The manor occupied 350–800 ha (900–2,000 acres) of arable land,

and owned other land as well. A large manor might have a mill for grinding grain, an oven for baking bread, a wine- or oil-press, fish ponds, orchards and gardens. Food, linen and woollen textiles, and garments and leather were produced. The arable land was cultivated under a three-field system: one field was sown in autumn, another in spring and the third left fallow. A four-year cycle of rotation of fallow land came into use around the eighth century, involving three periods of ploughing in the year.

1200s   THE SILK ROUTE REVIVAL

THE SILK Route was a series of land routes, altogether more than 6,000 km (3,750 miles) long, that connected the eastern Mediterranean with East Asia. It first opened about 100 BC when Emperor Wudi of the Han dynasty sub-dued large areas of Central Asia by conquest and alliance. Various routes ran from the Chinese capital Chang'an (now Xi'an, Shaanxi province) across northern China to the Mediterranean ports of Antioch and Alexandria. The Silk Route fell into disuse with the rise of militarised and belligerent Islamic states and the fragmentation of the Roman Empire but was revived under the Mongol Empire in the thirteenth century when Marco Polo travelled the route to China, taking three years. Shipments of Chinese silk travelled westwards along the Silk Route, while metals, glass and coins went in the reverse direction.

1240   MONGOL RULE

THE TURKISH advance into Europe and India, starting about AD 900, was temporarily halted in the thirteenth century by a Mongol whirlwind. Genghis Khan created a huge military alliance between the peoples of the Asian steppes and then raided in every direction. Mongol dominance lasted only about 150 years before the Turks mounted a new offensive. From this arose the Ottoman Empire, headed by a sultan. The sultan required not only a standing army, the famous janissary corps, but also several thousand slaves. At first most of these were war captives; additional numbers were purchased

▲ *Mongol warlords were a dominant force in Europe and India from the tenth century.*

from commercial slave dealers or obtained by conscription. One legacy of Mongol rule in the north (1240–1480) was the subcontracting of tax collection, first to corporations of Central Asian merchants and then to Russian princes, who created an enduring bureaucracy of tax gatherers.

1300s   FIREARM TECHNOLOGY

THE Chinese were the first people to make firearms, including cannon. This technology travelled to Europe in the fourteenth century, giving the users a great advantage over opponents armed only with swords. The barrels of early guns were made of iron strips fastened with iron hoops; or of cast brass and bronze. Later, bell-making foundries learnt how to cast cannon barrels and later still musket and handgun barrels from iron. The new technology had an impact on architecture and ship design. Forts were built in a star shape, which would help to deflect cannon balls and with their own emplacements for cannon. The acme of shipbuilding in this era was the galleon, which had guns on both flanks showing through gun ports.

1345   THE AZTECS AND THE INCAS

THE AZTECS founded their city of Tenochtitlán on swampy islands in Lake Texcoco (Mexico) in 1345. Canoes plied the lake and canals. Produce grown on the 'floating gardens', or *chinampas*, were taken to market. Food and clothing, pottery utensils, tobacco pipes and cigarettes were sold, along with luxury items – gold, silver, jade and feathers. Slaves, displayed in wooden cages, were also for sale. The Aztecs used fixed units of value, such as jade necklaces, for barter. The Incas of South America were the other most important contemporary American civilisation. Most Inca commoners worked under a

▲ *Wall and entrance gate of the Aztec city Tenochtitlán.*

communal system in which they had to farm fields designated for the gods and the emperor as well as their own. Inca cities had efficient drainage and water-supply systems.

Science and Technology

AD 500s THE USE OF THE ASTROLABE

BY THE ninth century the Arabs had perfected the astrolabe, a device first conceived by Ptolemy (AD *c.* 100–170), a scientist from Alexandria. It was a device by which the position of the stars could be used to determine a position at sea or on land, by knowing the date, and vice versa. Although it had obvious limitations, it became the most important instrument for navigation for several hundred years, partly because sailors usually remained within familiar waters and only travelled during a season of congenial weather, between May and September. By the late twelfth century the Arabs had knowledge of the loadstone compass, possibly invented in China. Suddenly it was possible to navigate without being able to see the sun or the stars, so confidence in navigating uncharted waters grew.

▲ *An astrolabe.*

AD 500s ROTATION FARMING

THE improvements made to farming, with the introduction of the mouldboard plough, resulted in surplus production, and the net effect meant more leisure time, or rather, time to learn the art of warfare. Nevertheless, people still suffered from malnutrition due to lack of food variety and productivity peaked off as the soils became exhausted of nutrients. There was a no-win situation until a new system of farming was introduced, which made it self-sustaining. The solution was the three-field rotation pattern. Fields were used for two years in succession and then left for a year. The first crop was used as a green fertiliser as well as a food source, and the second was grain, which tended to drain the goodness from the earth, thus requiring that the field lie fallow for 12 months to recover. Fields were grouped in threes so that each was subject to a different phase in any one year.

AD 751 PAPERMAKING

IN AD 751 a Chinese team set up a factory for making paper in Samarkand, east of the Caspian Sea. From there, the Arabs brought the technology to

Spain. By the end of the eleventh century water-powered paper mills were operating in Italy. It was old linen that supplied the principal raw material, flax fibre. This was soaked and pulped, ready to be lifted in uniform layers with mesh screens made from drawn wires. The drained pulp was then placed between layers of cloth to form a pile, which was then squeezed under a press to remove as much water as possible before hanging each leaf to dry. Paper was far cheaper than alternatives, such as parchment, so it quickly grew in popularity, and the net result was an increase in literacy as people became more interested in being able to read and contribute to the information that was being circulated.

▲ *Throughout the Middle Ages many thousands of manuscripts worldwide were written and illuminated.*

AD 765   THE REDISCOVERY OF EARLY SCIENCE

WHEN fanatical Christians, and then Muslims, sacked Alexandria at the beginning of the Middle Ages, a vast library of manuscripts was lost, which contained information about every manner of scientific discovery and theory. Amazingly, in AD 765 a Byzantine monastery in Persia was discovered to contain copies of many of the lost works. They were translated from Greek into Arabic in Baghdad and duplicate copies eventually found their way to Muslim-held Spain. By the mid-thirteenth century Spain had become Christian and the manuscripts were translated into Latin. Copies now found their way to all parts of Europe where they were the subject of intense interest, particularly because of the astronomical information, which had a directly practical application to navigation.

1044   GUNPOWDER AND SWORD

SOMETIME in the early eleventh century the Chinese chanced on the formula for gunpowder. The first recipe for making saltpetre, the main constituent, was recorded in 1044 by Ching Tsao Yao. The potential for gunpowder as a propellant was only fully realised when it got into the hands of warring Europeans looking for an edge over their

▲ *The Japanese shogun Yorimoto, with armed guards.*

enemies. It gained its familiar name when it was used in the first cannons, which were little more than upturned bells from which large stone balls were fired. Initially they were more feared for their display of noise and smoke rather than their accuracy, but before long cannon shot was ripping through soldiers and ramparts alike. In the late thirteenth century, Mongols had made repeated attempts to invade Japan. Thanks to a curved sword made from expertly tempered steel, the Japanese won against the odds. In 1274 the Mongols made their last assault, but hindered by a storm, the Japanese samurai were able to make an offensive move, getting close enough to massacre the Mongols while they fumbled with their own inferior weapons.

1066 STIRRUP AND LONGBOW

WARFARE played a significant role in asserting control over regions of Europe during the Middle Ages. There were two significant developments in warfare technology that came into play around the time of the Battle of Hastings in 1066: warhorses were an important means for gaining an advantage over heavily armed opposing infantrymen. This advantage was quickly lost however, if the cavalryman was dislodged from his horse by losing his balance or being pulled off. The solution was the stirrup. This simple

▲ *Warhorses provided a significant advantage over enemy armies during the Middle Ages.*

invention made all the difference, giving the rider a secure foothold whilst striking his lance or wielding his sword. The crossbow was a weapon favoured by Continental troops because it fired bolts at high velocity and could penetrate chain mail and armour. The British, though, had the Welsh longbow, which had a decisive advantage over the crossbow. A well-trained archer could send eight arrows in the time it took to load and fire just one bolt, and with an equal thrust each time.

1100s   WHAT A BLAST

IN THE 1100s Europeans at last mastered a technique for producing cast iron, some 1,500 years after the Chinese. This was by means of a blast furnace, so called because of the blasts of air required to achieve a high enough temperature to melt the iron. Water and sometimes wind power were used to operate the bellows and for crushing up the iron ore to increase its surface area. Blast furnaces gradually grew in capacity to meet the demand for the new cast iron, which had wider applications than wrought iron, but two distinct problems arose as a result. Charcoal began to run short as Europe's trees were increasingly felled, and slag impurities prevented as much as 50 per cent of the iron from being run off for casting. The introduction of coke and lime into the process, solved both of these problems, but not for several centuries to come.

▲ *Chain mail armour, in common usage in the eleventh century.*

1350s   A REGULATED EXISTENCE

THE END of the Middle Ages saw town clocks being introduced all over Europe. The concept of arriving for and leaving from work at certain times was just one example of the effect clocks had, particularly in towns and cities, where increased efficiency was the underlying motive for introducing clocks. By the middle of the fifteenth century, the steel spring had been introduced for powering clock mechanisms, instead of the weight drive. Smaller clocks could now be made, but springs lose their energy gradually as they unwind, so a device called a fusee had to be incorporated. It was a tapered or conical drive wheel that compensated for the loss of energy. In 1581 Galileo Galilei noticed the phenomenon of the pendulum. A hundred years later the pendulum would set a new bench-mark in time-keeping accuracy.

Religions, Belief and Thought

AD 500s NESTORIAN CHRISTIANITY

THE Christians of Jerusalem, following the destruction of the Jewish Temple in AD 70, fled mainly to Syria. Here Nestorius (AD 381–451) created the Syriac, or 'Nestorian' church, which taught (like Arius) that Jesus was not himself God but was a human made divine by God. After reaching Chaldea (Mesopotamia), Nestorian Christianity spread rapidly to Central Asia, China and India. By the third century a Christian sect, based on the teachings of St Thomas, was active in South India. Meanwhile, the hermits of Egypt gave birth to the Coptic Church, whose teachings soon spread to Ethiopia, where it has been the dominant faith for 17 centuries. Many of these churches survive to this day.

▲ *Different schools of Buddhism have appeared throughout Japan and China since the sixth century.*

AD 500s CHAN AND ZEN

THE Chan school was traditionally brought to China by the sixth-century Indian monk, Bodhidharma, and was systematised by Hui-neng (the '6th Patriarch') in the T'ang dynasty. The name derives from *Dhyana*, Sanskrit for meditation, and the central practice is the direct realisation of reality through meditation. Chan was influenced by the *Diamond Sutra* and also by the teachings of Taoism and the Hua-Yen school. Hui-Neng's Southern School taught that enlightenment was instantaneous whereas Shen Xui's Northern School taught that it was gradual. In Japan Chan was called Zen, this came from the Southern School and took two forms – the Soto Zen, taught by Dogen (1200–53), emphasise *zazen* meditation whereas the Rinzai Zen taught by Hakuin (1686–1769) used *koans*, unanswerable riddles to force the mind out of the delusory world of words.

AD 570   THE PROPHET MUHAMMAD

MUHAMMAD, the prophet of Allah, was born in Arabia in AD 570, and married a wealthy widow, Khadijah. In 610 he received his first revelations from the Angel Gabriel, whilst living in a cave undergoing a solitary retreat. To Muslims, Muhammad was the Final Prophet, the last in the line descending from Abraham and Moses, and

▲ *The Angel Gabriel, who appeared to the prophet Muhammad.*

his message was to have faith in the One True God. His first converts were his wife Khadijah and his cousin, Ali. He experienced grave opposition from poly-theists in Mecca, who used the Kaaba (the shrine towards which all Muslims must pray) for the worship of idols, but eventually he captured Mecca and rapidly spread his faith.

AD 622   FLIGHT TO MEDINA AND CAPTURE OF MECCA

MUHAMMAD'S teachings in Mecca led to hostility from the population – who were polytheists – and he therefore fled in AD 622 to Yathrib (later Medina), which had a sympathetic Jewish population, in an event known as the *hegira*, or 'flight'. This event is used as the starting point of the Muslim calendar. Over the next eight years he led raids on the camel caravans to Mecca, destroying the Meccan economy and enriching that of Medina. In 630 he captured Mecca and cleared the idols from the Kaaba. Returning to Medina, he died two years later.

AD 700s   VAJRAYANA: TIBETAN BUDDHISM

BY TRADITION, Buddhism was introduced to Tibet by the eighth-century Indian monk Padmasambhava, who founded the Nying-ma tradition and introduced Dzogchen meditation. Atisha (AD 982–1034), another Indian monk, was responsible for the second wave of Buddhism, resulting in the Kadam-pa order. The Tibetan scholar and householder, Marpa, founded the Sakya order. His disciple, the poet and ascetic monk, Milarepa (1040–1123), is seen as the founder of the Kagyu order, which was further developed by his disciple, Gampopa (1079–1153). The various schools of Tibetan Buddhism were synthesised and united by Tsongkapa (1357–1418) to create the Gelug-pa tradition, currently headed by the 14th Dalai Lama.

1000   MUSLIM INVASIONS

THE EXPANSION of Islam to the west had little impact on India for several centuries until the invasions by Mahmud, a king of Ghazni, a province in Afghanistan. Between 1000 and 1026 he led annual campaigns to capture Indian territories, such as the Punjab, and to destroy and seize the wealth of Hindu temples in the main holy towns of Mathura, Thanesar, Kanauj and Somnath, in the hope that the population would convert to Islam. At Somnath over 50,000 died in defence of the temple. This and the next two centuries were a 'dark age' for Hinduism as repeated Islamic invasions from

▲ *The Tibetan mystic and poet Milarepa, founder of the Kagyu order.*

the north-west, by Afghans and Turks, devastated the country. With the loss of the temples and academic centres, philosophy and religious thought declined, to be replaced by a vast jumble of superstitions.

1181   ST FRANCIS OF ASSISI

ST FRANCIS, the patron saint of ecology and founder of the Franciscan Order of Friars, has been called the Second Christ and he did more to re-establish the simple teachings and way of life of Jesus than anyone else since St Antony of Egypt. He was born into the family of a wealthy merchant in 1181, but following several religious experiences he abandoned this way of life and gave away all his possessions to become a

▲ *St Francis of Assisi, founder of the Franciscan order, and St Bernard of Clairvaux.*

wandering friar. His reverence for nature, as expressed in his Canticle to the Sun, is similar to that found in Celtic Christianity. When large numbers began to follow him, he created a simple Rule for them to follow. This included complete poverty, abstinence from meat and service to the poor. Today his Order is one of the largest in the Catholic and Anglican Churches.

1212   THE CHILDREN'S CRUSADE

IT IS one of the ironies of history that more than four centuries of war were dedicated to promoting the teachings of the prophet of peace. In all, there were eight crusades to attempt to free the Holy City of Jerusalem from

Muslim control – although the Muslims had generally allowed Christians to visit and worship in the city. These all ended either with temporary success, after bloody battles, or in complete chaos. The Fourth Crusade never reached Jerusalem and the soldiers, impatient to attack something, plundered the Christian City of Constantinople. The Children's Crusade of 1212 resulted in 20,000 children being sold as slaves in Egypt. In response to the crusades the Muslims abandoned their policy of appeasement and for several centuries slowly conquered Christian territory. They advanced eventually as far as the Danube, conquering Constantinople in 1453.

1274   EAST AND WEST DIVIDE

THE DIVISION of the Western Roman Catholic and Eastern Orthodox Churches was a gradual process. The real cause was probably the division of the Roman Empire into two halves, centred on Rome and on Constantinople. This led to dispute over the status of the Pope, the Bishop of Rome. Theologically this division was reinforced by dispute over the 'filiouie clause', a technical theological point that was probably given importance for political reasons. By the time that Thomas Aquinas's treatise *Against the Errors of the Greeks* was published in 1274, the division had become irreconcilable.

▶ *Saint Thomas Aquinas.*

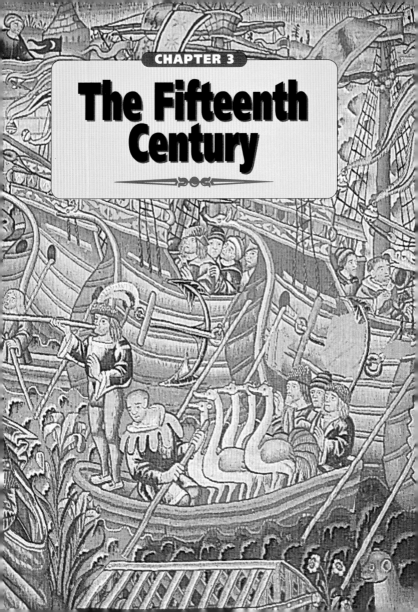

CHAPTER 3
The Fifteenth Century

Power and Politics

1453   THE RISE OF THE OTTOMANS

IN THE fourteenth century the Ottoman Turks conquered the Islamic Empire and began to advance into Europe. Mehmet II (1451–81) captured Constantinople in 1453 and then invaded the Balkans. For the next 200 years the Turks tried to invade eastern Europe. Belgrade was captured in 1521 and Vienna was besieged in 1526 and again in 1683, when it was only saved by the arrival of the Polish army commanded by John Sobieski. The Ottoman Sultans ruled a huge empire in the Middle East, North Africa and the Balkans. Their capital was Constantinople, but the empire was divided into provinces, each ruled by a governor. The extreme wealth of the empire led to increasing corruption and in the nineteenth century governors, such as Mehemet Ali in Egypt, began to try to break away from central control.

▲ *Henry VI, who lost much of England's empire in France.*

1471   THE END OF FEUDALISM

ONE OF the consequences of feudalism in England was that the barons came to see the king as little better than themselves. If the king was weak or unsuccessful, it was very tempting to try to overthrow him. When King Henry V of England died in 1422, his nine-month-old son, Henry VI, was unable to rule. When he eventually took power he was a poor ruler and failed to hold on to the English empire in France. His failures encouraged his enemies, the Yorkists, to try to seize power and eventually Henry was captured in 1461 and held prisoner in the Tower of London. He was almost certainly murdered in 1471. This was the final chapter of feudalism. Kings realised that they needed some greater degree of certainty in their control of the country and could not afford to allow powerful barons to challenge them.

1485   HENRY VII

HENRY VII became king of England in 1485. His immediate aim was to pacify England after the Wars of the Roses, which had lasted on and off for 30 years. His methods were simple and, at times, brutal. Any possible rivals to the throne were imprisoned and executed. The noble families, which had fought for the throne, were forced to give up their private armies. This

brought an end, once and for all, to the feudal system. Henry also built up a strong treasury, which gave him a high degree of independence. On the one occasion that he went to war in 1492, with France, he signed an armistice almost immediately. The French agreed to pay him £50,000, that more than covered his costs. Henry VII set a pattern which later monarchs followed, but few had his ability to manage their resources as effectively.

◀ *Henry VII, the first Tudor king of England.*

War and Peace

1406   INDIAN HILL FORTS

INDIAN hill forts were as good as anything built in Europe in the fifteenth century. A typical example of this is Mandu in Gujarat, built by Shah Hoshang Ghori (1406–35). Its powerful walls, bastions and gates stand 1,000 ft above the plain, with sheer sides to the south. The Indians were forced to accept the arrival of the Portuguese, the French, the Dutch and the British, but it was the latter that would expel the others and finally bring India into their own empire. In 1757, at Plassey, Clive with under 3,000 men defeated the Indians under Suraj-ud-Dowah, leading to the establishment of the British in the wealthy region of Bengal. Nevertheless, there was still much fighting before the British could dominate all of India.

1415   HARFLEUR AND AGINCOURT

THE English spent the latter half of the fourteenth century sending forces into France, in vain attempts to search for the elusive French army. A peace treaty was finally signed in 1396, but it did not last very long. Henry V, keen to press his claim to the French throne took advantage of French indecision and renewed the war in 1415. He captured Harfleur and marched on Calais. A huge French army was lured out in pursuit of his army of less than 6,000. The armies met at Agincourt, where the French showed that they had ignored

▲ *Henry V.*

the lessons of previous encounters with the English. In a little more than half an hour, Henry's archers slaughtered 6,000 of the 25,000-strong French army.

1452 THE USE OF CANNON

WHEN Urban, a Hungarian engineer was turned away by Constantine, the Byzantine Emperor, in 1452 he was employed by Mehmet II to construct a cannon 27 ft long and with a range of a mile. The Ottomans had already realised the importance of cannons and by 1364 had begun mass production, they had used field artillery at Kosovo in 1389. Mehmet arrived with his 100,000 men, a huge siege train and kept up a ceaseless bombardment of the city for six weeks. Within a week, the outer wall had been breached in several places, and when the Ottomans placed more cannon on a pontoon across the Golden Horn none of the city was safe from their bombardment. On two occasions, Mehmet thought that the bombardment had done enough, but was repulsed each time. On the third attempt, the city fell.

1479 FERDINAND AND ISABELLA

BY A chance of dynastic fortune – the accession of Isabella I to the throne of Castile in 1474 and of her husband Ferdinand II to that of Aragon in 1479 – the two most important kingdoms of Spain were joined. The 'Catholic kings' were exception-ally gifted, Isabella in internal politics and Ferdinand in foreign policy. Ferdinand turned his attention to the conquest of

▲ *Ferdinand II.*

▲ *Isabella I.*

Naples and to disputes with France over the control of Italy. In 1492 Granada was conquered, ending the reconquest of Spain from the Arabs. Isabella died in 1504 and upon Ferdinand's death in 1516 both of their crowns went to their grandson Charles I.

1494   ITALIAN WARS (HABSBURG-VALOIS WARS)

▲ *Charles VIII of France, during his invasion of Italy in 1495.*

AFTER the Peace of Lodi (1454), a precarious balance of power had been maintained among the chief Italian states: Florence, Milan, Naples, the papacy and Venice. This equilibrium was upset when Ludovico Sforza of Milan appealed to France for aid against a secret league of Florence and Naples. The French king, Charles VIII, descended into Italy with his army (1494), expelled the Florentine ruler Piero de'Medici and entered Naples in February 1495. Threatened by a coalition of Italian states allied with Emperor Maximilian I and King Ferdinand II of Aragon, Charles soon withdrew. A period of intermittent warfare followed, during which the Spanish general, Gonzalo Fernandez de Cordoba, conquered Naples (1503–04), bringing southern Italy under Spanish control whereas France dominated the northern half of the peninsula.

1495   GONZALO DE CORDOBA IN ITALY

GONZALO Fernandez de Cordoba was a Spanish general known as el Gran Capitan. He fought in the wars to drive the Muslims from Spain and helped negotiate the surrender of the Moorish kingdom of Granada (1492). He was sent to Italy with an army (1495) where he soon forced the French to withdraw. His brilliant victories at Cerignola and at Garigliano brought all of Naples under Spanish rule. He is credited with the introduction of the arquebusier, men armed with the latest handguns. Each had a bullet pouch; match, ramrod and powder in tubes hung on a bandolier. They also had a sword and helmet. He realised that these troops were perfectly capable of checking the assault of any enemy thrown at them.

Society and Culture

1400s   SLAVERY

SLAVERY has been called 'the greatest crime in the world'. It is also a very old one, probably as old as civilisation itself. There were slaves in ancient Judea, where Jewish law decreed that they should be released after a certain time. Ancient Rome teemed with slaves, nearly 21 million throughout Italy by about AD 50. Throughout the fifteenth century, Arabs traded in slaves across the Sahara Desert. However, a crime becomes a crime only when people become sufficiently shocked by it to call it so, and it was not until much later that an increasing level of dismay arose over the transportation of Africans across the Atlantic to work as slaves in the European colonies, established there in the previous three centuries.

1450   THE LEGACY OF ANCIENT GREECE

IN ABOUT 1450, at the start of the Renaissance, the Ancient Greeks and Ancient Romans (who had long ago emulated them) provided the models for this revival of art, architecture and learning.

▲ *The Greek physician Hippocrates.*

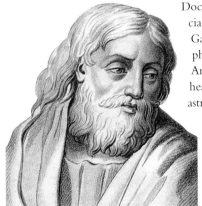

▲ *Greek physician Claudius Galen.*

Doctors looked back to the Greek physicians Hippocrates (460–377 BC) and Galen (c. AD 129–200), and philosophers to Aristotle (384–322 BC). Aristotle's theories on the motion of heavenly bodies were adopted by astronomers. The colonnaded buildings of Ancient Greece influenced architects. Mathematicians consulted the works of Euclid (330–260 BC). Artists and sculptors portrayed Greek mythical characters and other classical subjects. Though the ideas of Galen and Aristotle's theories of astronomy have been superseded, the Renaissance began a long period, which still continues today, when Greek ideas, including their democracy, retained – and still retain – an enduring influence.

1453   MEANWHILE, IN OTTOMAN TURKEY ...

WHILE Europe was moving towards a more enlightened, humanitarian concept of life, no such freedom existed in the Ottoman Turkish Empire, which was established after 1453 with the Muslim Turks' capture of Constantinople. The Ottoman sultan had numerous Christian and Jewish subjects; in the Balkans, Cyprus, Poland, the Crimea, and in Russia they were treated very much as second-class citizens. Organised into minority communities, and known as *rai'yah*, or 'the shepherded people', their lives, their property and their livelihoods depended entirely on the will of the sultan. They were not allowed to ride horses or carry weapons and they were barred from the Ottoman army and civil service. None of these rules applied to the majority, Muslim, subjects of the empire.

Exploration and Empires

1403   A TURNING POINT

THE second Ming emperor, Yung Lo (1403–24) for a time considered the possibility of expanding south-eastwards. He had assembled a huge fleet of 62 ships, which he sent into the Indian Ocean under Admiral Cheng-Ho. Cheng-Ho eventually made seven voyages around the Indian Ocean, visiting India, Sri Lanka and even the coast of East Africa at Mogadishu. He also sailed into the Red Sea and anchored in the Arabian port of Jedda, the traditional route for pilgrims to the holiest Muslim shrine at Mecca. After

▲ *Chinese explorer Cheng-Ho made seven journeys of discovery around the Indian Ocean.*

Cheng-Ho's death in 1434, and given the general preference of the Ming rulers for a self-sufficient economy, the great days of Chinese exploration came to an end. The tentative opening to the world had been closed off.

▲ *Portugese explorer Henry the Navigator.*

1420   SAILING INTO THE UNKNOWN

IT WAS believed that sailing beyond Morocco led to waters boiled by liquid flames from the sun. Sailing west led to swamps. To prepare crews for these hazards and to overcome fears, Henry the Navigator established a maritime centre to equip sailors with knowledge, instruments and vessels. Storms drove Henry's first expedition in 1420 to the Madeira islands. It was eventually colonised by Portugal, who introduced new crops and livestock. The islands of the Azores, reached in 1431, became a base for subsequent expeditions. By Henry's death (1460) his ships had sailed a third of the way down the African coast to present-day Sierra Leone. These ships stopped along the coast and sailed into river mouths to trade with African kingdoms, many of whom had grown rich trading with Arabs.

1480   MUSCOVY EMERGES

IN 1480, Moscow defeated an attempt to reassert the right to tribute made by the heirs of the Mongols, the Tatar khan of the Great Horde. Moscow had long been the most important principality in Russia in support of the rights of the Russian Orthodox Church and in dealings with the Tatars. Under Ivan III, the first of its rulers to call himself tsar, the territorial expansion of Muscovy moved rapidly. The great trading city of Novgorod, with its vast lands to the north, was annexed in 1478. Other states to the north-west of Muscovy were also added. By the end of the reign of Vasilii III in 1533, Muscovy was sufficiently powerful to be treated as an equal by the Habsburg dynasty.

1487   FINDING A ROUTE TO EAST AFRICA

JOHN II revived interest in exploration, leading to a series of voyages culminating in the first European sailing around the southern tip of Africa. Bartholomew Diaz left Portugal in 1487 with three

▲ *Portugese navigator Bartholo-mew Diaz, sailing to the Cape of Good Hope.*

vessels and sailed along the African coast until blown into open seas by storms. After sailing south for 13 days Diaz turned east, failed to sight land, so turned north and sighted mountains, and realised it was East Africa. A mutiny forced him to return home, sailing around Africa's southern tip. John II later called this the Cape of Good Hope. Diaz's critical discovery was not exploited as disputes over the Portuguese crown and hostility with Spain focused attention on domestic affairs. Despite this delay Spain had not found a route to Asia so explorations continued under Manuel I (1469–1521).

1492 SAILING TO THE NEW WORLD

COLUMBUS'S first expedition embarked in September 1492 with three ships carrying 100 men. In October they first landed on Watling Island and proceeded to sail round the Bahamas, Cuba and Hispaniola to find Asia, unaware of the significance of the discovery. Columbus was convinced that these were Asiatic islands leading to China. Relations with the indigenous peoples (mistakenly called Indians) deteriorated after the Spanish continually demanded provisions and thefts occurred. His second voyage carried 1,200 people, tools, seeds and animals to begin colonising the largest and most accessible Caribbean islands. Columbus's 1498 voyage found mainland Venezuela and the 1502 voyage found Central America. Columbus lost support as the elusive

▲ *Christopher Columbus landing at Watling Island.*

route to the East, and the anticipated riches, failed to materialise. Columbus died in 1506 convinced that the discovery of mainland Asia was imminent.

1492   SPAIN'S EMPIRE

THE Spanish crown exercised tight control over its fifteenth-century empire and its trade. All conquistadores gave a proportion of their profits to the royal treasury and crown representatives often followed their expeditions. All land was owned by the crown but the Encomienda system granted colonists control over particular areas (and all its indigenous inhabitants). In return the colonists helped the crown defend the empire and support missionary work within it. The crown also appointed colonial viceroys and legislators but was still the ultimate decision-maker. From 1503 a 'house of trade' in Seville, Spain, oversaw colonial trade and travel. All colonial exports were brought to Spain by royal 'treasure fleets' and taxes were imposed on imports.

1493   DIVIDING THE WORLD

IN 1493, Pope Alexander VI had used his spiritual authority to divide the world from North to South Poles between Portugal and Spain in an attempt to distribute the new colonies and to avoid conflict. Spain received the western hemisphere and Portugal the eastern hemisphere but disputes over the precise boundary line soon arose. After the Reformation, Protestant rulers would come to challenge the spiritual powers of Rome and begin competing for overseas empires. Although Spain continued to spend vast amounts controlling the colonies and defending the empire, it became weaker internally and consequently vulnerable to challenges from the

▲ *Pope Alexander VI split the world from north to south between Spain and Portugal.*

rising European powers. Spain's control over its overseas possessions weakened as the problems of communication and local efforts to assume greater autonomy across its vast empire grew.

1493   THE LURE OF INDIA

AT THE centre of all this travelling lay the Indian subcontinent. China, the Islamic world and Europe were all drawn towards it. Places such as Calicut, Cambay and the Coromandel coast were major cosmopolitan commercial centres, with Arab traders, Chinese merchants and spice dealers from the Malay archipelago, all conducting transactions in Indian markets. In 1493 two Genoese merchants, Hieronimo de Santos Stepahon and Hieronimo Adorno, travelled across Egypt and into the Indian Ocean. They reached Calicut and pressed on further east to Sumatra, but the hardships of the journey killed Adorno. Santos Stepahon only reached Tripoli in the Lebanon before writing his story in 1499. What happened to him afterwards is unknown.

1497   CROSSING THE INDIAN OCEAN

VASCO da Gama finally made the voyage by sea to India with four ships that sailed round the Cape of Good Hope in 1497. Explorations of Mozambique, Malindi and Mombasa revealed abundant trade with Indians and Arabs. Frictions between the Christian explorers and African Muslims led to clashes but Da Gama secured a pilot who guided them to Calicut, an Indian commercial centre, in May 1498. Da Gama had discovered a passage to Asia by finding the best Atlantic winds for sailing around the Cape of Good Hope, and had crossed to India in three weeks. Trading fleets emerged to carry cargo between India and Lisbon, which became a major commercial centre.

▶ *Tapestry showing Vasco da Gama's arrival in India.*

Trade and Industry

1400s EUROPEAN NAVIGATORS

THE European navigators of the fifteenth century sailed, usually at the command of their rulers, in search of gain. Fortunes were to be made from trade – in ivory from Africa, gold from Brazil, porcelain from China and tea and spices from India and Ceylon (spices were particularly sought after because they hid the taste of rotting food before the days of refrigeration). Among the early explorers were: Amerigo Vespucci (Italian), who sailed to the Caribbean and South America; Vasco da Gama (Portuguese), who pioneered the eastern sea route to India; Christopher Columbus (Italian), who made four voyages to the Caribbean; Ferdinand Magellan (Portuguese), who led the first expedition round the world.

▲ *Columbus sailing from San Domingo.*

1400s THE NATIVE PEOPLES OF CENTRAL AND SOUTH AMERICA

FROM a centre in the high Andes, the Incas developed a strictly centralised empire, which expanded to its greatest extent in the fifteenth century. The empire was linked together by a network of roads, of which the two main ones, running along the coast and inland, were each 3,600 km (2,250 miles) long. Potatoes and maize were the chief crops and the llama was an important resource. Practically every man was a farmer, producing his own food and clothing, which was made of llama wool and cotton. A relay service carried messages in the form of *quipu*, knotted cords, at a rate of 240 km (150 miles) per day. Inca communication networks greatly facilitated their conquest by the Spanish.

1400 THE KINGDOM OF BENIN

THE kingdom of Benin flourished from 1400 for three centuries in the area of modern Nigeria. The Oba, or king, performed ceremonies to ensure the rains and the harvests. The most important festival was the *agwe*, the feast of new yams, which took place at harvest time, in November. A number of slaves and animals would be sacrificed and this was followed by singing, dancing and 'magic' acts. Twice a year the villages had to send a tax to the Oba, consisting of yams, palm oil, pepper and kola nuts. The Oba alone was allowed to trade with the foreigners who began to visit Benin in the 1840s. Benin sold kola nuts

▲ *International trading in spices became a major industry once the New World opened up.*

to north Africans and palm oil (for soap), ivory, pepper and slaves to the Europeans.

1405 THE VOYAGES OF CHENG-HO

SOON after 1400 the Chinese emperor selected a
court eunuch named Cheng-Ho to be commander-in-chief of missions to the Western Oceans
to consolidate Chinese supremacy in trade and
the art of seafaring. In the course of his seven
voyages (1405–33) – on the first he commanded
62 ships and 27,800 men – Cheng visited
Malacca, Ceylon, Calicut, Sumatra, India,
Hormuz on the Persian Gulf and the east coast of
Africa. In 1424 the new Ming emperor forbade
the building of seagoing vessels and suspended

▲ *The Chinese briefly ventured
into trade and exploration at the
start of the fifteenth century.*

naval expeditions abroad. It was believed that imperial resources should not
be squandered on distant enterprises but mustered in defence against nomads.
In the wake of Cheng's voyages Chinese emigration increased, resulting in
Chinese colonisation, notably in South-East Asia, and the accompanying
tributary trade, which lasted until the nineteenth century.

1430s THE RISE OF JAPANESE SEAPOWER

AFTER about 1300 Chinese improvements in naval design penetrated Japanese
society: the compass, adjustable centreboards, keels, cloth sails and generally
larger, more serviceable ships. Sea voyaging was now practicable along the
Japanese coasts, across to China and South-East Asia and to the nearer Pacific
islands. Fishing soon developed into an important industry; and when the
Chinese withdrew from the seas in the 1430s Japan rapidly became the foremost naval nation in the region. Samurai (warriors), who had too little or no
land, took up piracy and quickly became the scourge of the China coast.
They brought back rich booty to their home ports, where the interchange
between merchants and warriors became intense and important and gave rise
to a warlike, self-reliant middle class.

1488 PORTUGUESE NAVAL ARTS AND INVENTIONS

IN 1488, Bartolomew Diaz discovered the Cape of Good Hope. Nine years later Vasco da Gama, another Portuguese sea captain, rounded the Cape and in 1499 he completed the first round trip to India. Both had the blessing of Henry of Portugal (d. 1460), nicknamed 'the Navigator', who prepared the way for the great voyages that opened up the entire habitable world to Europeans. Henry's motive was to circumvent and eventually overwhelm the realm of Islam. Henry commissioned astronomers and mathematicians to compile accurate tables of the Sun's declination at known latitudes, to help navigators determine their position. Thanks to these, da Gama spent 97 days out of sight of land, yet steered accurately to the Cape. The Portuguese also took the lead in shipbuilding, constructing stronger vessels with stouter hulls, more masts and several sails.

▲ *Japanese warriors took up piracy in the fifteenth century.*

Science and Technology

1450s   MOVABLE TYPE PRINTING

IT WAS the inventive genius of a German goldsmith called Johann Gutenberg (*c.* 1400–68) that ushered in the age of printing. During the late 1450s he devised a system for using individual type characters, cast in moulds from an alloy of lead, tin and antimony, which were interchangeable within a frame. The phonetic nature of writing in Europe, with its relatively few characters, gave it a distinct advantage over other writing such as Chinese, which comprised thousands of different characters and had been the language originally used to develop printing. It was quick and easy to assemble whole pages of type that could all be used time and time again for other jobs. As a result, printing took off rapidly. Within 30 years most of the western European countries had several printing works and by the early sixteenth century, most classical manuscripts were made available in print. The first newspaper appeared on sale in 1609 in Germany, where it had all started.

1473   THE BIRTH OF COPERNICUS

THE reinstatement of scientific inquiry led to an acceleration of progress, as it became the driving force in world

▲ *Polish astronomer Nicolas Copernicus revolutionised thought about the Earth's position in the universe.*

culture. As a result, theories began to surface that contradicted popular opinion, but were postulated simply because the scientific evidence suggested them to be tenable. Nicolas Copernicus (1473–1543), a Polish astronomer, was the first to suggest that the Earth was not the centre of the universe in post-medieval times. This came as a shock to European culture. His observations showed the Earth to be rotating around the Sun, which he in turn, mistakenly took to be the centre of the universe, but nonetheless, the solar-system hypothesis had been born. Christian beliefs were dominant at this time, so any idea which refuted the notion that the universe was centred around humanity was not well received. Copernicus's major treatise – *The Revolutions of the Celestial Spheres* – was not published until the year of his death.

1493   THE BIRTH OF PARACELSUS

A SWISS physician named Paracelsus (1493–1541) was the first scientist to make a nonsense of Galen's ideas about humours controlling the body and mind. He refuted the theory on the basis that the results of observation and experimentation should override the preconceptions of traditional lore, and that the results of his own studies had suggested scientifically based processes at work. He consequently established the practice of seeking external agents as explanations for disease and infection, making important progress in this area. By 1543 Vesalius, another great physician, had published his *On the Workings of the Human Body*, which opened the way for microscopic studies in the following centuries.

▲ *Paracelsus was the first to question Galen's theories on science and medicine.*

Religions, Belief and Thought

1440   THE BIRTH OF KABIR

KABIR was born in 1440 into a weaving family from the Hindu holy city of Benares. His father was a Muslim and his mother is believed to have been a Hindu. He sought to reconcile the mystical forms of Hinduism (in its Vaishnava form) and Islam (in its Sufi form) through worship of Rama/Allah as the one supreme God. He rejected the polytheism of popular Hinduism and taught that there was one God who had many names. He is known as the 'saint poet' and is remembered both for the many *bhajans* (devotional songs) that he wrote, and for being a teacher of Guru Nanak (1469–1539), the founder of the Sikh religion. His teachings helped to reduce conflict between Hindus and Muslims.

▲ *Krishna (left), one of the avatars of the Hindu god Vishnu.*

1450s   THE BEGINNINGS OF RENAISSANCE PHILOSOPHY

BY the end of the Middle Ages Western thought was in decline. It was confined to the monasteries and rigidly controlled by the Church. The teachings of the scholastics were other-worldly and were learned by rote in Latin. Corruption was rife and the popes had more interest in politics than spiritual practice. The liberal–intellectual revival that brought learning out of the cloisters was known as the Renaissance. This began in the city of Florence and slowly spread to northern Europe and England. It was sparked by two events – the introduction of printing in 1451 and the arrival of Greek scholars and classical texts following their expulsion from Constantinople by the Muslims in 1453. Study of Plato and other classical writers inspired humanist philosophies centred upon man and the world.

1472   WANG YANG-MING AND THE SCHOOL OF MIND

WANG Yang-Ming, a leading Neo-Confucian scholar, was the principal thinker in the School of Mind. This school challenged the older teachings of Chu His and the School of Principle. Wang Yang-Ming taught that the human mind was a perfect reflection of the Mind of Heaven and that humans should discover the Mind of Heaven only through study of the workings of their own minds. The school therefore encouraged self-cultivation through introspection and meditation

▲ *Confucianism is still widely practised throughout Japan and Korea.*

during daily activity and incorporated many Buddhist and Taoist ideas on meditation. These teachings spread rapidly to Korea and Japan.

1480s THE DECAY OF THE CATHOLIC CHURCH

THE corruption and decay of the medieval Catholic church and monasticism, which had its roots in the 1480s, had myriad consequences. It led to the humanist revival of the Renaissance, to the political breakaway of the Anglican church under Henry VIII and to the more fundamentalist and puritanical response of the Protestants under Martin Luther and John Calvin. This wide-ranging dissatisfaction eventually forced the Catholic Church to reform and from around 1550 there was a spiritual and institutional revival known as the Counter-Reformation.

1482 MARSILIO FICINO'S *THEOLOGICA PLATONICA*

MARSILIO Ficino (1433–99) played an important role during the Renaissance, in reviving the theories of Plato. He established a Platonic Academy near Florence for the purposes of studying the Greek philosopher. His commentaries and translations of Plato (from Greek to Latin), which he produced at his Academy, include *Theologica Platonica* (1482). In these, he explores Plato's religious thought, his theory of the immortality of souls and his views on platonic love. His particular interest was in integrating the thought of Plotinus and the Neoplatonists with Christianity, as he felt that these teachings existed in all religions.

1485 THE BIRTH OF LORD CHAITANYA

CHAITANYA was born in Bengal in 1485 and became the founder of a major Vaishnava sect – which is named after him. His teaching was that of passionate devotion, *bhakti*, directed towards Krishna, the latest avatar of Vishnu. His teachings follow on from the tradition of Ramanuja. The practice he taught of devotion and remembrance through continual chanting of the mantra Hare Krishna ('praise Krishna') is today principally associated with the International Society for Krishna Consciousness. Devotees live lives that are very simple, but which are also full of festivals and celebrations. The traditional Hindu teaching of *ahimsa* (non-violence) was given great emphasis, in

▲ *Although the fundamental beliefs of Christianity remained the same, the Church experienced division and dissention in the fifteenth century.*

particular in relation to a strictly vegetarian and healthy diet and the care of cows, which are sacred to Krishna.

1489   PICO DELLA MIRANDOLA'S *HEPTAPLUS*

COUNT Giovanni Pico della Mirandola (1463–94) was a Renaissance philosopher who studied at the University of Bologna, then became a wandering scholar, visiting universities throughout Italy and France. He later settled in

Rome, where he created one of the greatest libraries of his time. He was inspired by the writings of Plato and especially those of Plotinus and the Neoplatonists. These are explored in his *Oration on the Dignity of Man*, which presents man as a microcosm reflecting the order of the universe. In 1489, he published the *Heptaplus*, in which he gives a mystical explanation of the origins of the cosmos.

▲ *Desiderius Erasmus, Christian humanist leader.*

1492 DESIDERIUS ERASMUS AND HUMANIST CHRISTIANITY

ERASMUS was the central figure in the development of liberal-humanist Christianity in the Renaissance. Born in Rotterdam, he became a priest in 1492. He criticised the corrupt state of monastic life and scholarship, especially the stale dogmatism of the teachings of Aquinas, Ockham and Scotus – all derived from Aristotle. Instead, he advocated a return to the study of original texts such as the original Greek New Testament and the writings of Plato. His views were published in his satirical *In Praise of Folly* in 1511. Unfortunately his moderate criticisms were attacked as heresy both by the Catholic authorities and by their new opponents, the evangelical Protestants such as Luther and Calvin.

1492 EXPULSION FROM SPAIN

MANY of the Jews who had dispersed from Israel settled throughout Europe, where oppression by Christian governments occurred on a regular basis. Anti-Semitism grew during the Middle Ages and, in many cities, Jews were forced to live in separate enclaves or ghettos. A dramatic example of this occurred in Spain in 1492 when the Moors (Moroccan Muslims), who ruled the south (Andalusia), were defeated. The Moors had promoted religious tolerance and theological dialogue between the faiths. When they were defeated, all non-Christians, both Muslims and Jews, were expelled or sentenced to death by the Spanish Inquisition (and much of their money was used to finance Columbus's expedition to America).

▼ *The expulsion of the Jews from Spain: anti-Semitism was a rising concern in the fifteenth century, when they frequently suffered segregation or exile.*

CHAPTER 4

The Sixteenth Century

Power and Politics

1500s   THE RISE OF SPAIN

FERDINAND of Aragon (1479–1516) and Isabella of Castile (1474–1504) were the king and queen who united Spain at the end of the fifteenth century. Throughout the sixteenth century Spain became the most powerful force in Europe. The power of the nobles, especially in Castile was reduced and a centralised government set up. The Moors were driven from Granada, their last stronghold, in 1492. Ferdinand and Isabella also opened up a new field of power struggle when they sent Christopher Columbus to the New World in 1492. Their grandson, Charles I, who became the Holy Roman Emperor Charles V, played a key role in developing a new order in Europe. He set up a centralised administration for the whole empire and founded the Habsburg family, which was to rule the Holy Roman Empire and later Austria until the end of the First World War.

▲ *Holy Roman Emperor Charles V.*

1519   THE SPANISH EMPIRE

THE desire for wealth and power brought the Spanish Empire into conflict with the civilisations of Central America. The Aztec civilisation had evolved over a period of one thousand years and in 1519 had a capital city of perhaps 200,000 people. The Aztecs were ruled by a king who was elected and who appointed provincial governors. There was an effective system of law courts and a large army. Altogether the empire had about five million inhabitants. The Aztecs had developed the principles of architecture and engineering and by the sixteenth century were on the verge of developing a cursive script. In 1519 the Aztec Empire was attacked by the Spanish under Cortés and was destroyed within two years. Tenochtitlán, the capital, was completely obliterated.

1558 THE VIRGIN QUEEN

IN 1558, Elizabeth I became Queen of England. She was 25 years old. During her lifetime she had seen her father, Henry VIII, grow old and increasingly unhappy, her brother Edward VI die at the age of 15 and her elder sister Mary become very unpopular after she married Philip II of Spain and then tried to reimpose Catholicism on England. Elizabeth was determined to re-establish the authority of the crown. Traditionally the monarch in England was referred to as 'Your Grace'. This was the same title as was used for a duke and an archbishop. Elizabeth forced her courtiers, as they now became called, to address her as 'Your Majesty'. This implied that there was something different and remote about royalty. This set a pattern, that other monarchs were to follow.

▲ *Elizabeth I re-established Protestantism and the authority of the monarch in England.*

1568 THE DUTCH REVOLT

IN the sixteenth century the Netherlands were part of the Holy Roman Empire. Philip II of Spain planned to introduce the Inquisition into the Netherlands, where many people were Protestant, and this led to a revolt in 1568 by the Dutch. It was the first of a series of wars between Catholics and Protestants, which were to continue for almost a century. Philip tried to crush the revolt by force. He sent 20,000 troops and executed the leaders of the revolt. He managed to regain control of the southern provinces, but the north held out and eventually became independent as the United Provinces, often known as the Netherlands or Holland, after the largest province.

1578 ORGANISING THE MOGUL EMPIRE

THE Mogul Empire was founded by Babar (1526–30), but the organisation of the empire was the work of Akbar (1556–1605). He took control of all land and arranged for it to be administered directly by the crown. He also set up a state civil service to carry out his orders. Non-Muslims within the empire were treated as equals and were not subject to any special laws or taxes. In 1578, Akbar allowed public debates on religion involving all faiths, including Christians.

▶ *Mogul Emperor Babar invading Persia.*

Akbar strengthened the empire by conquering Gujarat and Bengal to the west and beginning the conquest of the Deccan to the south. This was the first time that a large part of India had been unified.

1598   PARIS IS WORTH A MASS

FROM 1562 to 1598 there was a series of eight wars between Catholics and Protestants (called Huguenots) in France. The Huguenots were concentrated

in the south-west of France, but Paris and the north-east remained Catholic. Henry of Navarre became King Henry IV in 1589. He was a Huguenot, but converted to Catholicism to ensure that the Catholics would accept him. In 1598 he issued the Edict of Nantes, which gave Huguenots equal political rights with Catholics and allowed the Protestant religion to be practised in some parts of France, but not in Paris and some other cities. It was the first example, however, of acceptance of Protestantism in a major Catholic country.

▲ *The expulsion of the Huguenots from France; one example of the conflict between Catholics and Protestants that occurred throughout Europe at this time.*

War and Peace

1500s   KEEPING ENEMIES CLOSE

VENICE seemed to pose the next threat, and in response France, the Habsburg Empire, the papacy and Spain formed the League of Cambrai (1508). Following its victory at Agnadello (1509), the League conquered all of Venice's mainland possessions. In 1512 the Habsburgs restored the Medici to Florence and in 1515 were defeated by the French at the Battle of Marignano. By the Treaty of Noyon (1516), France received Milan but renounced its claim to Naples. During the 1520s, France and the empire continued to fight over Lombardy. The French defeat at Pavia (1525) doomed French influence in Italy. The League of Cognac (1526) allied France, Florence, Milan, Venice and the papacy against the Habsburgs, but Spanish pikemen quickly conquered Milan and, in May 1527, sacked Rome.

1519   THE CONQUESTS OF MEXICO AND PERU

CHARLES I had hardly set foot in his new kingdoms when he was elected Holy Roman Emperor Charles V and departed for Germany. For the next two centuries, the fate of Spain was tied to that of the Habsburg dynasty. Charles spent most of his life defending his scattered domains against French,

◀ *The Battle of the Platform at Tenochtitlán in Mexico.*

Turkish and Protestant enemies. The conquest of Mexico (1519–21) by Hernán Cortés and the conquest of Peru (1531--33) by Francisco Pizarro resulted in the influx of gold and silver from America making Spain the greatest European power of the age. Charles abdicated in 1555–56, leaving Spain to his son, Philip II, and his German dominions to his brother, later Holy Roman Emperor Ferdinand I.

1522 SULEIMAN THE MAGNIFICENT TAKES RHODES

WHEN the Ottomans took Constantinople, they also captured one of the greatest shipbuilding centres in the world. The Turkish fleet grew enormously during the late fifteenth century, with notable victories against the Venetians (1463–79) leading to the occupation of Albania in 1478. In 1480, Mehmet failed in his attempt to take Rhodes from the Knights of St John of Jerusalem, but when Suleiman the Magnificent landed on the island in 1522, it was clear that they meant to stay. The town was surrounded by a wall 9 m (30 ft) high and 12 m (40 ft) thick, a formidable proposition. Four assaults were beaten off in September, but in December, the defenders had had enough and they departed to Malta, but this too was besieged in 1565.

1538 PHILIP II AND BARBAROSSA

BY THE mid-sixteenth century, Spain had become the dominant European sea power in the Mediterranean, but the western expansion plans were a key part of Suleiman's overall policies. His

▲ *Barbarossa, leader of the Barbary Corsairs.*

109

chief allies in this aim were the Barbary Corsairs, led by Khair-ed-din Barbarossa. They quickly built up a fleet and decisively defeated a Christian force off the Albanian coast in 1538. This meant that the Ottomans had sea supremacy east of Italy. Dragut captured Tripoli in 1559 for the Corsairs, but the massive Turkish attempt to capture Malta in 1565 failed. Philip II of Spain had by this time massively increased his fleets and after Suleiman died in 1566, the tide began to change in favour of the Christians.

1571   LEPANTO

WHEN the Christian fleet, under Don John of Austria, assembled at Messin in September 1571, it could boast 200 galleys, 6 galleasses, 24 large transport and 50 other craft. There were 50,000 seamen, most still shackled to their rowing positions and 30,000 fighting men. Against them, the Ottoman fleet, under Ali Pasha, mustered 250 galleys, 40 galliots and 20 other craft, with some 25,000 fighting men. The fleets spotted one another off Lepanto near the Gulf of Corinth on 7 October. The Turkish centre and right were destroyed, with a loss of around 200 ships and 30,000 men. This was the last time that oar-driven ships were used in a naval battle. Lepanto ended Ottoman naval supremacy in the Mediterranean.

1578   DUTCH WAR OF INDEPENDENCE

RELIGIOUS and political factors fuelled a revolt in the Netherlands in 1578. The revolt actually began in the southern provinces in 1566. In 1567 the duque de Alba was sent to quell the uprising, but the revolt spread under the leadership of William I of Orange (William the Silent). Under the treaty

▲ *Sixteenth-century map of the Netherlands.*

called the Pacification of Ghent (1576) all the provinces united to drive out the Spanish. Beginning in 1578 the Spanish governor Alessandro Farnese won back the southern provinces by political concessions. The northern provinces of Holland formed the Union of Utrecht (1579) and declared themselves a republic in 1581. The Dutch were aided by the war between Spain and England, which forced the Spanish to fight on two fronts and made England a valuable Dutch ally.

1588   THE SPANISH ARMADA

THE Armada was a great Spanish fleet assembled in 1588 as part of the attempt by Philip II to invade England. The plan was to send a fleet of 130

ships commanded by the duque de Medina Sidonia to cover an invasion force from Flanders under Alessandro Farnese. Lacking adequate ships of his own and block-aded by Dutch rebels, Farnese could not embark his troops. The Armada fought its way through the English Channel but, on 8 August, English fire ships drove the Armada out of its Calais anchorage. The Spanish regrouped and fought another action off Gravelines, but they were

▲ *The ill-fated Armada fleet, part of Philip II of Spain's plan to invade England.*

now out of ammunition. Realising that the situation was lost, Medina Sidonia sailed north around Scotland and Ireland and returned to Spain. He suffered heavy losses because of disease and shipwreck.

Society and Culture

▲ *A slave gang crossing the African desert.*

1500s TRADING IN SLAVES

SLAVERY was one of the most profitable trades in the sixteenth century. The sufferings of the slaves began when they were captured by raiding parties sent out by kings or chiefs of rival tribes. Sometimes the raiders ventured far inland for their 'booty', snaring unwary Africans in the forests or kidnapping them from their villages. The raiders took men, women and children; anyone who looked strong enough to stand the rigours of what lay ahead. Afterwards, a column of slaves might be marched, yoked and chained for 1,000 miles before they reached the coast. Many collapsed from exhaustion on the way, many died. Those who reached the coast were sold or traded for cloth, ornaments and other manufactured goods, which the slave traders had brought specially from Europe for the purpose.

1500s HUMANS BOUGHT AND SOLD

BY their own lights, the sixteenth-century slavers were not evil men. Nor did they necessarily feel the need to justify the fact that they were selling other human beings. They did not, in fact, regard black Africans as properly human at all, since they were, in their eyes, uncivilised heathens. These beliefs may lie behind the fact that the British laid down no rules about the humane treatment of slaves. The French and the Spaniards did, and the Spaniards also forbad the breaking up of families. The British, however, had no qualms and terrible scenes of grief and violence took place at slave markets, for instance in Jamaica, when husbands, wives and children were sold to different owners, never to see each other again.

1500s   SAILORS AND GEOGRAPHERS

MUSLIM seamen and navigators had a great deal to teach Europeans, even long after the crusades were over. European vessels, for instance, routinely used square sails until they discovered how the Muslim triangular lateen sails made better and faster of the wind at sea. Muslim maps were preferable by far for those venturing out to sea out of sight of land, since Muslim geographers had a more accurate and comprehensive view of the layout of the earth. In the early sixteenth century, the Muslim map-maker Pir Muhyi al Din Ra'is drew a chart of the South Atlantic Ocean showing West Africa and South America.

◀ *Native Africans were captured while out hunting and shipped to Europe.*

1519 THE CITY OF THE AZTECS

THE thin air and freezing cold made the Spaniards' journey through the mountains a gruelling one, but on 8 November 1519, Cortés and his conquistadore entered Tenochtitlán, the Aztecs' capital city, to

▲ *Aztec warriors defending the temple at Tenochtitlán.*

be greeted by a gorgeously garbed Montezuma, the Great Speaker, and treated like gods. Tenochtitlán was a revelation, with its massive palace and sacrificial towers, the metals which decorated statues and images of the Aztec gods, and its sheer size and complexity. However, the Aztecs, too, were due for a revelation. They had never before seen soldiers mounted on horseback and thought soldier and horse was a single animal. They had never seen, either, the Spanish arquebuses and muskets, which breathed fire and destruction.

1521 THE DOWNFALL OF THE AZTEC EMPIRE

ONCE the Aztecs realised the Spaniards' aggressive intent, they drove them out of Tenochtitlán. However, soon the Spaniards returned, this time aided by vast numbers of the Aztec Empire's long-misused subjects. After a ferocious struggle, which reduced Tenochtitlán to ruins, the city fell on 13 August 1521. What followed was the total destruction of Aztec society – the end of human sacrifice, which disgusted the Spaniards, forcible conversion to Christianity, the break-up of the Aztec *calpulli* (clans) and the enslavement of the people. The allies who had helped the Spaniards to their triumph – Tepanecs, Mixtecs, Totonacs, Zapotecs, Mayas – received the same treatment. Mexico became New Spain, and part of the Spanish American Empire, which lasted 300 years.

1532 THE CONQUEST OF THE INCAS

HISTORY repeated itself, though with extraordinary variations, in the South American Andes, where, in 1532, Spaniards under Francisco Pizarro (*c.* 1475–1541) reached Tahuantinsuyu and imprisoned the Sapa Inca, Atahualpa. These Spaniards, too, had come for gold and Atahualpa, realising it, made them an amazing offer: whole rooms full of gold and silver in exchange for his freedom. The Spaniards could hardly refuse, but they soon realised, and feared, Atahualpa's near-mesmeric power when, without demur, his subjects filled the rooms as ordered. Atahualpa could just as easily have commanded the Spaniards' slaughter, but they moved first, contriving a murder charge and executing him on 29 August 1532. At that, the Incas, supine as always before authority, awaited the orders of their new, Spanish, masters.

▲ *Spaniard Francisco Pizarro, who conquered the Inca Empire.*

1550s EXCHANGING DISEASES

MEDICAL knowledge in Europe in the sixteenth century did not yet encompass the causes of disease or, in the case of fatal infections, their proper cure. Yet, within the new Spanish American Empire, realisation dawned before long of the disaster that the conquerors had brought with them. When Orellana voyaged the Amazon, he noted how many people there were on its banks. Native America was clearly crowded, but not after thousands of people began to die from smallpox and other European diseases to which they had no resistance. Spanish priests who tended the sick realised what had happened, but disease worked both ways. Spaniards began to die, in their turn, of strange fevers and infections that Spanish physicians had never seen before.

1550s MEDICINE AND MERCY

IN medieval medicine, the cure had often been worse than the disease. For instance, bleeding patients to expel evil 'humours' weakened and often killed them. Though this savage approach to medical care did not disappear, more intelligent methods began to appear in the mid-sixteenth century. There was a determined quest to understand disease and the processes of human anatomy. The Italian Girolamo Fracastoro (*c.* 1483–1553) did important work on how contagion spread. Another Italian, Andreas Vesalius (1514–64), investigated the workings of

◄ *'Bleeding' patients was believed to expel evil 'humours' and restore balance in the body.*

the human body. In Britain, in 1628, William Harvey (1578–1657) discovered the circulation of the blood. The French army surgeon Ambroise Paré (*c.* 1509–90) dressed wounds with soothing balms rather than cauterising them and prevented profuse bleeding in amputations by tying off the blood vessels.

1550s   SCIENCE AND INVENTION

SCIENTISTS, too, were seeking better methods that would lighten workloads, improve working conditions and promote efficiency. The German Georg Bauer or 'Agricola' (1494–1555) investigated mining technology and described diseases that affected miners. Such work had added importance because of the increasing use of coal to replace the wood formerly used for fires. Later, in 1712, Thomas Newcomen (1663–1729) invented the 'atmospheric engine' designed to pump water from mines and so reduce the danger of

▲ *Georg Bauer, 'Agricola', made pioneering investigations into mining diseases.*

flooding which would otherwise overtake workers underground. He was preceded by Thomas Savery (*c.* 1650–1715), inventor of the water-driven steam engine in 1696. In manufacturing industry, new techniques in glassmaking were introduced and the first frame knitting machine was invented by William Lee (d. 1610).

Exploration and Empires

1519   DISCOVERING A NEW CONTINENT

AFTER failing to find sufficient riches in the Caribbean, explorers began to search the interiors of the Americas in the hope of greater reward. These were named after the Italian Amerigo Vespucci, who had travelled to the

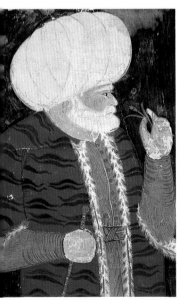

▲ *Suleiman the Magnificent, one of the greatest Ottoman emperors of the sixteenth century.*

New World between 1497 and 1504. Conquistadores (military adventurers) launched privately funded expeditions to these areas and settlements were established from 1509. Vasco Nuñez de Balbosa's 1519 journey across the Isthmus of Panama between North and South America to the Pacific Ocean was one of the most significant expeditions. Until then, Europeans did not know this 'Great South Sea' existed and that Asia must be beyond this new continent.

1520   THE EXPANSION OF THE OTTOMAN EMPIRE

AN energetic young sultan became Ottoman emperor in 1520. Suleiman, who was called 'the Magnificent', extended Ottoman power deep into Europe and across the Mediterranean. His victories over Hungary in 1526 led to a failed attempt to capture Vienna in 1529. In 1538, an Ottoman expedition even threatened the Portuguese trading post of Diu in India. Suleiman's empire, however, had reached its limits. The Habsburg dynasty in Spain managed to stall the Ottoman offensive in the Mediterranean during the 1540s. The failure of the siege of Malta in 1565, and the defeat of the Turkish fleet at Lepanto in 1571, six years after Suleiman's death, ended the immediate Turkish menace towards Europe.

1540s EXPLORING THE AMAZON

CONQUISTADORES like Gonzalo Pizarro and Francisco de Orellana continued overland expeditions in South America. They finally crossed the continent during an expedition to find the legendary golden kingdom of El Dorado. After being carried by a current down the Napo river, a branch of the Amazon, the expedition travelled almost 5,000 km (3,000 miles) down the Amazon to the Atlantic. Orellana named the Amazon after the legendary Greek female fighters as he had encountered female warriors during the expedition. Indigenous cultures were often destroyed by the introduction of the language, architecture, customs and religion of Spain. Colonists married indigenous nobility who liaised between the Spanish and the local population.

1542 FRANCIS XAVIER SPREADS THE FAITH

PORTUGAL marked each 'discovery' with a *padrãos* – a cross built on a stone pillar. This represented the arrival of the new power and its faith. These Christian symbols were soon followed by missionaries responsible for religious conversion. Diogo Cão crossed the Equator in 1482 with four Franciscans and left them in the Congo, in

◀ *The death of the Jesuit missionary Francis Xavier at Sancien in China.*

an attempt to convert the natives to the Christian faith. This practice was repeated along the entire route to Asia. Jesuit Francis Xavier who arrived in Goa in 1542 moved through South-East Asia to Japan on a 10-year ministry to achieve Portugal's spiritual ambitions in a region of Hindus, Muslims, Buddhists and Annamites.

1558   WARS IN THE WEST

IVAN the Terrible turned his army west in 1558 when he invaded the state of Livonia. This was the beginning of a long series of wars with the powers of the region that gradually extended the border of Muscovy westwards. The struggle was with the Baltic powers of Sweden and the united kingdom of Poland-Lithuania. At the time of Ivan's death in 1584, however, there was little to show for these wars. The most important gain was the port of Narva on the Baltic, but this was lost to Sweden in 1617, after a chaotic period known as the Time of Troubles that saw a Polish army occupy Moscow itself.

1568   ENGLISH PIRACY

ENGLISH traders wanted to participate in the valuable commerce with the Spanish colonies in the New World. But the Spanish government sought to maintain a monopoly, so that any exchange would take place in Spain. As a result, an undeclared maritime war broke out between

▶ *Sir Francis Drake, who practised piracy in Spanish waters during his voyages.*

England and Spain in 1568. Initially this was confined to the Atlantic, but in 1576 one English captain, Sir Francis Drake, began planning a voyage to the Pacific. He left Plymouth in 1577, sailed around South America pillaging Spanish ports along the coast, and reached the Spice Islands in November 1579. He took on a cargo of cloves and continued eastwards, returning to Plymouth in September 1580. Drake's profitable voyage produced several imitators.

1592   JAMES LANCASTER

THE knowledge that Drake brought back to England would probably have been exploited more energetically were it not for the demands of a war with Spain. The defeat of the Spanish Armada in 1588 required virtually every seagoing warship that English ports could muster. A sustained assault by the English on the Portuguese spice trade was delayed until 1592, when James Lancaster reached Penang, in the Malay peninsula. From here he sailed into the Strait of Malacca and attacked every

▲ *Drake brought many goods, including spices, back to England.*

Portuguese ship he came across, before sailing for home. Unfortunately for Lancaster, part of his crew mutinied in Bermuda, and made off with his ship. Lancaster's voyage itself was a failure, but the knowledge he gained contributed to the foundation of the Honourable East India Company in 1600.

Trade and Industry

1500s PAPER MONEY

MONEY was invented in many different countries around the same time, 2000 BC. Many different objects have been used as money. Paper was first introduced as money in China, probably as early as the seventh century. Being rare, paper was precious. Paper money was widely used during the Ming dynasty, 1368–1644. Not until the sixteenth century did Europeans discover the value of paper money. A merchant would store his money with a goldsmith, against a receipt promising to pay back the money when it was needed. The merchant could use the receipt to buy goods from another trader, who would then use it to reclaim the money from the goldsmith. In due course, the receipts were used instead of coins. Goldsmiths soon formed organisations called banks to issue notes worth fixed amounts of gold or silver. The first European bank to print its own paper money was the Stockholm Bank, Sweden, in 1661.

▲ *Modern tea picking in Indonesia; tea was one of the earliest exports from this part of the world.*

1500s   EUROPEAN EXPANSION

FROM the early sixteenth century the Europeans became world superpowers. Their discoveries had taken them all over the world, where they had established trading companies and laid claim to territory. They exported many things: finished goods, notions of law and governance, enterprise and inventiveness and diseases. Among their imports were tobacco, foodstuffs, coffee and tea, manufactured goods such as cloth, gold and silver and profits. Although European influence did not predominate everywhere in the world, for example in Africa, it was only a matter of time before European requirements made inroads into other civilisations. Trade, commerce and finance began to be subjected to principles and controls superimposed from above.

1500s   FINDING THE MARK

DEVELOPMENTS with cannon and firearms, with the introduction of gunpowder, were rapid. Soon it became possible to attack from considerable distances, which was just as well if the enemy had similar fire power. Reaching a distant target could no longer depend on trial and error, so a new science was introduced, called ballistics. Ballistics involved the use of geometry and physics in calculating the required trajectory of a projectile. The calculations were based on a number of key factors, so that the incline and azimuth (vertical and horizontal) angles of the gun barrel were correct. They are – direction, distance, elevation, wind interference and velocity of projectile. A

▲ *A French grenadier setting off a grenade.*

number of devices for making the necessary measurements were invented and developed during the sixteenth century. They also found useful service in surveying land for more accurate map-making.

1500s CONSEQUENCES OF EUROPEAN DISCOVERIES

EUROPEAN naval supremacy had three major consequences. The flow of massive quantities of silver and gold from the Americas made prices rise – by four times in Spain – adversely affecting buyers on fixed incomes while profiting sellers. A second consequence was the spread of American food crops such as maize, the sweet potato and the potato. New food crops increased local food supplies and swelled the population, not least in West Africa, the source of the millions of slaves who were taken to America in the seventeenth and eighteenth centuries. The third major impact was the spread of disease. In the Spanish New World the population in 1500 was about 50 million; by about 1650 it had shrunk to only four million – despite Spanish immigration.

▲ *Tobacco was an early export from the New World once trade routes began to open up.*

1500s MERCANTILISM

WITH the establishment of empires and colonies by European countries, after about 1500 trade became an arm of governmental policy. Each empire tried to acquire as much wealth as possible for as little outlay as possible. This form of international trade, known as mercantilism, embodied the belief that foreign exports are preferable to both internal trade and imports, that the wealth of a nation depends on its stock of gold and silver and that governmental interference in the national economy towards such ends is justified, even desirable. The earliest mercantilist efforts were directed towards eliminating internal trade barriers, that had been in place since the Middle Ages. Governments helped industries to grow because they were a promising source of taxation. Colonies were inevitably exploited as sources of raw materials and prevented from trading with other nations.

Science and Technology

1500s   GLASS AND COAL

GLASS for making windows was in increasingly high demand by the end of the sixteenth century in Europe. Broad and crown glass were the two main types used, which were still made using glass-blowing techniques. The enormous growth in the industry had led to a shortage of charcoal because forests had yielded all of their timber. At the turn of the seventeenth century things had got so desperate that alternatives were being sought. Coal was a familiar domestic fuel but too dirty for glass smelting, until a new underfed furnace was invented that kept the glass free from soot and smuts. This was hailed as such an important event that the use of charcoal for making glass was banned. The coal-mining industry took off in one quantum leap. Soon it was the driving force behind copper, brass and lead production and only a few years away from powering the industrial revolution.

▲ Coal mining increased in importance during the sixteenth century, when coal began to be used in glass-making.

1539   CARTOGRAPHY

WHILE many map-makers were developing ways to portray the lands and oceans of the world on to flat maps, others were directing their attentions toward detailed mapping of more familiar territory. In 1539, Richard Benese, the man who defined the area of an acre, issued a comprehensive volume of instruction on surveying and the use of associated tools and instruments. He had set a precedent, which marked the way for modern cartography. In 1592 the first fully surveyed map of England was published by Saxton, showing villages, market towns and rivers. 1592 saw the first surveyed map to include the courses of all principal roads. By the mid-seventeenth century, precise distances were being added to maps, meticulously recorded using foot wheels. The first world atlas of maps became available in France in 1658.

1551   MAKING MEASUREMENTS: THE THEODOLITE

EDMUND Gunter (1580–1626) was the man who made detailed mapping possible by inventing his Gunter's chain. It was a simple device, comprising a series of 22 yard sticks linked together. The chain was used to take the dimensions of areas of land, which could then be used to calculate larger tracts and areas by triangulation. The theodolite, invented in 1551, was a military ballistics instrument that was used in conjunction with Gunter's chain for measuring the relative elevations of locations. By contrast, Pierre Vernier (c. 1580–1637) of France, invented a device for taking very accurate width and thickness measurements of small objects. It was called the Vernier after its inventor. In 1621 came the invention of the slide rule, which was used as a standard means for performing mechanically certain arithmetic calculations, such as multiplication, division, addition, subtraction and square roots, up until the invention of the calculator.

1580s   MAPPING THE GLOBE

FOLLOWING the great voyages of discovery by Columbus, da Gama, Magellan and others, the world had been charted to show a considerable number of land masses and oceans spread out fairly evenly over a spherical surface. The curvature of the Earth's surface presented itself as a practical problem when it came to drawing maps on to flat pieces of paper. A Flemish map- maker named Gerardus Mercator (1512–94), hit on the idea of inventing a

▲ *Flemish cartographer Gerardus Mercator introduced the idea of a cylindrical plan to map the globe.*

cylindrical projection to solve the problem partially. Mercator's projection displayed the lines of longitude and latitude (parallels and meridians) as a grid, which became immediately popular because it meant that courses could be plotted in straight lines with a pair of compasses. All map projections distort reality, however they work, and the flaw in Mercator's was that exaggerations in width occurred moving away from the equator north and south, until the poles were stretched to equal the length of the equator itself.

Religions, Belief and Thought

1500s COUNTER-REFORMATION AND CATHOLIC MYSTICS

THE RECOVERY of the Catholic faith was aided by the emergence of several spiritual thinkers including three Spanish saints, St Teresa, St John and St Ignatius Loyola, the founder of the Jesuit Order. St Teresa of Avila (1515–82), the Carmelite mystic, is famous for her ecstatic visions, and St John of the Cross (1542–91), who was inspired by her, wrote of his own mystic experience of abandoning self in *The Dark Night of the Soul*. Ignatius Loyola (1491–1556) was a Spanish theologian and military leader. After serious injury he adopted a religious life and studied spiritual practices – as described in his *Spiritual Exercises*. His highly intellectual Jesuit Order, of which he was the general, was organised along military lines with the objective of rooting out Protestant heresy and restoring the true faith.

▲ *Niccolo Machiavelli.*

1513 MACHIAVELLI'S PRINCE

NICCOLÒ Machiavelli (1467–1527) was responsible for a revolution in political thought as a result of the publication of his *Il Principe* ('The Prince') in 1513. In common with other Renaissance thinkers his views are secular; they centre on man and the world and they are inspired by Classical literature. His advice to the Italian city states and their princes was based not upon religious principles, such as the divine right of kings, but simply upon doing whatever worked. This empirical and pragmatic approach can be seen as a precursor to the Scientific Revolution. He looks at past events, such as the lives of Romulus, Theseus and Brutus, as described in Livy's *Histories*, for lessons about the most effective ways for a state to maintain its power.

1517   MARTIN LUTHER

IN 1517 the German monk and theologian, Martin Luther (1483–1546), nailed to the door of his local church a long condemnation of the church's practice of selling 'indulgences' – documents that promised the buyer a reduction of time in purgatory. He declared that salvation came through faith and not through such acts. This practice was just one of many examples of the corruption of the church at that time. Erasmus responded to this situation by promoting humanism, but Luther instead called for a strict adherence to the basic teachings of the Bible, which he translated into German, and a rejection of everything else – monks, ritual, the decoration of churches and the veneration of saints.

▲ *Martin Luther (left) with others leaders of the Reformation.*

1518   THOMAS MORE'S *UTOPIA*

SIR THOMAS More (1478–1535), Lord Chancellor of England, was the principal figure in the English Renaissance. He was a humanist Christian and, like his contemporary, Erasmus, regarded the happiness and well-being of humanity as the highest Christian ideal. His beliefs and his critique of the political and religious situation of his time are to be found in his *Utopia*, published in 1518. This depicts an imaginary society, inspired partly by Plato's *Republic*, that lives in accord with basic Christian teachings such as the absence of private property, non-violence, the abolition of hunting, religious tolerance, humane penalties for crimes and the rejection of wealth. More was executed for treason against Henry VIII in 1535.

▲ *John Calvin.*

1533   JOHN CALVIN

JOHN Calvin, born in France, was inspired by the Protestant teachings of Luther. Expelled from France in 1533 he moved to Geneva, where he turned the city into a repressive theocratic dictatorship. Worship, beliefs and morals were imposed by force and opponents were excommunicated or executed. His follower, John Knox, introduced a similar regime into Scotland. Fanaticism during this time took many forms – approximately 100,000 women were tried as witches, music and festivals were banned and persecution of Jews was widespread. Calvin's teachings, whilst they shared the simplicity of Lutheranism, differed in that he believed in predestination and opposed the ordination of bishops. These differences later became the basis for several wars between the Protestant states of Germany.

1540s   HENRY VIII AND THE ANGLICAN CHURCH

THE ORIGIN of the Anglican Church was not primarily theological or religious, but resulted from Henry VIII's anger at the Pope's refusal to allow him to divorce. Secession from the Catholic Church, which controlled the whole of western Europe, was only possible because of the very low esteem in which it was generally held. Whilst its clergy were Catholic by education and theology it was supported by the new Protestant movement in northern Europe and this wide range of theological views remains in the Anglican Church to this day. Protestant influence was a significant factor (or excuse) behind Henry's decision to dissolve the monasteries and seize church treasures.

1570s   GIORDANO BRUNO
DISCOVERS PROTESTANTISM

FILIPPO Bruno was born in northern Italy and took the name Giordano when he became a Dominican monk. As a monk he studied the works of

Aristotle and Thomas Aquinas, but, in the 1570s, fearing prosecution for heresy, he fled and spent a number of years wandering throughout Italy and Switzer-land – where he encountered Protestantism. His writings, such as *On the Infinite Universes and World* (1584), attracted the attention of the Inquisition, and he was imprisoned for eight years. After this time, he still refused to recant, and was burned at the stake by the Church in 1600. Although many of his ideas seem strange today, his freedom of thought and his views on the unity of the world had much influence on the philosophy that developed over the following century.

1572   ST BARTHOLOMEW'S DAY MASSACRE

REFORMATION in northern Europe and Counter-Reformation in southern Europe split France down the middle. As the church was seen as part of the state this led to civil war. A massacre of Huguenots (French Protestants) at Vassy in 1562 led to seven civil wars over the next 18 years. These were fuelled by German and British support for the Huguenots and Spanish and Italian support for the Catholics. On 23 August 1572, over 8,000 Huguenots were killed in the St Bartholomew's day massacre in Paris. The shocked response from other European nations forced a truce but conflict continued to flare up. In 1627 Cardinal Richelieu, on behalf of the French government, led the siege of the Protestant stronghold of La Rochelle, and from 1618 to 1648 Austria and Germany were engulfed in the devastating Thirty Years' War.

▲ *The massacre of the Huguenots.*

CHAPTER 5

The Seventeenth Century

Power and Politics

1600s   THE DIVINE RIGHT OF KINGS

THE Divine Right of Kings was a concept, which developed in the late sixteenth century and early seventeenth centuries. It simply stated that kings were appointed by God and could only be punished by God. Opposition to the monarch was, therefore, impossible. In France, Spain and the Holy Roman Empire, all Catholic countries, Divine Right was accepted almost as a matter of course. It was a further source of royal authority and power. It also gave the church a privileged position. In Protestant countries Divine Right was not popular. Charles I's belief in it in England was one factor in the outbreak of Civil War in 1642 and also in Charles's execution in 1649. Overall, Divine Right stabilised but also ossified politics. Opposition became more difficult and the development of democracy was virtually impossible.

▲ *The execution of Charles I of England.*

1649   THE DEATH OF A KING

THE Stuart kings, James I (1603–25) and his son Charles I (1625–49), both tried to avoid dealing with Parliament as much as possible. By being frugal, James was able to avoid summoning Parliament for many years. Charles I also did not summon Parliament from 1629 until 1640, but he did not realise that if he was to do without Parliament he also needed to reduce expenditure. When he summoned Parliament in 1640 to pay for a war with the Scots, he was faced with a barrage of complaints. For two years Charles and Parliament argued, then, in August 1642, Charles lost his patience and declared war on Parliament – a war he was to lose. In 1646, Charles surrendered to Parliament and after three more years of arguing, in January 1649, the Parliamentary leaders reluctantly put Charles to death.

1658 AURANGZEB

AURANGZEB was the last of the Mogul Emperors. He seized power in 1658 when he rebelled against the Emperor Shah Jahan, the builder of the Taj Mahal. Under Aurangzeb the Mogul Empire began to break up. This was partly the result of his attacks on Hinduism, which led to rebellions by Hindus and Sikhs. It was also brought on by Aurangzeb's failure to control his own regional governors, who increasingly began to ignore his authority and raise taxes for themselves. Aurangzeb faced opposition from the Hindu Maratha princes from southern India and from the British, who had arrived in India in the early seventeenth century. When he died in 1707, the Mogul Empire began to disintegrate.

1660 RESTORATION OF CHARLES II

CHARLES II was restored to the English throne in 1660, after the 11 years of the Republic. He was a very popular king, but as he grew older it became clear that he would have no legitimate children. Charles's successor would be

▶ *Charles II, restored to the English throne after the Civil War.*

his brother James, Duke of York. But James was a Catholic and many people were afraid that this would lead to a Catholic revival in England. Some Members of Parliament tried to prevent James becoming king, others supported him. His supporters became known as Tories, his opponents as Whigs. Both names were terms of abuse. These were the first political groups in Parliament. They were not really political parties, but they became the basis of the Liberal and Conservative Parties of the nineteenth century.

1661 THE SUN KING

THE Sun King was Louis XIV, King of France (1643–1715). He made France the most powerful country in Europe. Louis was only five when he became

king and did not rule in person until 1661. He followed the practice of centralising power into his own hands. Louis also established a dazzling court at his new Palace of Versailles, just outside Paris. The bishops and nobles of France flocked there to pay court to the king. Their days were often spent watching the king get up, the *levée*, or go to bed, the *couchée*. They were also expected to watch him have

◀ *Louis XIV, 'the Sun King', established French supremacy in Europe.*

breakfast, lunch and dinner. Extra privileges were carrying the king's bedrobe or walking before him with a candle as he went to his bedroom. This ensured that the French nobility were kept where Louis could keep an eye on them.

1688   THE GLORIOUS REVOLUTION

JAMES II was forced to flee from England in 1688, and was replaced by his daughter Mary, who became queen. Her husband, William of Orange, became king. In the years after 1689 a series of Acts of Parliament were passed to limit the power of the Crown.

Parliament had to meet every year. Taxes could only be collected for one year at a time. The monarch had to be a Protestant and could not leave the country without Parliament's knowledge. These were attempts to place some limits on the power of the king, but the king could still appoint and dismiss ministers and decide all policy. But William III, and his successors Queen Anne and George I, became less involved in the government of Britain and the post of prime minister developed, as well as the beginnings of the Cabinet. Britain was becoming a constitutional monarchy.

▶ *William and Mary, joint rulers of the English throne after James II fled the country.*

War and Peace

1600s   STATES IN CONFLICT

THE striking development in seventeenth-century warfare was the sheer scale of armies. Gustavus Adolphus allocated half of Sweden's budget to military expenditure. Smaller states, such as Scotland and Switzerland sold their man-

▲ *Oliver Cromwell, leader of the English Civil War.*

power to the greater nations. The Thirty Years' War (1618–48) marked the beginning of modern warfare. During that conflict King Gustavus II Adolphus of Sweden greatly improved army organisation and discipline, introducing more powerful artillery and a lighter infantry musket that permitted soldiers to load and fire faster. During the wars of the English Civil War (1642–49), Oliver Cromwell raised an extremely effective fighting force by conscription. Law fixed pay, supplies, and discipline, and for the first time, the scarlet coat became the badge of English troops.

1618   THE THIRTY YEARS' WAR

THE Thirty Years' War was the last major European war of religion and the first all-European struggle for power. Hostilities broke out on 23 May 1618, when a number of Protestant Bohemian noblemen threw two royal governors of their country out of the windows of the Hradcany Palace in Prague.

The Bohemians appealed to the Protestant prince of Transylvania, who, with the encouragement of his overlord, the Ottoman sultan of Turkey, was hoping to win the crown of Hungary from the Habsburgs. They also elected Frederick V of the Palatinate as their new king. They hoped that Frederick's father-in-law, James I of England, and his uncle, Maurice of Nassau, virtual ruler of the United Provinces of the Netherlands, would lend him support.

1630s   THE LION OF THE NORTH

IN July 1630 the Swedish king, Gustavus Adolphus, landed in Pomerania to begin a series of victorious campaigns against the imperial armies. At Breitenfeld (17 September 1631) and at the Lech River (15 April 1632) he defeated Tilly, and at Lutzen (16 November 1632) the Swedes defeated Wallenstein, although Gustavus Adolfus was killed. The intervention of France (1635) on the 'Protestant' side cut across the religious alignments of the combatants. In 1640 both Catalonia and Portugal rebelled against Spain, although all three were Catholic. In 1643, the Protestant Christian of Denmark, fearing the increasing power of Protestant Sweden, restarted the old Danish-Swedish rivalry for the control of the north-western entrance to the Baltic. Once more the Danes were heavily defeated and lost their monopoly control over the Sound.

1633   BIRTH OF THE FIRST ENGINEER

THE effectiveness of citadels for defence was greatly enhanced in the seventeenth century by the work of a French military engineering genius named Sébastien de Vauban (1633–1707). Retaining the basic features of the citadel

▲ *Sébastien de Vauban.*

structure, he devised a means of extending the outer-works so far that no enemy could begin siege operations at close range. De Vauban was also a master of offensive siege-craft; he developed the concept of using parallel trenches to connect the zigzag trenches used by besieging troops and the use of the ricochet shot from cannons plunging over the walls to drop on the defenders beyond the walls. The best examples of de Vauban's work can be seen at Neuf Brisach and Lille, typical of his 'star fort' designs.

1640s   THE ENGLISH CIVIL WAR

AFTER a drawn battle at Edgehill in Warwickshire (1642), the Royalists threatened London. In 1643 the Royalists were victorious in most parts of England except London and the east. Charles was defeated at Newbury (20 September 1643) and the tide turned for the Parliamentarians for good in 1644, when the Royalists were beaten at Marston Moor in Yorkshire (2 July). In 1645 the Royalists were defeated by Thomas Fairfax's New Model Army at Naseby, and in 1646 Charles, who had surrendered himself to the Scots, was turned over to Parliament and became a prisoner. After Charles I's execution (30 January 1649), his son Charles II renewed the war, sustained by royalists in Ireland and Scotland; but Cromwell defeated the Irish and then invaded Scotland, where he crushed the Scots at Dunbar (1650).

▲ *The Battle of Edgehill during the English Civil War.*

1650   THE BATTLE FOR MARITIME SUPREMACY

THE leading maritime nation of the first half of the seventeenth century was the Netherlands. From 1650, at the height of their prosperity, Spain ceased to be a menace to the French and the British. Consequently, the Dutch were thrown into direct competition with the British. Between 1650–52, the British passed three Navigation Acts excluding the Dutch from their trade. By 1652 the British had over 60 large warships with over 100 guns each. Three Anglo-Dutch Wars were fought (1652–54, 1665–67 and 1672–74), after which the British overtook the Dutch as the major maritime power. As a result of the wars, the British gained New Amsterdam, which became New York (1667).

1667   MARLBOROUGH

JOHN Churchill, 1st Duke of Marlborough entered the army in 1667; he first distinguished himself by helping defeat the rebellion of the Duke of Monmouth (1685). James raised him to the peerage and promoted him to lieutenant general. Churchill soon shifted his allegiance to William of Orange, who deposed James and ruled as William III. Churchill campaigned for William during the war against France in Flanders and Ireland. When Anne became Queen in 1702, she appointed Marlborough Commander-in-Chief and First Minister. During the long war against France, he won victories at Blenheim (1704), Ramillies (1706), Oudenarde (1708) and Malplaquet (1709). Marlborough is acknowledged as a master military strategist and as one of the great generals in British history.

▲ *John Churchill, 1st Duke of Marlborough.*

Society and Culture

1600s   LIFE EXPECTANCY

DESPITE improvements in medicine and a new understanding of the human body, life expectancy in Europe was a great deal shorter than it is today. Although the stirrings of improvement were already there in the seventeenth and eighteenth centuries, it was to be a very long time before the risks to life lessened. Many infants died either at birth or soon after. Many women died in childbirth. Infectious diseases created epidemics in which thousands died, especially in the unhealthy and overcrowded districts of large cities. Since Roman times, life expectancy had barely moved above 40, less than that for women and even lower for others, for example, French peasants, who could rarely hope to live for more than 22 years.

▲ *In 1601 the Poor Law was introduced in England, creating a better environment for the lower classes.*

1601   A LAW FOR THE POOR

IN Britain, vagrants and beggars wandering the roads seeking shelter and sustenance had long been both a scandal and a security problem for the better-settled population. These miserable outcasts from society created fear and trepidation, since what they were not given, they stole. In 1601, the government of Queen Elizabeth I took official action, and created a Poor Law, signalling for the first time that the state had assumed responsibility for the less fortunate. The law imposed a poor rate to fund poor relief, and appointed Overseers of the Poor in every parish to buy materials to provide work for the unemployed. The price of grain was controlled, and if famine struck, imported grain from abroad was distributed in the affected areas.

1607   ENGLISH SETTLERS IN NORTH AMERICA

A REPEAT of history was inevitable after Europeans settled in North America. Just as the Spaniards destroyed the Aztecs, Incas and others further south, there could be only one ending to the clash between the ambitious, enterprising but intolerant and ruthless newcomers and the semi-nomadic first Americans living their simple, traditional life in the north. When the first English settlers established themselves in Virginia in 1607, the natives helped them survive their first winter, teaching them how to hunt and trap animals and raise crops of corn and tobacco. In time, as the United States, which evolved from the early settlements, set out to claim the country from coast to coast, this was something the native Americans would come to regret.

1631   THE TAJ MAHAL

'A DREAM in marble' and 'a poem in stone' are two of the many attempts to express the phenomenal beauty of the Taj Mahal which the Mogul Emperor Shah Jahan (1592–1666) built for his favourite wife Mumtaz who died in

1631. The Taj, a marvel of intricate sculpture and mosaics, with walls, floors and screens studded with

◀ *The Taj Mahal.*

precious stones, stands on the bank of the River Jumna near Agra and took 22 years (1631–53) to construct. More than 20,000 workmen were employed to build it together with the surrounding gardens and fountains. Nearby stands a mosque where Shah Jahan was able to see the Taj reflected in a stone set in the wall before him as he prayed.

1636   SAMURAI JAPAN

THE Japanese world, frozen into stasis by the Decree of 1636, was based on duties and obligations from which there was no escape. Often brutally controlled by Shogun warlords and the samurai since the tenth century, the strictly disciplined Japanese lived in a hierarchical society in which failure, or perceived failure, to honour the warrior overlords could mean instant execution, and the Emperor, though a figurehead, was regarded as divine. The strict samurai Code of Bushido, in which loss of honour could be assuaged only by *seppuku* (ritual suicide) imbued the civilian mindset, producing a culture of great formality in which observing proper rituals and expected behaviour and above all, automatic obedience to all authority, was paramount.

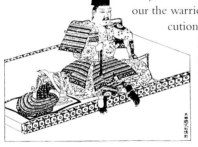

▲ *Warlords had been exercising strict control over Japan since the first shogun, Yorimoto.*

1670   THE TRIAL OF WILLIAM PENN

THE jury system, brought to England by the Normans after 1066, was often abused by judges bullying juries for the verdict they wanted. This threatening behaviour finally met its match in 1670, when the Quakers, William Penn and William Mead, were charged with riot for preaching their faith in public. The judge was intent on a 'guilty' verdict, but the jury disagreed. What was

▲ *A Quaker meeting; William Penn was put on trial for preaching the faith in public.*

...ore, they refused to give in despite imprisonment, fines and threats. ...ltimately, the Lord Chief Justice, Sir John Vaughan, ruled that judges could ...ot 'lead (juries) ... by the nose'. The 'not guilty' verdict stood and the case, ...nown as 'Bushell's Case' from the name of the foreman, Edward Bushell, ...stablished the right of British juries to independent verdicts.

Exploration and Empires

1602   BEGINNINGS OF CONFLICT

THE English East India Company also sought profits in South-East Asia, and in 1602 the company established a base at Bantam. The Dutch were already located there, but they were unwilling to share in the wealth of the spice trade. Conflict sprang up between the traders, and the English traders left in Bantam were prevented – sometimes by violence – by the Dutch, Portuguese and even the Javanese, from engaging in commerce. The Portuguese had a fort at Amboina, one of the main ports in the Spice Islands, but the Dutch seized it immediately after the English had reached a treaty with its governor in 1606, rendering the deal void.

1610   THE MUSLIM WORLD AND ITS NEIGHBOURS

TO ISLAM, the world had always been divided into two camps: the House of Islam, representing the lands ruled by the faithful, and the House of War, which includes everybody else. While Muslim states tended to ignore going out to the rest of the world, they did welcome visitors who brought useful technology, especially if they chose to accept Islam. A combination of events in about 1610 led to a substantial number of English and Dutch pirates settling in the lands of the Barbary corsairs of North Africa. These immigrants provided navigational and shipbuilding information that helped transform the corsairs into the terror of the seas. Jewish physicians who had studied in the West were also much sought after at this time.

1619   COEN IN THE EAST INDIES

THE DUTCH East India Company had started its life committed to trading alone, avoiding the commitments a proper empire would require. However,

◄ *The mosque of Muhammed Ali in Egypt.*

▼ *Naval battle between Barbary galleys and ships.*

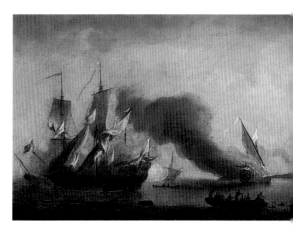

after a few years it became apparent to the Board of Directors that a monopoly of trade would ensure higher profits than free competition. In 1619, the Dutch sent Jan Pietszoon Coen to the East Indies. Coen had very clear ideas of what he wanted to do. First, he founded the Dutch post at Batavia (modern Djakarta) to serve as a centre for all inter-Asian trade. Then, he forced all rival traders out of the islands of South-East Asia. The attacks on the English culminated in 1623, with a massacre at their main post at Amboina.

1632   THE WAY TO THE PACIFIC

RUSSIAN explorers learned of a comparatively advanced Siberian tribe, the Yakuts, in about 1620. The high-quality furs the Yakuts brought to Russian trading posts stimulated the greed of the traders. In 1632, Pyotr Beketov took an armed force to the Lena and conquered the Yakuts. He built a fort on the site of modern-day Yakutsk, and then carried on southwards to the country of another Siberian tribe, the Tungus, and conquered them, too. A post in the land of the Tungus, at Butalsk, was the base for a journey eastwards in 1639 by a party of 20 men led by Ivan Moskvitin. This little band followed the Ulya River downstream to its mouth, where it emptied into the Sea of Okhotsk. These were the first Russians to reach the Pacific coast overland.

1643   TO THE CHINESE BORDER

THE expedition to the Ulya River uncovered news of large silver deposits along another river to the south. In 1643, Vasiliy Poyarkov travelled to the Amur to find out the truth of this but behaved so badly towards the local tribe that another expedition led by Yerofey Khabarov in 1649 had a hostile reception. Khabarov returned in 1651 ready for war. The Amur tribes paid tribute to the Chinese emperor, but that did not deter the Russians. A fort was built at the confluence of the Amur and Sungari rivers. Khabarov and his Cossacks defeated a Chinese assault in April 1652. An uneasy peace between China and Russia in the Amur country continued until the Russians agreed to withdraw in a treaty between the two empires in 1689.

1654   EXPANSION OF THE DUTCH EMPIRE

COLLECTION and dispersal points of slaves became important targets in wars. Dutch forces seized posts or constructed new ones in Brazil, and the need to supply slaves to these territories caused the seizure, in 1654, of one of the oldest Portuguese bases in Africa, Elmina, near the mouth of the Volta River. Other European states built their own posts on the coast nearby, including the Swedes, the Danes and the Prussians, countries almost entirely without American possessions. The islands of the Caribbean were handed round European states like real estate in a modern city. The Dutch had captured Curaçao in 1634 from the Spanish. The French settled Guadeloupe and Martinique, and in 1697 the French forced Spain to grant them half of the island of Hispaniola, which eventually became Haiti.

1682   PETER THE GREAT'S WARS OF EXPANSION

IN 1682 the 10-year-old Romanov heir Peter became tsar. In 1695 he embarked on a campaign of expansion that resulted in wars with the Turks and Sweden. Although initially Peter experienced more defeats than victories, by the end of his reign, in 1725, the Russian Empire had regained the lands around Narva that they had previously held during the reign of Ivan the Terrible, and also Estonia and Livonia. This had enabled the construction of a new city, christened St Petersburg. Peter's campaigns had also led to the acquisition of land around the Caspian Sea, including the strategic city of Baku. However, his two wars against the Turks produced no lasting gains.

1699   THE TURKISH RETREAT

IN 1683 the Turks made a second attempt to capture Vienna. This too failed, but this time the Habsburg Empire was able to recover substantial areas conquered by the Turks 150 years before. Even at the time, the peace treaty signed in 1699 was recognised as a turning point in relations between the Turks and Europe. The eighteenth century was an era of continuing retreat by the Turks under Russian and Habsburg pressure until, in 1798, the fringes of their empire became, like India, the battleground for outside

▲ *The defeat of the Turks outside Vienna, an event that marked the beginning of the Ottoman decline.*

powers. The French invasion of Egypt in that year, led by Napoleon, was an attempt to threaten the British position in India.

Trade and Industry

1600s THE INVENTION REVOLUTION OF THE SEVENTEENTH CENTURY

A SCIENTIFIC revolution took place in the 1600s, with the invention of many items that had industrial, agricultural or commercial uses. Among these were: the telescope (1608, Hans Lippershey, Dutch); the steam turbine (1629, Giovanni Branca, Italian); the adding machine (1642, Blaise Pascal, French); the barometer (1643, Evangelista Torricelli, Italian); the air pump (1650, Otto von Guericke, German); the reflecting telescope (1668, Isaac Newton, English); the calculating machine (1671, Gottfried Wilhelm Leibniz, German); and the steam pump (1698, Thomas Savery, English).

1600s THE DUTCH AND ENGLISH EAST INDIA COMPANIES

THE establishment of the Dutch (1600) and English (1602) East India Companies gave great power and organisational strength to their respective nations. The Dutch dominated in East Asia. By the 1640s they had driven the Portugese from Malacca and Ceylon and established themselves in Java, becoming masters of the spice trade. In the Americas the English colonies in Virginia (1607)

▲ *Hans Lippershay, inventor of the first telescope.*

and Massachusetts (1620) soon overtook the Dutch colony in New York (1626). The French began to colonise Canada, starting at Quebec (1608).

The most lucrative European ventures were in the smaller islands of the Caribbean, where plantations – worked by imported African slaves – yielded sugar, a commodity much in demand at home. English, French and Dutch entrepreneurs had, by the 1640s, taken the bulk of this trade away from the Portuguese and the Spanish.

1609   BANKS

THE first bank opened in Amsterdam, Netherlands, in 1609. By the mid-seventeenth century banks were commonplace in Europe. In Japan feudal clans ran banks, which issued their own paper money. As paper money became more widely used, the gold it represented generally stayed

▲ *The founding of the Bank of England in 1694.*

in storage. Goldsmiths here saw an opportunity: they could lend a little of the actual gold out and make money by charging the borrower for it. Many of the early banks failed because they lent too much gold. If many savers came to collect at the same time there was not enough to go round. To prevent this, most governments now regulate the amount a bank can lend. The world's first central bank, the Bank of England, was established in 1694.

1630   THE BEGINNINGS OF THE SLAVE TRADE

AN Englishman, John Hawkins, piloted the first slave ship to Spanish waters in 1562–63. Negro slavery and agricultural plantations began to become important only after about 1630 when sugar plantations became firmly established. The entrepreneurs of the slave economy in America were, in the end, mainly Portuguese, English, French and Dutch. Their impact on the native inhabitants was huge. The colonists brought disease, their own religions, culture and styles of life that penetrated from the initially mainly coastal settlements right across the continent. The horse, for example, a Spanish import into America, became the basis of a nomadic lifestyle in which buffalo were hunted. This so-called Plains Indian culture spread across the North American prairies in the seventeenth century.

▲ *Sir John Hawkins, who traded with the Spaniards in kidnapped negroes.*

1649   RUSSIAN RUNAWAYS

IN RUSSIA in the mid-seventeenth century the idea of being tied to the land took on an almost literal meaning. The tsar had insufficient money to pay salaries to his officials and to army personnel. Instead, he rewarded them with grants of land. Of course, land without peasants to work it was valueless. To prevent peasants from running away, the tsar had laws passed authorising landholders to chase and capture runaways. A law of 1649 required each man to remain at his post, in the place and walk of life in which he had been born. The practice never quite matched the theory: runaways often escaped from Russian society altogether and settled elsewhere in Asia. Exceptionally, one might rise to a top official post.

1650s   SUGAR PLANTATIONS

THE impetus for the slave trade came from the fashion in the 1650s for drinking tea, coffee (first introduced to Europe in 1516) and chocolate.

People liked to stir in some sugar to disguise the natural bitterness. The sudden demand led to phenomenal growth in sugar plantations in the West Indies, the ideal place to grow sugar cane. And slaves seemed the ideal means of providing the labour. During the sixteenth century about 1,000 slaves were imported from the west coast of Africa into the West Indies. Within the next hundred years, another 800,000 were imported. The sugar barons of the eighteenth century were a powerful elite. British slave merchants accounted for 40 per cent of Europe's trade in slaves and made an estimated overall profit of £12 million out of trading more than 2.5 million Africans.

▲ *The rise of the slave trade was caused by increasing demand for workers on sugar plantations.*

1694   THE NATIONAL DEBT

THE rapid rise of England's power was facilitated by the invention of a new instrument of credit, the national debt. This allowed public borrowing for emergencies on very advantageous terms. The central idea was that Parliament should be responsible for repayment. Previously, governmental borrowing had been in the king's name and debts were regarded as his personal obligation. In 1694 Parliament established the Bank of England, one of whose principal functions was to lend money to the government on the understanding that Parliament would guarantee repayment and raise the necessary funds by levying taxes. This meant that costs could be spread over several years. Moreover, as repayment became a near certainty, interest rates would fall and the English government was able to borrow from foreigners as well as from its own subjects. Foreign governments were not so well placed.

Science and Technology

1600s   GALILEO

INFLUENCED by Copernicus, an Italian scientist called Galileo Galilei (1564–1642) was the founder of a new scientific method. By deducing laws to explain the results of observations and experiments, he was reinforcing Copernican theory and treading new ground of his own. He is duly thought of as the first modern scientist. He showed that different-sized objects with the same density would display the same constant acceleration when released to fall simultaneously, and that, allowing for friction, a body moving on a horizontal smooth surface will neither accelerate nor decelerate. These demonstrations angered contemporaneous orthodox scientists, because they seemed to contradict logical or instinctive preconceptions about physics. He also used the newly invented telescope to observe that the Moon was not a perfect sphere, and that the planets did indeed revolve around the sun, for which he was forced to recant by the Catholic Inquisition.

▲ *Italian Galileo Galilei, whose experiments founded a new era in scientific understanding.*

1600s   GLASS SHEET

A PROCESS was developed in the 1600s that enabled the production of sheet glass for the first time. This meant that large single-pane windows and mirrors could be made, and a whole new industry rose up around the process. It involved pouring the required quantity of molten glass on to a casting table, where it was carefully spread and rolled out to an even thickness and allowed to cool slowly, to prevent it cracking. The development of larger, coal-fuelled, furnaces had proved essential for supplying molten glass in sufficient quantities for good-sized sheets. Techniques for making high-quality optical glass were improved in the 1700s allowing for considerable improvement in optical instruments such as the telescope and microscope, which required very precise and accurate lenses.

1600 MAGNETISM

JUST AS some scientists were experimenting with the mysterious qualities of electricity, others were approaching the field of study from the other side, by playing around with magnetism; although no one had yet linked the two. William Gilbert, a friend of Sir Francis Drake (c. 1545–96), was fascinated by the natural magnetism of loadstone, used as a compass by the great navigator. In 1600 he published a book called *On Magnets* following 18 years of

▼ *Early experiments with magnetism.*

experimentation. He believed that magnetism was the force attracting everything to the Earth and therefore, that space must be a vacuum. Otto von Guericke (b. 1602) extended Gilbert's ideas. He demonstrated how to create a vacuum with his famous horse experiment in 1652, showing that 16 animals could not pull two evacuated brass hemispheres apart until air was let in. He then made a sulphur ball which, when rubbed, would attain magnetic qualities, mysteriously glow in the dark and make crackling noises.

▲ *An early pendulum clock, invented by Christian Huygens.*

1608   THE FIRST TELESCOPE

THE advances in scientific understanding pursued by the likes of Galileo were aided by the invention and development of instruments. The telescope was invented in 1608 by Dutchman, Hans Lippershey (*c.* 1570–1619), as a military reconnaissance device. Galileo had adapted it within a year, and began to change the human view of our position in the universe radically, by what he saw in the skies. The fundamental effect that the telescope had was to call orthodox scientific beliefs into doubt and initiate a revolution in thinking, where every aspect of science and technology was required to be fully investigated. It is held also that Galileo noticed the phenomenon by which a pendulum takes the same time to complete a swing, whatever the length of the arc. This led another Dutchman, Christian Huygens (1629–95), to develop the pendulum-regulated clock, which in turn enabled scientists to measure time accurately enough to verify Galileo's astronomical theories.

1609   THE FIRST MICROSCOPE

JUST as some scientists were interested in the study of the universe, so others were interested in studying the minutiae of things around and within them. The telescope, which might have been called the 'macroscope', spawned an *alter ego* in the form of the first optical microscope in 1609. The invention of a Dutchman, Zacharias Janssen (1580–*c*. 1638), the microscope transformed scientific knowledge of the way things are designed and function at a cellular level. Study by magnification initiated various new approaches to biology, chemistry, geology and so on. William Harvey (1578–1657), an English physician, discovered the circulation of blood thanks to the microscope. This in turn, led to more dynamic and progressive approaches to medicine, now that blood was understood to be the medium for transporting vital chemicals to parts of the body.

1643   TORRICELLI'S GENIUS

THE introduction of pumps for removing flood water from mines revealed a strange phenomenon. It was found that water could only be sucked up a tube for some 10 m (32 ft) or so, after which it would simply go no higher. This meant having to pump the water in stages to the surface. An assistant of Galileo, called Evangelista Torricelli (1608–47), set to work on this problem in 1643. He had a moment of

▲ *The invention of the microscope led to many discoveries about the nature of blood, although the practice of bloodletting continued.*

genius, reasoning that the air was in fact like a lake, which asserted a pressure that increased with depth. Cleverly, he opted to experiment with mercury instead of water, as it was 14 times more dense, which meant being able to scale down his apparatus. He filled a long glass test tube with mercury and then inverted it with the open end held submerged in a dish of mercury to keep an air seal. He found that the mercury column dropped to a length of about 76 cm (30 in) and stopped, with a small space above it. This was clear evidence that the weight of air, or air pressure, was supporting the column of mercury, and that the space above must be a vacuum.

1670   NEWTON'S REFLECTING TELESCOPE

BY THE time Isaac Newton started his astronomical observations it was very difficult to make telescopes any larger. The design developed by Galileo was a refracting telescope, which required lenses to become bigger and bigger if a greater magnification of the stars was desired. Making larger lenses was becoming prohibitively expensive because of the level of expertise involved, so an alternative design needed to be invented. It was Isaac Newton himself who first built the new type of telescope, called the reflector telescope. A

concave mirror was used to focus the light collected, instead of a lens. Large mirrors were cheaper and easier to make, and they had the added advantage of being far less heavy and so easier to mount than lenses. Newton's first reflector telescope was made in 1670; it led to the construction of some very large instruments, which effectively opened up the skies for closer scrutiny.

▶ *Isaac Newton – philosopher, mathematician, scientist and astronomer.*

1682 STEAM ENTERS THE PICTURE

THE first practical application of steam was in Papin's pressure cooker of 1682. He noticed and recorded the physical forces created by steam as it expanded and contracted, which inspired Thomas Savery to build a steam operated mine pump between 1698 and 1702. By 1712, Thomas Newcomen (1663–1729) had invented the first 'proper' steam engine, featuring a piston and cylinder, and this design was widely used for pumping the water from mines for several decades. A mathematical instrument maker named James Watt (1736–1819) was repairing a Newcomen engine when he realised that the design could be improved by incorporating a separate condenser. This allowed the working cylinder to remain hot and increased the efficiency of the engine considerably. The Watt steam engine was such an improvement that it went on to power the Industrial Revolution. The late eighteenth century saw it adopted in all sorts of ways for driving machinery in factories.

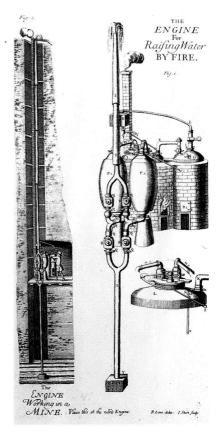

▲ *Thomas Savery's steam pump, known as the 'Miner's Friend'.*

Religions, Belief and Thought

1600s   THE BIRTH OF MODERN SCIENCE

BACON (1561–1626) and Descartes (1596–1650) are generally seen as the founders of modern science. Bacon stated that science should be about the collection and organisation of observed facts so that general principles could be derived from them. Before him, the tendency was either to indulge in theoretical speculation or simply to describe the world without explaining it. Descartes argued that all matter ultimately consisted of measurable particles and that all we need to do is to measure how these particles behave. All other properties, such as colour and texture, are unreal or can be reduced to the basic quantities of size and shape.

1602
CAMPANELLA'S
CITY OF THE SUN

TOMMASO Campanella (1568–1639) was born in southern Italy and became a

▲ *Tommaso Campanella was imprisoned for nearly 30 years for his 'heretical' ideas.*

Dominican monk when he was 14 years old. He rejected the scholastic and Aristotleian philosophy that he was taught and claimed that all knowledge of the world was obtained directly through the senses. This strictly empirical position contrasts with his later interest in astrology and white magic. Although denounced as a heretic and imprisoned for almost 30 years for holding these views he spent several of his final years acting as astrological adviser to the pope. His *The City of the Sun* (1602) depicts an imaginary society governed by philosophers, in which the state provides education for all, there is no private property and all things, including wives, are held in common.

1646 GEORGE FOX AND THE QUAKERS

THE Society of Friends, or 'Quakers' was founded in England by George Fox (1624–91). Following his own inner experiences in 1646 and 1647 he rejected the formal institutions of the Church and emphasised direct awareness of the divine. Quaker meetings involve no liturgy or ritual and are characterised by long periods of silence and contemplation – during which they were once said to 'quake' in awe of God, hence their name. Quakers are renowned for their active concern with peace issues and social justice and for the democratic way in which they run their affairs. An American offshoot, the Shakers, was founded by Mother Ann Lee in 1774.

▲ *George Fox, founder of the Society of Friends, a strict puritanical religious group.*

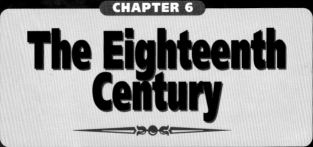

CHAPTER 6

The Eighteenth Century

Power and Politics

1700s   THE BRITISH IN INDIA

THE British landed in India for the first time in 1603. They were representatives of the East India Company for which a charter had been granted by Elizabeth I in 1600. For more than a century they occupied coastal trading posts, such as Madras, but in the mid-eighteenth century they were able to defeat both the Dutch and the French and take control of the trade of the subcontinent. In 1784, Pitt's India Act prevented the East India Company from interfering in the affairs of Indian states, but in the early nineteenth century, after the Maratha Wars, the company acquired more and more influence across India. By the 1820s, almost all of India was governed, directly or indirectly, by the East India Company.

1763   THE TREATY OF PARIS

THE Treaty of Paris in 1763 brought to an end the Seven Years' War, called in America the French and Indian War. The war had resulted in a comprehensive victory for Britain over France. The French forces had been driven out of America and India and the French navy had been crushed at

▶ *Present-day India; the country was subject to European colonisation from the seventeenth century.*

Quiberon Bay in 1759. The British army had even won a victory on the continent at Minden in the same year. The end of the war had two principal effects. Firstly, it built up resentment in France against Britain, which led to the search for an opportunity to gain revenge, and secondly, and much more importantly, it led to increasing opposition from the colonists to British rule, especially when this involved increased taxes to help pay for the cost of the war.

1773   THE BOSTON TEA PARTY

THE centre of resistance to British rule in the 1760s and '70s was the port of Boston in Massachusetts. Because they relied on trade, Bostonians were far more affected by restrictions imposed by the British government than other, more agricultural colonies to the south. In 1770 this led to an attack on a group of soldiers that resulted in the deaths of five Bostonians. In December 1773, when tea from India arrived in Boston, it was dumped into

▲ *Tea being thrown into the sea by disguised Bostonians, in retaliation against British trade restrictions.*

the sea by Bostonians disguised as Indians. This protest became known afterwards as the 'Boston Tea Party'. In June 1774 the port of Boston was closed and the colony of Massachusetts lost many of its rights of self-government and justice. Representatives of all of the colonies, except Georgia, met at Philadelphia in September 1774 in the First Continental Congress. They agreed to refuse to import British goods from December 1774.

1775   THE MARATHA WARS

THE Marathas were Hindu princes from southern India who attacked the remnants of the Mogul Empire in the mid-eighteenth century. They were organised into a loose confederacy and competed amongst themselves for leadership. Their success against the Mogul Empire brought them into conflict with the British, leading to the first Maratha War from 1775–82. A second war broke out in 1802, which resulted in the Marathas being defeated at the battles of Assaye and Argaum by Sir Arthur Wellesley (later the Duke of Wellington). This led to the collapse of Maratha power. They retained control of their lands, but were under the indirect control of the British.

1776   THE DECLARATION OF INDEPENDENCE

WAR broke out in America between the colonists and the British in April 1775. Much of the early fighting centred on Boston, which the British were forced to evacuate in March 1776. Congress then announced that the authority of the British crown was at an end. The Declaration of Independence was drawn up by Thomas Jefferson on 4 July. The actions of the Americans set a new

▶ *The Declaration was the basis for a new way of life in America.*

precedent in power and politics. They asserted the right of a people to throw off their allegiance to their king and establish for themselves a new and different form of government. The next step was the Articles of Confederation and Perpetual Union, which were signed in November 1777. This set out the basis for a United States of America, which came into being in 1781 when the British forces in America surrendered.

1787 CONSTITUTION

THE Constitution of the United States of America was signed on 17 September 1787. Until then the states had only been united by the Articles of Confederation. The Constitution came into effect in June 1788 when the ninth state, New Hampshire, ratified it. The drafting of the Constitution had proved difficult. Until the 1770s the states had all had their own governments and it had been opposition to British rule that had united them. Once the British left, some of the old rivalries reappeared. States were reluctant to raise taxes for the Federal Government, there were disagreements over trade and between the agricultural states of the South and the more industrialised in the North. In addition, the smaller states, such as Connecticut and Rhode Island feared that they would be swamped by the larger states such as Massachusetts and New York. What resulted was a compromise.

1789 THE BASTILLE

IN May and June of 1789, while the Estates-General was arguing at Versailles, bread prices in Paris reached record levels. On 14 July 1789 a crowd of Parisians attacked the Bastille, a royal fortress in Paris, that was used as a prison and an arsenal. They were looking for weapons to defend Paris against a possible attack by Louis XVI's forces. The attack was a complete success and the governor of the prison surrendered, but the mob killed him immediately. The fall of the Bastille was a symbol that the power of the king could be challenged, and it had been the working people of Paris who had played the most important role in the events. It was an ominous step for the aristocracy.

▲ *The siege of the Bastille, one of the first steps towards Revolution in France.*

1792   THE JACOBINS

IN September 1792 the National Assembly was set up in France. This soon
fell under the control of the Jacobins, who were members of a club, that met
in a monastery in the rue St Jacques. Their leader was Maximilien
Robespierre. The monarchy was abolished and Louis XVI was put on trial
and executed in January 1793. Robespierre then initiated the Reign of
Terror, in which all of his political opponents, including members of his own
party, were brought before revolutionary tribunals and then executed, particularly by the guillotine, a new device used for beheading people. Robespierre
became virtual dictator of France, even introducing a Law of Suspects, which
allowed people suspected of planning crimes to be tried.

War and Peace

1700   THE GREAT NORTHERN WAR

SWEDEN, the dominant power in northern Europe when the war began,
fought against an alliance intent on seizing its empire. After Charles XII
inherited the Swedish throne (1697), Denmark, Saxony and Russia attacked
Sweden (1700). Charles defeated the Danes, then turned his attention to
Russia, destroying the Russian army that was besieging Narva (1700).
Charles toppled Augustus from the throne of Poland (1704) and broke his
power in Saxony (1706). In 1707, Charles was decisively defeated at Poltava
(1709) by Peter the Great and fled to the Ottoman Empire. Russia seized
Livonia, Estonia and the Gulf of Finland. Charles returned to the north in
1714, but was killed during a campaign against Danish-ruled Norway (1718).
This signalled the emergence of Russia as the strongest power in the Baltic.

1713   UTRECHT AND BEYOND

THE Treaty of Utrecht (1713) ended
France's attempts to dominate Europe.
However, there was still the question of
colonies and trade. The Dutch were no
longer a problem and the Spanish were
content to ally themselves with France
when it suited them. The Anglo-
Spanish War of Jenkins' Ear (1739–48)
proved to be the first flashpoint,
followed by the Austrian War of

▶ *The signing of the Treaty of Utrecht in 1713.*

Succession (1740–48), in which Britain and France fought from 1743. After a brief pause, France and Britain clashed in the Seven Years' War (1756–63), which carried on as the American War of Independence (1775–83), although this was effectively over after Cornwallis surrendered at Yorktown in 1781.

1740   THE WAR OF THE AUSTRIAN SUCCESSION

IN 1740, Emperor Charles VI died without a male heir, and his lands passed to a daughter, Maria Theresa. Two months later, Frederick II of Prussia,

anticipating a partition of Habsburg domains, invaded Silesia. A Prussian victory at Mollwitz in 1741, hastened the formation of an anti-Habsburg coalition that included Bavaria, Spain and France, as well as Prussia. Illustrious victories by Frederick II in 1745 compelled Maria Theresa to sign the Treaty of Dresden on 25 December 1745, reaffirming Prussian control of Silesia. In 1745, the French had won a tremendous battle over a combined Austrian, English and Dutch force at Fontenoy, but had lost Canada. A general peace was finally concluded at Aix-la-Chapelle on 18 October 1748.

▲ *Frederick II, king of Prussia.*

1756   THE SEVEN YEARS' WAR

THE Seven Years' War pitted Britain and Prussia against Austria, France, Russia, Saxony, Sweden and (after 1762) Spain. On the European continent, hostilities began in 1756, when Frederick II (the Great) of Prussia, anticipating an assault from Maria Theresa of Austria and Elizabeth of Russia, launched a surprise offensive through the electorate of Saxony, a minor Austrian ally. Sweden aligned itself against Prussia, and Frederick's advance into Bohemia led to a Prussian defeat at Kolin in June 1757. A Russian army marched into East Prussia in August, and Austrian troops occupied Berlin for several days in October. Only Frederick's outstanding victories at Rossbach in November and at Leuthen a month later prevented the allies from overwhelming his kingdom.

1763   PRUSSIAN SOVEREIGNTY

COSTLY Prussian successes at Zorndorf in 1758 and again at Leignitz and
Torgau in 1760 only drained Frederick's limited resources. He suffered
another defeat, against the Russians, at Kunersdorf in 1759. By the end of
1761 the Austrians had moved into Saxony and Silesia, and Russian troops
held Prussian Pomerania. With enemy armies closing in around him,
Frederick seemed incapable of further resistance. At this critical moment the
Russian empress died (January 1762) and was succeeded by Peter III, one of
Frederick's devoted admirers. Peter immediately withdrew from the war, and
Austria, unable to defeat Prussia alone, was compelled to end the fighting in
Germany. A treaty confirming Prussian sovereignty over Silesia was signed at
Hubertusberg in 1763.

1775   AMERICAN REVOLUTION
(WAR OF INDEPENDENCE)

THE American Revolution was caused by colonial opposition to British
economic exploitation and anti-monarchist sentiment. The spark that
ignited wholesale revolution, came at Lexington, Massachusetts, on 19 April
1775. General Gage despatched a small force to seize illegal military stores at
Lexington. The local colonists' militia, known as minutemen, exchanged fire
with the British troops and the Battle of Lexington and Concord began the
Revolution. The second Continental
Congress met in Philadelphia May
1775 and adopted the rebel militias in
the field as the Continental Army;
George Washington was appointed
commander-in-chief. The British
were reinforced by the arrival in

▶ *The Battle of Bunker Hill, near Boston,*
during the American War of Independence.

Boston of William Howe, Sir Henry Clinton and John Burgoyne with additional troops raising their total force to 10,000.

1790s   VALMY AND JEMAPPES

THE nations of Europe began moving against revolutionary France even before the execution of Louis. In August, 1792, a joint Prussian-Austrian army invaded north-eastern France. They were met at Valmy, the day being won by the French. Other French forces pushed back the Austrian army at the Battle of Jemappes. In January 1793, the revolutionary government in Paris issued the infamous orders to execute King Louis and Marie-Antoinette. Britain was transformed from a concerned observer to an implacable foe. The Austrians were driven from the Netherlands, and The United Provinces (northern Holland) were annexed. By 1795, Prussia, Spain, Hanover and Saxony had all opted out of the coalition, leaving Britain and Austria to continue the fight against France's revolutionary government.

▲ *Napoleon Bonaparte.*

1799   THE RISE OF BONAPARTE

AUSTRIA was now fighting a lone war on the Continent. In Italy, Napoleon Bonaparte expelled the Austrians from northern Italy in a lightning campaign. They then joined up with Joubert's troops marching out of southern Germany and advanced on Vienna, forcing the Austrians to sue for peace. An Egyptian campaign in 1798 was a strategic failure. Back in Europe, a joint Austrian-Russian army managed to wrest most of northern Italy away from the French. Napoleon seized power in 1799 and a fresh French army defeated the Austrians at Marengo in Italy. By the end of 1800, the French were driving into southern Germany and the Austrian government sued for peace, bringing the French Revolutionary Wars to a close in early 1801.

Society and Culture

1759   THE CANALS

INCREASE in industrial production created problems; it meant that increased transport was required to carry goods to shops and markets and in the mid-eighteenth century, Britain's roads were not capable of standing the strain.

They were dusty, pitted, muddy, icy and dangerous depending on the time of year and factory owners had no faith in their carrying a regular supply of goods safely. The solution was water transport and after 1759, an artificial waterway, the Bridgewater Canal, was built connecting Manchester to the coal mines on the Duke of Bridgewater's estate at Worsley. A network of canals followed, built by gangs of strong, but rough-living navvies (navigators) who lived like nomads, moving from one location to the next.

▲ *The Bridgewater Canal, the first of many canals built to open up trading routes between the major cities in Britain.*

1770s   DANGER IN THE MINES

MINES were even more unhealthy than the mills and factories, if that were possible. Damp, cold, dark, dangerous, they were nevertheless the workplace for many men, women and children who spent long hours underground. Children of four or five sat all day opening and shutting doors. Pregnant women hauling trucks loaded with coal risked miscarriages or worse. The railways inside the mines could be death traps if, for instance, workers lost their hold on a truck and were knocked down and run over. Gas escaping from the coalface could choke them to death. Ceilings could cave in and bury or trap them. Yet there was no protection and if mineworkers could not work, they faced dismissal and starvation.

1770s   THE AGE OF ENLIGHTENMENT

THE humanism of the Renaissance had its effects on philosophy and politics, and gained its most powerful impetus in the eighteenth century. This was the Age of Enlightenment, which sought to remake society and its institutions in the light of pure reason. The Ancient Greek concept of democracy came to the fore with revived ideas about representative government. The French political philosopher Jean-Jacques Rousseau (1712–78) set out his own theories of democracy, of the right to elementary education. The Scots economist Adam Smith (1723–90), author of *The Wealth of Nations* (1776), advocated the untrammelled workings of free enterprise and the importance of free trade. All these ideas were revolutionary, given the traditional social and economic values they sought to replace.

▲ *Granville Sharp, one of the earliest philanthropists to fight for the abolition of slavery.*

1787   THE ABOLITION SOCIETY

BRITAIN had become the greatest slave-trading nation in Europe, yet it was here that positive moves were made to get the trade banned. In 1787 philanthropists, driven by religious belief, formed the Abolition Society. Abolitionists toured ports and interviewed slave-ship captains and crews to build up a picture of the horrors being perpetrated.

They faced violent objections, from plantation owners, from those who believed black savages to be 'natural' slaves, and from others who maintained that the slave trade was a training ground for sailors. Parliament finally banned the trade in 1807, 20 years later. Another 26 years went by before slavery itself was abolished in all British possessions.

Jacques Rousseau
28. VI. 1712. +2. VII. 1778.

▲ *French philosopher, author and liberal thinker Jean-Jacques Rousseau.*

1789   IDEAS OF REVOLUTION

THE French Revolution was well primed with liberal ideas through the writings of Voltaire (François-Marie Arouet) (1694–1778) and Jean Jacques Rousseau (1712–78). Its rallying cry 'Liberté, Egalité, Fraternité' ('Liberty, Equality and Brotherhood') largely encapsulated their principles. The people became paramount in French revolutionary thinking, which also required a complete break with the repressive past. Now, France was not the king's property, as before, but belonged to all who lived there. A new calendar was introduced, with 1789 as Year One, as well as a new religion, and the Cult of the Supreme Being, to replace the old Catholicism. These innovations did not last, but the primacy of the people, which the Revolution promoted, had come to stay.

1790s   THE DECLINE OF EUROPEAN FEUDALISM

THOUGH feudalism died in Britain after 1350, it persisted in France and Russia. In France, the liberalising revolution of 1789 brought it to an abrupt and bloody end. Russia was more isolated from European trends and it was not until 1861 that Tsar Alexander II (1818–81) abolished feudalism and freed the serfs. Russian feudalism had taken a particularly harsh form, and the serfs had been 'property', sold along with the feudal estates they worked. The tsar was assassinated by anarchists in 1881, but even 20 years of freedom had not released the serfs from their servile mindset. When anarchists called for rebellion against the tsar, they refused, clinging pathetically to their traditional belief that he was the 'Little Father', their protector and friend.

1790s   BRITAIN STANDS BACK

IN Britain, French revolutionary concepts made little headway. The British, in fact, gave sanctuary to French 'aristos' who fled across the English Channel to escape the revolutionaries' slaughter of their class. British kings were not absolute monarchs, but constitutional sovereigns, subject to the will of Parliament. Though most ordinary people had no voting rights, they were not brutally suppressed like the French feudal peasants. There was also a degree of religious toleration in Britain, although anti-Catholic and anti-Nonconformist laws persisted. There was no deep-seated popular resentment on which revolution could flourish in Britain.

▲ *Many French aristocrats fled to Britain to escape the Revolution.*

Exploration and Empires

1730s   THE TURKS AND POLAND CRUSHED

SUCCESSIVE Russian rulers from the Empress Anna to Catherine the Great initiated wars against the Turks and took part in wider European conflicts throughout the eighteenth century. The first war against the Turks, launched in 1735, ended in a humiliating political settlement in 1739, in which the tremendous gains the Russians had made were given up when their Habsburg allies signed a peace treaty. But during the reign of Catherine the Great (1762–96) further gains were made at the Turks' expense. Russia also participated with the Habsburgs and Prussia in three partitions of Poland, which extinguished that once-powerful eastern-European state.

1741   THE WAR FOR NORTH AMERICA

THE growing wealth of the British colonies along the Atlantic coast of North America, in part based on the profits from slavery, attracted more and more settlers. These newcomers were desperate for land, and this resulted in a series of wars with French colonies in the St Lawrence river valley and around the Great Lakes. Although these coincided with the wars in Europe,

▶ *Conflict sprang up between British and French colonists in North America in the 1740s.*

they were fought independently. Fighting broke out in 1741, halted briefly in 1748, and resumed in 1754. At the end of the conflict in North America, in 1760, the British had pushed the French out of their main colony on the mainland, Quebec.

1757   THE END OF ISLAMIC INDIA

A NEW Hindu power that could withstand the advance of the Mogul armies arose in southern India during the end of the seventeenth century: the Marathas. The strength of the Marathas, combined with internal unrest in the Mogul empire, helped to overthrow the effective power of the sultan in Delhi. He became effectively a figurehead ruler, and India was once more divided into warring states. These included the European traders, who brought the conflicts from home to India. In 1757, the army of the East India Company, led by Robert Clive, defeated the army of the Naxab of Bengal at Plassey. The effect of this victory was to make England the strongest political power in India.

▲ *Captain James Cook, whose expeditions into the Pacific opened up the world to further settlement.*

1769   JAMES COOK

THERE remained many unresolved questions about the Pacific, and the Englishman James Cook (1728–79) helped answer many of these through his forages into the unknown seas in those parts. He plotted many unexplored areas in this part of the world from 1769 on. Cook produced a chart of New Zealand and, after landing in Botany Bay, he claimed the Australian south-east coast for Britain, calling it New South Wales (1769). Cook also made an exploration of the Great Barrier Reef, and proved that New Guinea was not connected to Australia. He made another voyage to New Zealand between 1772 and 1775, before being killed in Hawaii in 1779.

1780s   DEFINING THE BOUNDARIES

FRENCH aid to the United States, starting from 1778, tipped the balance of the war in favour of the Americans. In 1781, a large British army trapped at Yorktown, Virginia, surrendered. Fighting an alliance of France, Spain and the United States was beyond British resources. In 1783, a treaty ended the war. But enforcing this independence was not easy. Britain saw no reason to give up valuable fur trading posts around the Great Lakes, while Spain hoped to gain territorial advantages in the lands north of Florida and east of Louisiana. It took a major war with the Native Americans of the Midwest and the aggressive deployment of soldiers in the South to secure the 1783 borders. By 1796, the borders of the United States had finally been firmly fixed along the Great Lakes and the Mississippi river.

1788   THE PENAL COLONY

ALTHOUGH Spanish and French missionaries, traders and whalers increasingly colonised the Pacific, Australasia was left to Britain, who decided to use New South Wales as a penal colony. Eleven ships carrying 700 convicts, 36 women and guards, plus provisions for two years, arrived in Botany Bay in 1788 and settled around Sydney Cove. Few people travelled beyond the Great Dividing Range that stretches for 4,800 km (7,000 miles) up the east coast. The British had no powerful neighbours to threaten the colony, but faced the problem of economic viability and a population composed largely of criminals. In 1801, however, Napoleon Bonaparte (1769–1821) sent Thomas-Nicholas Baudin to the Australian coast. In response Britain sent Matthew Flinders to survey the entire coastline of the country, which he called Australia.

▶ *The governor of the newly established penal colony in New South Wales, inspecting convict settlers.*

1793   CHINA IN CHAOS

CHINA'S rulers rejected an attempt by Britain to widen the scope for traders in the East Asian empire in 1793. Trade took place on a controlled basis only, in a few ports. But the most popular import was an addictive drug, opium. The social havoc this wreaked led the Chinese to attempt blocking the supply, and caused the First Opium War (1839–42). At the end of this conflict, Britain had acquired Hong Kong, and freer trade had been agreed. China now tipped into chaos. In 1850 a dangerous revolt that threatened the ruling Manchu dynasty broke out in the south of the country. The Tai-ping rebellion eventually took control of central China for many years, until it was suppressed with European help in 1864.

▲ *A meeting between the British and the Chinese during the first Opium War.*

1798   FRANCE AND EGYPT

DURING the wars between Revolutionary France and the rest of Europe, the French government decided to threaten Britain's link with India by invading Egypt. In July 1798 the attacking force arrived off the Egyptian coast. The French conquered Egypt, but abandoned these gains following the defeat of their fleet and army by the British. In 1802 the French army left, and after several years of instability, Mohammed Ali came to power in 1809, nominally as the viceroy of the Turkish sultan. Mohammed Ali wanted to be an in-dependent ruler, and pursued this aim single-mindedly, frequently with French support. At the time of his death in 1849, Egypt controlled the Nile valley as far as Khartoum, and both sides of the Red Sea coast.

Trade and Industry

1700s   TARIFFS

A TARIFF is a schedule of customs duties, sometimes called imposts, generally imposed by a government on imports, and sometimes also on exports. Tariffs were originally levied to raise revenue. In the sixteenth and seventeenth centuries, when national economies and nation states were coming into being, they were imposed mainly as instruments of government economic policy. The purpose might be to protect domestic industries against foreign competition. It was common for a government to levy high, discriminatory tariffs as a means of displaying hostility towards another. Equally, friendly nations might be accorded preferential treatment. Almost every peace treaty concluded between warring powers in Europe after 1700 contained a most-favoured nation clause compelling the two sides to extend to each other tariff treatment as favourable as that accorded to any other nation.

1709   COAL AND IRON

ABRAHAM Darby (*c.* 1678–1717) independently developed the use of coal (in the form of coke) for blast furnaces to increase their output. This turned Europe and then North America into the workhouse of the world for the next two centuries. Darby, who had used coke in smelting

▶ *The iron bridge over the Severn at Coalbrookdale.*

copper, founded the Bristol Iron Company in 1708. He acquired premises at Coalbrookdale, on the Severn, near supplies of low-sulphur coal. In 1709 he made marketable iron in a coke-fired furnace. Soon he was able to demonstrate the superior cheapness and efficiency of coke by building much larger furnaces than were possible with charcoal as a fuel. The quality of the iron permitted the manufacture of thin castings, which were as good as brass for making such items as pots and other hollow wares. It was at Coalbrookdale that one of the world's first cast-iron bridges was built (1799).

1750s   CHANGE IN EUROPE

IN western Europe the most important change in agriculture in the mid-eighteenth century was the spread of potato cultivation. In the environment of, for example, Germany, the calorie content of a potato crop was about four times that of a grain crop. In the Balkans and Hungary, maize played a similar role in enlarging food-production capacity. In communications France led the way in developing all-weather roads and a system of canals that connected with natural waterways. In manufacturing England took the lead, offering plenty of scope for private enterprise and hands-on inventiveness. New crafts were also created by imitation of the products of other countries. By trial and error, Europeans learnt how to replicate Chinese porcelain.

1760s   THE COTTON INDUSTRY

RICHARD Arkwright (1732–92), an inventor and businessman, invented the spinning frame, which could produce strong cotton thread. Arkwright was the first person to use one of James Watt's steam engines to drive machines, for spinning and weaving, in a cotton mill. These machines could spin not just one thread, as on a hand-powered spinning wheel, but hundreds of threads.

WILLS'S CIGARETTES.

ARKWRIGHT'S SPINNING MACHINE.

▲ *Richard Arkwright's spinning machine.*

Manchester became the centre of the cotton industry in Britain and was sometimes known as 'Cottonopolis'. It grew rapidly during the Industrial Revolution, but the people who worked in the factories lived in unhealthy, filthy, overcrowded slums, without running water, on unpaved streets lacking drains or mains sewers.

1776   FREE-TRADE THEORY

THE first free-trade theorists were a group of eighteenth-century followers of the economist François Quesnay, known as the physiocrats. They maintained that the free movement of goods accords with the principles of natural liberty. Government intervention is justified only to the extent necessary to ensure free markets. This is because a nation's well-being is best secured if individuals are allowed complete freedom to pursue their economic interests. The national advantage represents the sum total of individual advantage. The free-trade system, which prevailed during the nineteenth century, received its most eloquent expression in *The Wealth of Nations* (1776), by the Scottish economist Adam Smith. The policy stands in opposition to mercantilism, which put a high value on national self-sufficiency, guaranteed, if necessary, by high protective tariffs.

1782   WATT'S STEAM ENGINE

JAMES Watt (1736–1819) was the most important engineer of the Industrial Revolution. While working at the University of Glasgow, he was asked to repair a working model of a steam engine used for pumping water that had been

▲ *James Watt's steam engine.*

invented by Thomas Newcomen in 1705. Realising he could build much better engines, from the 1760s onwards he applied himself to this. Using only a quarter of the coal needed by earlier engines, these were cheaper to run and more powerful. In partnership with Matthew Boulton in Birmingham, Watt built steam engines that could drive all kinds of machinery, for example to lift coal to the surface in mines. In Watt's first steam engine, a coal fire heated water to make steam. In 1782 he built the first rotary steam engine, with cogs and wheels, so that the engine could turn wheels and drive machinery. The watt, the unit of electrical power, is named after him.

1789   AN END TO SERFDOM

SERFDOM in Russia was a system in which the peasants were theoretically free tenants but were in fact in servitude to the landowners, who exploited them mercilessly, demanding ever-larger shares of the crops. By the late seventeenth century serfs were usually heavily in debt to their masters and were virtually chattel slaves. The system persisted until the mid-nineteenth century in Russia and other parts of eastern Europe. Tsar Alexander II (r. 1855–81) abolished serfdom throughout Russia in 1861. In western Europe feudalism and serfdom had almost disappeared by the eighteenth century and the French Revolution of 1789 put the final nail in their coffin. Former serfs had by then attained a degree of economic independence and even become small landowners in their own right.

1793   THE COTTON GIN

TWO notable agricultural inventions of the eighteenth century were the seed drill, developed by the English agriculturalist Jethro Tull (1674–1741). The seed drill cuts a furrow in the soil and then drops the seed through a tube. It sows the seed in rows, permitting cultivation between the rows and thus reducing the need for weeding. The seed drill featured a rotary mechanism on which all subsequent sowing implements were based. The cotton gin, invented in 1793 by the American inventor Eli Whitney (1765–1825), cleaned the cotton by separating the seeds from the fibres of the short-staple cotton plant (work hitherto done by hand). The efficient design remains in use today almost unchanged.

Science and Technology

1700s   ELECTRICITY ENTERS THE PICTURE

VARIOUS experiments were conducted over the early half of the eighteenth century in an effort to understand the nature of electricity, more out of curiosity than through any recognition of its potential. One of Newton's pupils, Francis Hauksbee, invented a device called an Influence Machine in 1706. It was a glass globe that demonstrated the glow of air molecules by friction and the way electricity would attract various items of metal and threads. Stephen Gray discovered in 1729 that a thread would carry the attractive force down its length from the machine. In 1745 the Leyden jar was developed by Kleist and Musschenbroek as a means for storing electricity, and by 1749 electricity saw its first practical application, firing mines and other explosives. In 1786, Luigi Galvani showed that electricity stimulated movement in frogs' legs by inventing the cathode and anode cycle, which led in 1796

▲ *The eighteenth century saw the discovery and first uses of electricity; today it is an integral part of our lives and landscape.*

to fellow Italian, Alessandro Volta, building his Voltaic Pile battery, comprising layers of copper and zinc.

1700s   NEWTON'S MATHEMATICS

ISAAC Newton (1642–1727) was an English physicist and mathematician who laid the foundation for the discipline of modern physics by demonstrating that scientific principles are of universal application. He investigated various phenomena during his lifetime, making some notable discoveries and developing explanatory laws. In the 1700s, he developed theories on calculus, based on the work of fellow mathematician John Wallis. He also described three laws of motion and defined the nature of weight, mass, force, acceleration and inertia. His most famous work concerned gravity, on which he expounded in 1685, saying – 'Every particle of matter in the universe attracts every other particle with a force whose direction is that of the line joining the two, and whose magnitude is directly as the product of the masses, and inversely as the square of their distances from each other.'

▲ *Sir Isaac Newton, whose scientific principles paved the way for modern physics.*

1720s   CALCULATING MACHINES AND COMPUTERS

SEVERAL calculating machines were conceived before the Industrial Revolution. John Napier (1550–1617), Blaise Pascal (1623–62) and Gottfried Von Liebnitz all came up with devices. In the 1720s, Basile Bouchon devised a machine that worked on the punched-card principle of the Jacquard Loom. In 1835, Charles Babbage (1792–1871) conceived and drew up plans for his computer named the 'Analytical Engine'. It was never made, but it embodied the principles on which modern digital computers are based. Herman Hollerith, an American, made a tabulating machine that was used to take a census in 1890. It introduced individual punched cards as a means for sending or blocking signals, which could then be counted to calculate the census results.

▲ *Sir Richard Arkwright, inventor of the first automated spinning machine.*

1733   TEXTILE AUTOMATION

AS the Industrial Revolution gathered pace, one of the first large-scale industries to be affected by technological developments was the textiles industry. Many thousands toiled in textile mills where processes had traditionally been very labour-intensive.

Then suddenly, engineers started introducing machines for automating processes that obviated the need for large workforces. The machines introduced included John Kay's (1704–64) Flying Shuttle in 1733, James Hargreaves's (d. 1778) Spinning Jenny in 1767, Richard Arkwright's (1732–92) Spinning Frame in 1769, Samuel Crompton's (1753–1827) Spinning Mule in 1779 and Edmund Cartwright's (1743–1823) Power Loom in 1785. Added to these, James Watt's steam engine was introduced in 1769 as a power supply, instead of water.

1757   ORIGINS OF PRECISION ENGINEERING

ONE of the key factors in the success of new industrial processes leading into the Industrial Revolution, was the ability of engineers to make very precise components for their machines and apparatus. One area that demanded extreme accuracy, and therefore spearheaded such techniques, was instrumentation for navigation. The sextant was an instrument for calculating position by aligning the horizon with a specific star or the Sun. When it had a telescope added to it in 1757 its potential for accuracy was improved considerably, but the divisions scribed on the scale (six for each degree) now needed to be marked far more accurately. The solution came in 1774 with the Ramsden dividing engine. It introduced the concept of using a tangent screw

► *James Hargreaves's Spinning Jenny, a machine that could spin eight bobbins at one time.*

or worm-gear for making minute adjustments. The worm-gear was then incorporated into lathes and other machinery and hailed the beginning of mass production of precision-made components in all areas of industry. The concept of interchangeable parts was also born, because the new machinery would now make things to exactly the same specifications every time.

1770   THE FIRST STEAM VEHICLES

AS WELL as driving the wheels of industry, the steam engine was recognised before long as a means for propelling vehicles. The first recorded example was a carriage designed for pulling field guns. Nicolas Cugnot designed and constructed it in 1770 in Paris. It was a cumbersome machine; difficult to steer and constantly running short of steam. Richard Trevithick (1771–1833) was the first to build a steam-powered locomotive, which he ran on the Penydarren railway in Wales in 1804. By the 1820s locomotives were becoming a familiar sight and the brittle cast-iron tracks had to be replaced with wrought iron, as the locomotives became heavier and more powerful. The first steam-powered boat was made by Claude d'Abbans and took to the water in 1783. The engine, made by Frèrejean et Cie, rotated a large paddle wheel.

1781   THE DISCOVERY OF HYDROGEN

WORK on gases eventually led to the realisation that materials are either made up of pure elements or they are made from molecules, which comprise combinations of elements. Henry Cavendish (1731–1810) discovered hydrogen by experimenting with acids on metals. In 1781 he ignited a mixture of hydrogen and air and was amazed to find that he had created water, which was thought to be an element. By 1814, a Swedish chemist called Jöns Berzelius (1779–1848) had devised various symbols to represent elements and compounds, and he went on to publish tables indicating atomic and molecular weights of over 2,000 chemicals. The 'Periodic Table', based on atomic mass, was devised in 1869 by Russian chemist, Dmitri Mendeleyev (1834–1907). The table grouped similarly massed elements together vertically and ranked them horizontally according to characteristics. It had to include blank spaces as well, indicating that there must be elements as yet undiscovered, which have since been found or artificially created by scientists.

▲ *English chemist Henry Cavendish, who discovered hydrogen.*

1792   COAL REFINING AND APPLICATIONS

IN 1792, William Murdoch (1754–1839) invented an apparatus for processing coal by 'destructive distillation'. By heating coal to very high temperatures without the presence of air, it would break down into component fractions, including gases, liquids and solids, all of which proved to have useful applications during the Industrial Revolution. Coal gas was used for lighting and as a fuel for the internal-combustion engine. Coal tar was used for waterproofing canvas to make tarpaulin. Naptha was used as a solvent for rubber in the Mackintosh process. Pitch, bitumen and asphalt were used for building road surfaces and other sealing applications, such as in roofing. Coke was the carbon content of the coal, bereft of all the other hydrocarbons listed above, and was used as fuel industrially and domestically. Its most important role by far was as the fuel in blast furnaces for producing the vast quantities of iron and steel consumed in the Industrial Revolution.

1796   INOCULATION AND VACCINATION

INOCULATION from smallpox had been practised for many years before the Industrial Revolution, by using infected tissue from a sufferer to induce a mild form of the disease in a healthy person, who would then develop resistance to the full-blown disease. There were inherent risks though, which actually resulted in a higher overall mortality rate. In 1796 a British scientist called Edward Jenner (1749–1823) managed to inoculate a boy against smallpox by using cowpox vesicles. Cowpox was a related disease, which caused the boy to develop the antibodies in his system necessary to fight off smallpox. This became known as a non-variolous vaccination, and established the practice of using either dead or related pathogenic organisms for inoculating against serious diseases.

▲ *Dr Edward Jenner giving the first vaccination against smallpox.*

Religions, Belief and Thought

1700 THE BA'AL SHEM TOV AND HASIDISM

RABBI Israel ben Eliezer, The 'Ba'al Shem Tov' or 'Master of the good name', was born in the Ukraine in 1700. After living in Spain, he worked as a lime digger in Romania. He became a herbalist and earned the title of 'ba'al shem', and whilst practising herbalism he promoted his religious teachings through simple stories and parables. His teachings of joy in response to the immanence of God in the world and of the superiority of spiritual emotion over intellectual religious understanding proved highly popular amongst the uneducated Jews of eastern Europe. He meditated in the forests, taught that God was present in nature, and was prone to spontaneous singing, dancing and storytelling. The emphasis upon sincere prayer and continual awareness of God's presence differed markedly from the legalistic and oppressive Judaism of his time.

1748 JOHN WESLEY AND THE METHODISTS

JOHN Wesley was the founder of the Methodist movement, an offshoot of the Church of England. The name derives from the methodical approach he

▲ *Founder of the Methodist movement, John Wesley.*

applied to studying the Bible for developing personal devotion. He promoted his approach at outdoor sermons throughout Britain, to which he dedicated 12 years of his life. His decision to employ lay preachers in support of his mission, then to ordain them, led to a split with the Church of England and in 1748 he created the Methodist Church. Reinforced by the profuse production of hymns by his brother, Charles, the movement spread rapidly in America and Wales.

1762   ROUSSEAU'S *EMILE*

JEAN-JACQUES Rousseau was renowned as the greatest liberal thinker and advocate of democracy and freedom in the eighteenth century. His writings covered every discipline from education to politics and from theology to science, but all were held together by his underlying belief in the innate goodness of human nature and the natural world and the corrupting influence of artificial culture. In his *Emile* (1762) he presented healthy education as a result of

innate curiosity about the world and not as a result of coercive lessons. The only healthy governments were those that emerged from a social contract between free and equal citizens. Christian living involved allowing God to act in our lives and in nature and in minimising our ignorant interference with this process.

1770s JEREMY BENTHAM AND UTILITARIANISM

JEREMY Bentham's utilitarian theory of ethics is that an act is good to the degree that it contributes to the greatest

◀ *English Utilitarian philosopher Jeremy Bentham.*

happiness of the greatest number. If an act gives one unit of pleasure to three people and causes two units of pain to another person then it is better to do this act than not to do it. This 'scientific' approach to ethics distinguishes it from approaches, such as the Christian one, which are based on justice or on the intentions of the person acting. This position was developed by his student, John Stuart Mill (1806–73), in his book, *Utilitarianism* (1861).

1770s GOETHE'S CRITIQUE OF REDUCTIONISM

JOHANN Wolfgang Goethe (1749–1832), Germany's greatest literary figure, was one of the foremost critics of reductionist science in the eighteenth century. He argued that as the natural world can only be known through subjective and qualitative experience, the process of reducing these experiences to mathematical quantities was not empirical. He felt that scientists were deliberately blinding themselves to the reality of the natural world and replacing it with an abstraction. This allowed them to treat nature as an inanimate object and to exploit it for their own ends. To counter this problem he attempted to develop a theory of colour that incorporated the direct sensory experience of different colours. It is generally felt that his critique is of more value than the alternatives he developed.

▶ *Bust of Johann Wolfgang Goethe.*

1776 ADAM SMITH: *THE WEALTH OF NATIONS*

ADAM Smith (1723–90) was a Scottish economist and philosopher and the founder of modern economics. His most important publication, *An Inquiry into the Nature and Causes of the Wealth of Nations* (1776), explores the function of the market and explains how free trade, free enterprise and the free

division of labour can work for the benefit of all. He describes this as the action of a 'hidden hand'. In common with the French *laissez-faire* economists, he advocated free international trade. He is seen today as a politically 'right wing' thinker who advocated the selfish pursuit of profit. However it is often forgotten that he also wrote and lectured extensively on social ethics, justice and meaningful work. He was the author of the *Theory of Moral Sentiments* (1752) and donated the majority of his own wealth to charity.

▲ *Scottish economist Adam Smith.*

1789 THE FRENCH REVOLUTION

'LIBERTÉ, Egalité et Fraternité' was the rallying cry of the revolutionaries who stormed the Bastille in 1789 and overthrew the monarchy. The French Revolution was a series of political events that abolished the absolute power of the king and the rich landowners and replaced it with a Republic elected by all the people. The new Government adopted the 'Declaration of the Rights of Man and of the Citizen' declaring everyone equal and free and subject to fair taxes. Perversely this was imposed through a reign of terror. The Revolution, despite its violence and tyranny, inspired political radicalism across Europe.

1792   ROBERT OWEN AND NEW LANARK

ROBERT Owen (1771–1858) a manager of a spinning factory in Manchester, disillusioned with poor working conditions, became a practical utopian. He sought in 1792 to create a new type of community in the village of New Lanark, where originally children as young as five worked 13 hours a day. He created schools, increased the minimum working age to 10, decreased the working day and supported trade unions, factory reform and votes for all. Disillusioned with the slow results he started another community, New Harmony, in the United States, which his son then managed. His ideas were published in *A New View of Society* (1814) and he addressed parliament on this subject in 1816.

▶ *Cartoon depicting English philanthropist Robert Owen.*

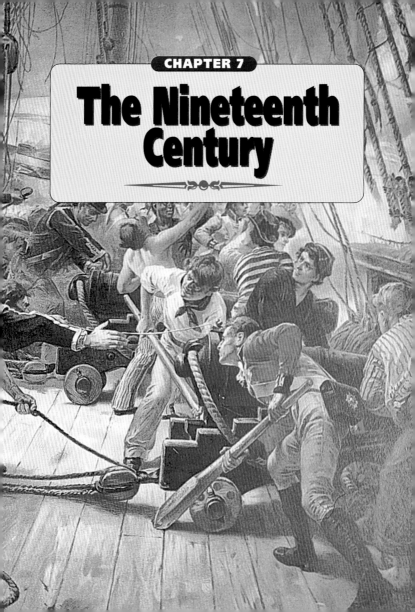

CHAPTER 7

The Nineteenth Century

Power and Politics

1800s   NATIVE AMERICANS VS SETTLERS

THE States of the Union in America began to expand as soon as the Constitution was ratified. This began the long period of conflict between the

▲ *The Native American way of life was to change irrevocably with the arrival of European settlers.*

colonists and the Native Indians, who found themselves being forced further and further west. In Georgia the Cherokee Indians, who had developed an advanced culture with newspapers, schools and libraries, were evicted from their homelands. President Jackson forced them to move west of the Mississippi, which was to become the final home for the southern Indians. The journey west became known as the Trail of Tears. But

this was to be only the first of a whole series of evictions, culminating in the obliteration of the Sioux at the battle of Wounded Knee in 1890.

1815   THE HABSBURGS

THE Habsburgs, the Austrian royal family, ruled a large empire, that covered much of central Europe. At the end of the Napoleonic War they had been given, in addition, most of northern and central Italy. Their empire was governed from Vienna by the emperor, but was very multinational and multi-lingual in character. To the east there were Hungarians, Czechs, Slovaks and Ruthenians, to the south there were Italians, Croats and Slovenes and to the north there were Poles. The Habsburgs knew that, of all the empires of Europe, theirs was the most vulnerable to nationalism. For 33 years, from 1815 to 1848, any sign of nationalism was eradicated without mercy.

1820s NATIONALISM

NATIONALISM, the concept of the nation state, was uncommon in the eighteenth century. Then autocratic power was exercised by hereditary royal families, not by the people whom they ruled. The French Revolution and Napoleon's Empire created a new sense of national identity in France and abroad, and as early as the 1790s there were demands for reform in both Britain and Austria. The demands in Britain succeeded in the 1830s, but elsewhere, autocracy struck back using repression. In the 1820s radical movements throughout Europe were crushed by the armies of Russia, Austria and Prussia.

▲ *The Austrian Habsburgs dynasty ruled one of the largest empires in Europe.*

1844 THE *ZOLLVEREIN*

THE *Zollverein* was an economic union set up by Prussia in 1819. The Rhineland had been given to Prussia at the Treaty of Vienna in 1815 and the Prussians decided to set common tariffs for all their territories, creating a customs union, or *Zollverein*. Other German states joined and by 1844 almost all of Germany was included. Although the *Zollverein* was not a political force, it led to Prussia being seen as the leader of Germany with the result that many German states were drawn into a Prussian sphere of influence and away from Austria. It laid the basis for the nation state of Germany and challenged the German Confederation, set up in 1815, and dominated by Austria.

1857　　THE INDIAN MUTINY

IN 1857 there was a revolt against the East India Company by members of its army. To the British it was seen as mutiny; to Indians it marked the beginnings of Indian nationalism. The revolt began when a new cartridge was introduced. Muslims came to believe that it was smeared with pig fat. Hindus came to believe that it was smeared with cow fat. East India Company control broke down in many parts of northern India and in 1858 the British Government took over the government of India. In the 1860s and 1870s a number of nationalist movements were set up, culminating in the Indian National Congress in 1885. It was this organisation which led the fight for independence in the twentieth century.

▲ *The Indian Mutiny, which eventually led to British government over India.*

1862   BISMARCK

OTTO von Bismarck became Chancellor
of Germany in 1862. He was a conservative Prussian politician, who
wanted to extend Prussia's dominance in Germany by uniting the
country under the king of Prussia.
He followed the policy of
realpolitik, which meant that he was
ready to use any means to achieve
his ends. In 1864 Bismarck, in
alliance with Austria, declared war on
Denmark and took Schleswig. In 1866
he firstly signed a treaty with France and
then picked a quarrel with Austria. The
French remained neutral, but the Austrian
army was crushed in seven weeks. When the
peace terms were discussed, Bismarck insisted on
being lenient to Austria; he knew that he would want its support in the future.

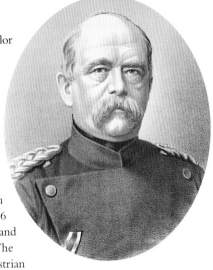

▲ *Otto von Bismarck*

1871   ALSACE-LORRAINE

THE provinces of Alsace and Lorraine were taken by Germany at the end of
the Franco-Prussian War. They became part of the new German Empire. This
was bitterly resented in France. For more than 40 years the statue in Paris,
which represented the city of Strasbourg, the capital of Alsace, was draped in
black cloth. *Revanchisme*, 'revenge', became important in French politics. The
French actress, Sarah Bernhardt, refused to appear in Germany. When she was
asked to name her fee by a theatre manager, she sent a telegram with the
words 'Alsace-Lorraine'. It was obvious that sooner or later France would
attempt to regain the lost provinces and the main battle plan of the French
Army, 'Plan 17', involved a direct assault from Champagne into Germany.

1878   AUSTRIA VS RUSSIA: SEEDS OF WAR

TURKISH power in the Balkans began to collapse in the middle of the
nineteenth century. Greece became independent in the 1820s, and Romania,
Bulgaria and Serbia emerged at the end of the nineteenth century. This
created an area in South-East Europe in which there were many small states,
but no dominant great power. Both Russia and the Austrian Empire tried to
advance into the Balkans. Austria was given control of Bosnia and
Herzegovina in 1878 and annexed the territories in 1908. Russia formed an
alliance with Serbia. They had a common script and the same religion. It was
to be the clash between these two powers, that was to lead to the outbreak of
the First World War in 1914.

1882   THE DUAL AND TRIPLE ALLIANCES

THE Dual Alliance was signed
between Germany and Austria in
1879. It became the most important part of Bismarck's attempts to
give Germany security. It was
aimed at Russia. If either power
was attacked by Russia, the other
would declare war immed
iately. In 1882 the Dual Alliance
was extended to become the
Triple Alliance with the inclusion
of Italy. While these agreements
gave Bismarck some security, they

▶ *A meeting between Bismarck
and Napoleon III.*

isolated Russia, so in 1881 he had arranged the Alliance of Three Emperors, between Germany, Austria and Russia. This was based on the DreiKaiser-Bund, but this time contained a series of terms. This agreement was renewed in 1884, but in 1887 Russia refused to sign. Bismarck quickly concluded a secret treaty with Russia, the Reinsurance Treaty, which was designed to prevent Russia forming an alliance with France.

1894 THE DUAL ENTENTE

IN 1887, Wilhelm II became emperor of Germany. He soon disagreed with Bismarck and demanded his resignation in 1890. As a result, Russia refused to renew the Reinsurance Treaty in 1890. Instead, relations between Russia and France grew much closer. In January 1894 they signed the Dual Entente, which was intended to be a counterweight to the Triple Alliance. Both powers agreed to defend the other if attacked by Germany

▲ *Emperor Wilhelm II of Germany.*

and to mobilise their forces immediately if the powers of the Triple Alliance mobilised. The Dual Entente created the situation that Bismarck had tried for so long to avoid, the possibility of a war on two fronts, with Germany caught between the armies of France and Russia.

War and Peace

1805   TRAFALGAR AND AUSTERLITZ

IN one of history's most famous military manoeuvres, Napoleon marched his main Grande Armée into Germany and surrounded the Austrian army. With their strategic centre breached, the Austrians were unable to prevent the French occupation of Vienna, and in December 1805 the remaining allied army catastrophically lost the Battle of Austerlitz to Napoleon, knocking Austria out of the wars for several years. In the Atlantic, the French and Spanish Navies were caught by the British fleet after their attempt to secure the English Channel for Napoleon. The resulting naval battle off Cape Trafalgar was one of the greatest in history, for its time, and resulted in the destruction of both the French and Spanish fleets, but at the cost of Nelson's life.

▼ *Nelson on deck at the Battle of Trafalgar.*

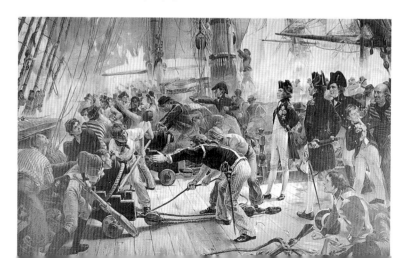

1813   THE BATTLE OF LEIPZIG

THE new allied coalition of Great Britain, Russia, Prussia, Spain, Portugal, Austria and Sweden slowly ground down the remaining French armies. Austria especially had not suffered a significant military defeat in eight years, and her relatively intact armies were to form the backbone of the 1813 and 1814 campaigns. Despite victories at the battles of Lutzen, Bautzen and Dresden, the French Army suffered a crushing defeat at the huge three-day Battle of Leipzig in October 1813. By 1814 allied armies were advancing into France from every direction and despite continuing French resistance, Paris surrendered on 31 March 1814. A few days later, Napoleon surrendered unconditionally, and was exiled to the island of Elba in the Mediterranean.

1835   THE TEXAN WAR OF INDEPENDENCE

IN November 1835 a convention of Anglo-American settlers set up a provisional state government and declared that Texans were fighting for the rights due them under the Mexican Constitution. A Texan army was quickly gathered and marched to attack the Mexican garrison at San Antonio. For 13 days the small force defended the Alamo against more than 5,000 Mexican troops. On 6 March, the Alamo fell. The Texans had almost 800 men when they faced Santa Anna's force of about 1,600 soldiers at San Jacinto. Taking the Mexican Army by surprise, most of Santa Anna's troops were killed or wounded. Santa Anna was captured the next day, and in Velasco on 14 May, he was forced to recognise Texas's independence and to withdraw south of the Rio Grande.

▲ *The Mexican army taking the Alamo.*

1845 MAORI WARS

IN 1841 New Zealand became a separate colony of Great Britain, and British government and settlements were established. The resultant loss of Maori tribal lands triggered the Maori revolts against British rule from 1845 to 1848 and again from 1860 to 1870. At Gate Pah, in 1864, the British attacked the Maori stockade with an overwhelming force. After a bombardment and several assaults the stockade fell with the loss of over 100 men. The Maoris had lost just 30, having abandoned their defences just before the final assault. Peace was permanently established in 1871, however, after which the Maori gained representation in the New Zealand Parliament that had been established in 1852.

▲ *Florenmce Nightingale's work in the Crimea paved the way for more sanitary nursing conditions.*

1854 CRIMEAN WAR

IN 1853 Tsar Nicholas I of Russia demanded the right to protect Christian shrines in Jerusalem, then part of the Turkish Empire. As a first step, his troops moved into the Turkish Balkans. By August 1854, Turkey, with the help of Britain, France and Sardinia, had driven the Russian forces out of the Balkans. The allied troops landed in the Crimean peninsula on 16 September 1854, and laid siege to the Russian fortress of Sevastopol. Battles were fought at the Alma River, at Balaklava and Inkerman. During the siege of Sevastopol disease took a dreadful toll of French and British troops. Florence Nightingale's heroic work as head of the hospital service did much to improve conditions. By September 1855, Sevastopol was in allied hands.

1865   UNION

THROUGHOUT the American Civil War, the South were disadvantaged in terms of manpower and materials. The more populous and industrialised North could always deploy larger and better equipped armies in the field. The South, however, boasted some of the most talented commanders of the century; Stonewall Jackson, J. E. B. Stuart, Jubal Early and their senior commander, Robert E. Lee. Lee sustained the South

▲ *Florence Nightingale receiving the wounded in the Crimea.*

far beyond their true capacity, defeating numerous Union generals in decisive and well-managed battles. He failed to defeat the Union army at Gettysburg, and in 1864 faced Grant, the new northern commander. Forced on to the defensive, he nevertheless inflicted heavy losses on Grant at the battles of the Wilderness, Spotsylvania and Cold Harbor. Early in April 1865 he met Grant at Appomattox and surrendered the Army of Northern Virginia.

1874   INCREASES IN MILITARY EXPENDITURE

BETWEEN 1874 and 1896 European military expenditure increased by 50 per cent. The tsar, fearful of the horrors of modern warfare and concerned by the rise in spending and the expansion of the armies, called a disarmament conference at the Hague in 1899. Even the Americans, who had only just recovered from a devastating civil war, took the position that any reduction in arms and troops should be considered potentially dangerous to peace. In the event, the conference was doomed to failure and no meaningful agreements were reached.

1879 THE ZULU WAR

CONVINCED that the independent Zulu kingdom adjoining the new British possessions in South Africa was a serious threat, an ultimatum was delivered ordering the Zulus to disband their army. Knowing that the Zulus would refuse, a British and colonial army under Chelmsford crossed the Buffalo River in January 1879. Hopelessly underestimating the tactical ability of the Zulus, Chelmsford split his forces and left the way clear for the enemy to attack the British camp. A full six British companies were slaughtered, in addition to several hundred black and white colonial troops. A

▲ *British forces defending the hospital at Rorke's Drift against the Zulus.*

wing of the huge Zulu army crossed the Buffalo, but was driven off at high cost by a small force at the hospital station at Rorke's Drift.

▲ *Muhammed Ahmed – the Mahdi.*

1881 THE MAHDI

IN 1881, Muhammad Ahmed declared himself the Mahdi, the prophesied Muslim messiah who would rid the world of evil, and launched a holy war on the infidel occupiers of Sudan. The Mahdi led a victorious attack on Al Ubayyid in 1883, and went on to capture all of the Darfur region of western Sudan, defeating an Egyptian army led by British Colonel William Hicks. In 1884 British General Charles George Gordon was dispatched to Khartoum to evacuate Egyptian troops. The Mahdi's forces surrounded Khartoum and besieged the city for 10 months, while Gordon begged the British government for reinforcements. On 26 January 1885, two days before British reinforcements arrived, Khartoum fell and Gordon and his entire garrison were massacred. The British reconquered Sudan in 1898.

Society and Culture

1800s   LIFE AS A CONVICT EXILE

IN 1788 a convict fleet of 11 ships sailed for Botany Bay in Australia. The worst punishment for convicts after the death penalty was transportation to an unknown land as far from Britain as possible. Fortunately, when they reached Australia, the convicts were able to use their work skills to build houses and lay out streets. They even built prisons. Others were put to work labouring on the land to produce food. Some, however, resorted to crime and were sent as prisoners to nearby Norfolk Island. The conditions there were so frightful that prisoners about to be hanged told a visiting priest that they welcomed the punishment since it would 'take them out of this terrible place'.

1825   THE END OF
SPANISH AMERICA

BY 1810, Spaniards, natives and the mixed-blood 'mestizos', the products of intermarriage, were united in one stern purpose: to end tyrannical Spanish rule in America. Led by 'El Liberador', the Venezuelan Simon Bolivar (1783–1830), Colombia (1819), Venezuela (1821), Ecuador (1822), Peru (1824) and Bolivia (1825) fought savagely against the Spaniards, neither side giving any quarter. Bolivar and his fellow liberators, José San Martin of Argentina and Bernardo O'Higgins of Chile were defeated several times before the rulers suffered disastrous defeat at Boyacá, Colombia on 7 August 1819. Virtually the whole Spanish army surrendered. Meanwhile, Mexico and other Central American states also wrenched their freedom from the Spaniards and by 1825, Spanish rule had been brought down.

1840s   CHINA HUMBLED AND REVIVED

IN 1839–42, the British went to war with China over Chinese reluctance to open its ports to the trade in Indian opium, which the British sought to use

as currency for valuable imports such as Chinese porcelain, silk and tea. China, hopelessly outclassed by modern weapons, had to yield Hong Kong and open five 'treaty' ports. Another Opium War, in 1860, wrested more concessions from the Chinese emperor who had to allow the British, French and other foreigners to create enclaves on Chinese territory, where they were immune from Chinese law. Later, wiping out this

▲ *The refusal of the Chinese to open their ports to the British opium trade led to war in the 1840s.*

humiliation became a strong motive for the Communist Mao Zedong (1903–76), who became ruler of China in 1949 and made it a power in the world once again.

1864   THE RED CROSS

IN 1859, Henry Dunant (1828–1910), the Swiss philanthropist, drew the same conclusions about medicine in war as Florence Nightingale when he witnessed the Battle of Solferino, at which there were 40,000 casualties. Dunant saw soldiers lying ignored on the battlefield, bleeding from wounds and in agony as the fighting raged around them. Dunant, like Nightingale, was shocked and appalled but refused to shrug off a situation that had been accepted in war for centuries. In 1864 he founded the Red Cross Organisation for the care of battle casualties on both sides in a conflict and this humanitarian work extended before long to protection for prisoners-of-war and ultimately to the relief of suffering throughout the world.

1865   FREEING THE SLAVES OF THE AMERICAN SOUTH

THE southern states of the USA had relied heavily on slaves to work on the cotton and other plantations and by 1860, the South quarrelled with the non-slave North especially over what southerners felt was undue federal interference from Washington. The matter was settled by the victory of the North in the Civil War (1861–65) after which the slaves were freed. Some southerners refused to accept that slaves were no longer slaves and in 1866, the Ku Klux Klan secret society was founded to reassert

▲ *The Battle of Solferino, which shocked Henry Dunant into founding the Red Cross.*

white supremacy. The Klan aimed at terrorising the former slaves and anyone who supported them. The Klan disbanded in 1869, but was revived and still persists, though in minor form, to this day.

1872   NEW ARMED FORCES

THE Japanese had long been a warlike nation and had even turned war into sport, with the martial arts kung fu, ju-jitsu and kendo. Modern technological warfare, however, was entirely new in their experience when, after 1872, their army was trained by the Germans and their navy by the British.

All this meant that modern battleships and weapons were acquired by a people who, barely 20 years earlier had been so terrified by Perry's steam-assisted sailing ships that they called them *kurofune*, 'smoking dragons'. What was more, before modernisation, so that no one could escape the bonds of isolation, the Japanese had been forbidden to build vessels that could sail more than a certain distance out to sea before they sank.

1880s   MORE WESTERNISATION

ANY other nation but the obedient Japanese might have suffered cultural collapse at the pace and extent of changes that, ultimately, enabled them to leap from medieval to modern within 40 years, a tenth of the time it had taken in Europe. By 1882 the Bank of Japan had been established. The Cabinet was reorganised along German lines. Government papermaking and cotton-spinning plants were established, with steam-power introduced into some 200 factories by 1890. Railways, steamships and electric power plants were constructed. The Japanese were soon catching up so fast that they were absorbing innovations not long after they first appeared in the West – for example, telephones, invented in the US in 1869 and the cinema, first introduced in France in 1895.

1885   THE MOTOR CAR

MACHINES can liberate. This was certainly true of the bicycle which, after about 1890, enabled women, who took up cycling with especial enthusiasm, to travel further than had ever been possible before, with or without the bifurcated 'knickerbockers' designed to preserve their modesty.

▶ *Gottlieb Daimler.*

The same could be said of the motor car pioneered in Germany after 1885 by Gottlieb Daimler (1834–1900) At first a plaything for the rich, the car enabled many townsfolk to venture out into the countryside for the first time. Country folk were not always pleased at the invasion, but when the car gave thousands the sort of mobility that the horse could never offer, it increased knowledge and understanding of rural life and brought people, however reluctantly, closer together.

1895 POPULAR ENTERTAINMENT

THE brothers Auguste (1862–1954) and Louis (1864–1948) Lumière gave the first film performance in Paris in 1895. The images were so realistic that the audience, seeing a train coming towards them on screen, panicked and ran out of the cinema. Despite this unfortunate beginning, the cinema became the first mass entertainment medium, and a rival in Britain to the music hall. The music hall, sentimental, tuneful and rowdy, not only entertained, but expressed working-class aspirations in a particularly touching way. The better life for which they now felt able to hope was tempered by sadness at their distance from it. 'With a ladder and some glasses', ran one song 'You could see to Hackney Marshes, if it wasn't for the houses in between'.

▲ *Louis Lumière, one of the pioneers of cinematography.*

Exploration and Empires

1800s SHEEP AND SETTLEMENT

BY 1800 there were 5,000 convicts around Sydney and the introduction of Merino sheep from South Africa (1794) had given the colony an export product to attract free settlers. Coastal settlements increasingly sprang up including Perth (1829), Melbourne (1835) and Adelaide (1836). By the 1830s there were 100,000 settlers. A regular steamship service between Sydney and Britain from 1856 increased the population to one million by the 1860s, by which time convict transportation had ceased. The discovery of gold in Victoria (1851) led to an influx of settlers but wool remained the main export commodity. Australia's colonies became self-governing in 1850 and British troops left in 1870.

1801 AFRICA VS AMERICA AND EUROPE

▲ *The French naval invasion of Algiers.*

THE Muslim countries of western North Africa had always derived part of their income from what to European eyes was piracy, but to Islamic ones was the duty of fighting the infidel. In 1801, the ruler of Tripoli declared war on the United States. This opened a series of minor military engagements between the North

African states and European and American powers that culminated in 1830 with a full-scale French invasion of Algiers. The French combined military might with a policy of settling French colonists in pacified regions. By 1847 the whole of the coastal strip and the fertile land between the Mediterranean Sea and the Sahara Desert had fallen under French control.

1815 THE AGE OF IMPERIALISM

IMPERIAL expansion was continuous after 1815 as nations sought the prestige of overseas conquest. In Africa this became a 'scramble' as new colonial powers (like Germany and Italy) increased the momentum to secure territories before their rivals. Peace was maintained between the colonists through the Berlin Conference (1884–85), which helped divide Africa into 'spheres of influence'.

▲ *The Berlin Conference, at which Africa came under European imperial power.*

Great Britain made the greatest gains including Egypt (1882), Nigeria (1884), British Somaliland (1884), Southern Rhodesia (1890), Northern Rhodesia (1891) and Sudan (1898). France also made significant gains, mainly in North and West Africa, including the French Congo (1875–92), French West Africa (1886–98) and Madagascar (1895–96). During the 'scramble' Germany quickly built up an African and Pacific empire, covering one million square miles and Italy seized Tripoli (1861), Eritrea (1889), Somaliland (1893) and Libya (1912).

1830s   DARWIN'S VOYAGES OF DISCOVERY

THE growing value of overseas trade caused governments to demand ever more accurate information about destinations in the far corners of the world. One British voyage to survey the South Atlantic and Pacific coasts of South America carried the naturalist Charles Darwin (1809–82). His studies of South American plant and animal life during the 1831–35 voyage of HMS *Beagle* contributed to his theory of evolution. Darwin's researches encouraged the exploration of the Amazon Basin between 1848 and 1861 by the naturalists Alfred Wallace (1823–1913), Henry Bates (1825–92) and Richard Spruce (1817–93). The information acquired by scientific expeditions like these was of great use to investors seeking new natural resources to exploit, and contributed to the development of a colonial economic relationship between South America and Europe.

1846   THE SUEZ CANAL

IN 1846, a group of Austrian, French and British investors agreed that the time had come to cut a canal between the Mediterranean and the Red Sea, thereby providing a shorter sea route between Europe and the Far East. Mohammed Ali was uninterested in this project but his successors were more enthusiastic. In 1858, a stock issue raised the money, work began in 1859, and the canal opened 10 years later. The canal was vital to Britain, and Britain now chose to interfere in Egypt's internal politics. In 1881, a group of Egyptian army officers seized control of the country, and the threat to the canal caused the British to occupy Egypt in 1882.

▼ *The Suez Canal, built to provide a passageway between Europe and the Far East.*

1853　JAPAN AND CHINA RESIST

IN 1853 a squadron of American warships arrived in Tokyo Harbour. They forced the Japanese government to sign a treaty opening Japanese ports to trade. The leaders of Japan made a determined effort to catch up with the European powers. The deferential discipline of Japanese society enabled the process of modernisation to proceed rapidly. In 1894, Japan fomented a war with China, and emerged victorious in 1895. As part of the peace settlement, Japan acquired Korea, thus becoming one of the powers exploiting China. In 1899 a resistance movement popularly known as the 'Boxers' began a rebellion in China that resulted, in 1900, in a siege of the foreign diplomats' compound at Peking. An international army including a Japanese contingent crushed the rising, ending imperial China's last hope of regaining control of its borders.

▲ *The Chinese Boxer Rebellion.*

1860s   CROSSING AUSTRALIA

THE first crossing of Australia (1860–61) was completed by Irishman Robert Burke and ex-miner William Wills riding on camels, the first use of the animals in the country. Both perished on the return journey. British surveyor John MacDonnell Stuart completed the first south-north crossing (1860–62) on his third attempt after overcoming water shortages, Aborigine hostility and oppressive heat. During the 1860 trek Stuart found and named the MacDonnell Ranges and came within 240 km (150 miles) of the centre of Australia. Such crossings enabled the government to begin linking Australia by telegraph and railway. By 1900 explorers had reached most of the 'outback' but the demanding terrain and temperatures they experienced had confirmed the belief that much of the interior was unsuitable for settlement.

1885 THE FIRST STIRRINGS OF NATIONALISM

VIOLENT resistance to colonial rule had been commonplace for centuries but the first systematic political challenge arose with the Indian National Congress (est. 1885). This aimed to further the powers of Indians who were already entering local government and the civil service. Similar movements later emerged elsewhere, such as the National Congress of British West Africa (est. 1918) and the South African Native National Congress (est. 1912). Despite these movements only Britain offered any measure of self-government to its colonies by making Canada, New Zealand, Australia and South Africa into independent 'dominions'. Such freedoms were, however, restricted to colonies where white settlers were a large or dominant section of the population.

1899 THE BOER CHALLENGE TO THE BRITISH EMPIRE

THE greatest challenge to British power in this century arose in South Africa, in the form of the Boers (Dutch settlers). Two Boer republics had become enclosed by British territories, and conflict between the settlers began to arise. Increasing friction between the Boers and the British escalated into war after Cecil Rhodes (1853–1902), Prime Minister of Cape Colony 1890–96, attempted to seize the diamond and gold areas of the Boer republics. Throughout the Boer War (1899–1902) the British suffered serious defeats at the hands of the Boers, until many of the Boer communities were placed in concentration camps. Their property was destroyed, denying the soldiers vital supplies, and thus turning the fortunes of the war.

◀ *Explorers Burke and Wills crossing Australia in 1861.*

Trade and Industry

1802   TELFORD'S ROADS

THOMAS Telford (1757–1834), nicknamed 'the Colossus of roads', was one of the most important civil engineers of the Industrial Revolution. From 1793 he built canals, including the Ellesmere Canal, to carry raw materials and finished goods from Wales to the River Mersey. In 1802 he was made responsible for building and repairing a network of roads in the Scottish Highlands. He invented a new solid-gravel road surface, that could take wheeled vehicles and withstand harsh weather. The 1,400 km (875 miles) of new roads and 11 bridges he built changed the whole way of life in the Highlands. Telford's supreme achievement was the building of a road from London to Holyhead, north Wales, which took 15 years. He used explosives to blast away rock to make new passes. Of the several bridges along the route, the Menai Straits suspension bridge is the most famous.

▲ *Thomas Telford.*

▶ *Suspension bridges were one of the great engineering feats of the Industrial Revolution.*

1803 THE OPENING UP OF AMERICA

IN 1803 the United States bought the lands west of the Mississippi River from France for $11,250,000. The Louisiana Purchase doubled the country's size. Thousands of people now began to move westwards to settle in and cultivate the new territories. The new settlers drove out the Native Americans who lived on the Plains. The move west picked up speed after the American Civil War in the 1860s. The first American railway was opened in

▲ *The Railroad joins East and West in America.*

South Carolina in 1830. By 1880 America's rail network was bigger than that of Europe. Rail transport made the development of America possible in spite of the great distances between places. Goods could be sent cheaply and easily to market in exchange for factory-made equipment for farm use.

1824 TRADE UNIONS BECOME LEGAL

TRADE unions are organisations of employed workers, formed mainly for the purpose of collective bargaining. Journeymen's guilds existed in the Middle Ages (journeymen being workers hired on a daily basis) but modern trade unionism was a product of the Industrial Revolution. In 1799 the Combination Law made all unions illegal and they had to function largely as secret societies until 1824, when the law was repealed and unions became legal for negotiating wages and hours of labour. The movement grew steadily in numbers and influence. The Trade Union Act of 1913 allowed a trade union to pursue any lawful purpose. The London dock strike of 1889 was the first instance of the organisation of unskilled labour by trade unions.

1830   THE SCRAMBLE FOR AFRICA

FRANCE, whose first major African territory was acquired with the conquest of Algeria in 1830, dreamed of 'civilising' Africa, while building a vast empire across the top of the continent. Britain championed a scheme for a 'Cape to Cairo' railway. British motivation was mixed: trade, territorial power, missionary zeal to Christianise the continent and the wish to populate much of the world with British settlers so as to guarantee the future of the Anglo-Saxon race. The Germans arrived late on the scene (1884) but thereafter expanded rapidly. The Italians tried but failed to take Ethiopia in 1896. The Belgians and Portuguese also staked claims, essentially to African resources. Clashes inevitably occurred between the European imperialists and indeed contributed to the international tensions that precipitated the First World War.

1839   OPIUM WARS

IN the 1830s many Chinese had begun to smoke opium and the British and other Europeans were happy to supply the drug, which was produced mainly in India. When Chinese officials forbade its import, European traders got round this by smuggling and bribery. In 1839 the Chinese sent a commissioner to Canton to clamp down on the illegal importing of opium. When the Chinese destroyed a large cargo of the drug, war broke out. The British landed troops and took the city of Shanghai. By the Treaty of Nanking (1842) four ports in addition to Canton were opened to European trade and Hong Kong was

▼ *The British taking Chin-keang during the Opium Wars.*

ceded to the British. Fighting resumed in 1856, and in 1860 an Anglo-French force seized Peking. Other Western nations received privileges and even went one better, gaining exemption from Chinese law for their nationals living on Chinese territory.

1848 GOLD RUSHES

JAMES Marshall was building a mill on the banks of the Sacramento River, California, in 1848, when a sudden gleam caught his eye. It was gold. Within a year thousands of people, gripped by gold fever, were rushing to California, even from Europe, in the hope of making their fortunes. The same thing happened after gold was found in the Australian outback in 1851. Most of the prospectors were unlucky. Eventually the

▲ *The nineteenth-century gold rush was not confined to the US; gold was also mined in Australia and South Africa.*

demand for coins outstripped the amount of gold being produced in the world. Minted coins were given a symbolic value unrelated to the amount of metal they contained. Nowadays most gold is stored, nearly half of it at Fort Knox Gold Depository, USA. Only exceptionally is the precious metal used for coins.

1850s   MASS PRODUCTION

THE American Civil War created a demand from the government for guns with interchangeable parts, which could be repaired quickly on the battle-field, as well as being assembled more rapidly and cheaply in the first place. Whereas hitherto all parts had been made in workshops, now they were made in engineering factories. All the parts were standardised. Finishing was no longer done by hand but instead by machine tools. Once these systems were in place, mass production became possible. The skilled craftsman was replaced by the unskilled or semi-skilled worker whose job was to 'mind' a machine or be responsible for one small, specialised operation. This was the basis for the production line, which Henry Ford developed in the United States in the 1920s for motor-car manufacture.

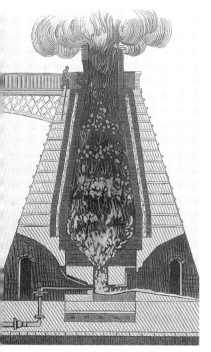

▲ *Improvements to the blast furnace opened up engineering possibilities during the Industrial Revolution.*

1850s   THE INDUSTRIAL REVOLUTION IN EUROPE

IN Europe machine shops developed in Liège, Belgium, after 1807, and soon afterwards in France. Germany took the lead in the 1850s in the new tech-nologies of chemicals and steel. The firm of Krupp, founded in 1811 in the Ruhr region, produced armaments as well as steel wheels for rolling stock on the expanding German railway system. Before the First World War Krupp pursued a benevolent social policy towards its workers. A major contribution to the steel industry was the invention of the blast furnace for refining ore. This furnace operated on the principle that a blast of air forced through a mixture of solid fuel and ore burns away impurities and converts them to slag, which is insoluble and can be skimmed off.

1895   RUBBER

RUBBER seeds were brought from Brazil in 1876 but the founder of the natural-rubber industry was H. N. Ridley of the Singapore Botanic Gardens. Ridley's tapping experiments showed that cultivated trees could produce latex continuously without themselves being seriously injured or even killed. The first commercial plantings of rubber in Malaya occurred in 1895 and development was rapid in the European-controlled territories of South-East Asia. Here

▲ *Tapping rubber trees in Indonesia.*

the temperature and humidity are high all year round and there was a large, cheap and skilled labour force. The rapid growth of the motor-vehicle industry after 1905 greatly stimulated natural-rubber production. The Japanese occupation of South-East Asia in the Second World War, however, blocked much of the world's natural-rubber supply and boosted the development of a massive synthetic-rubber industry, particularly in the United States.

Science and Technology

1800s MASS-PRODUCTION TECHNIQUES

THE most crucial development in the latter half of the eighteenth century was mass production. Textiles, and ceramics saw huge expansion of their industries, bringing a shift of labour force, from working the fields to working in town factories. Henry Maudslay introduced a new lathe in 1800, dubbed the 'go-cart', that revolutionised the production of precision parts. Championed by Marc Isambard Brunel (1769–1849), Maudslay went on to develop a production line for the mass-production of ships' blocks. By 1808, he had perfected five machines, which only needed 10 unskilled men to operate them. In America Elisha King Root began developing mass production techniques associated with farming. In 1832 he established a factory for producing steel axe heads, and in 1837 John Deere began mass producing the steel ploughshare. Both tools were essential for clearing and dressing vast tracts of land for agricultural use in both America and Russia during the second quarter of the nineteenth century.

1820s ASPHALT AND CONCRETE

IN the late 1820s, John McAdam (1756–1836) devised a new process for making road surfaces using a mixture of heated bitumen or asphalt and stones, which would set by cooling to provide a smooth durable top layer. His invention was dubbed 'Macadamising' and has remained a ubiquitous form of road surfacing ever since. Portland cement was invented by Joseph Aspdin of Yorkshire, in 1824. It proved to be a very versatile building material indeed. By 1867 steel-reinforced concrete had been patented by Joseph Monier of France. The first reinforced concrete building was erected in America in 1872 and the first concrete road was laid in 1892, also in America.

1826   PHOTOGRAPHY AND CINEMATOGRAPHY

THE first photographic image was taken in 1826 by Joseph Niepce (d. 1833) in France. His assistant, Louis Daguerre (1789–1851) made an improvement known as the daguerreotype in 1839. The first photographic print-making process, using the negative-positive method on paper, was invented in 1835 by William Henry Fox-Talbot, which meant being able to produce duplicate copies. The first colour photograph, taken by James Clerk-Maxwell (1831–79), and the invention of the single-lens reflex camera, by Thomas Sutton occurred in 1861. The first successful attempt at producing a moving photographic image was made by Louis Aimé Augustin Le Prince in New York 1885.

▲ *French photography pioneer Louis Daguerre.*

1835   TELEGRAPH TO TELEPHONE

IT was the inventor of the Morse code, Samuel Morse (1791–1872), who built the first electric telegraph in 1835. Electrical pulses were sent along the telegraph wire using his code; at the receiving end, a series of clicks were heard which had to be deciphered by the operator. This was the first modern form of telecommunication. In 1876, Alexander Graham Bell (1847–1922) made an assemblage of components devised in part by other electrical scientists which he had improved upon for practical application. He had invented the telephone by doing so, and was able to transmit the first-ever spoken message via an electrical wire. Important in their own right were the microphone and loudspeaker he had developed, which found plenty of other applications.

▼ *Alexander Graham Bell, inaugurating the New York – Chicago telephone system.*

1859   EVOLUTION AND INHERITANCE

TWO Englishmen were responsible for the theory of evolution. Both of them were aware that the variety in species, including humans, seemed to suggest an ability to change over time. Charles Darwin (1809–82) spent five years as a naturalist on board the HMS *Beagle*, 1831–36. He visited South America and the Galapagos Islands and what he saw led to the development of his theory, but he spent many more years looking for tangible evidence. Alfred Russel

Wallace (1823–1913) was 14 years younger than Darwin. He became a professional naturalist, making a living by collecting specimens of plants and animals to send back to Europe from South America and South-East Asia. By 1858 he had arrived at the same idea of 'evolution by natural selection' as Darwin, and sent an outlining essay to Darwin. When Darwin received this he was shocked to realise that he had spent too long expounding his own theory and published *The Origin of Species by Means of Natural Selection or the Preservation of Favoured Races in the Struggle for Life* in 1859.

◀ *Alfred Russel Wallace.*

1867 ANAESTHETIC AND ANTISEPTIC

ONCE scientists began to understand that micro-organisms were responsible for infection and disease, a whole new approach to medicine and surgery was initiated, thanks to the microscope and the accidental discovery that it was possible to sterilise food by heating it. Joseph Lister (1827–1912) was the first surgeon to introduce an antiseptic into his routine, in 1867. He used a spray of carbolic acid (phenol), an extract from coal tar, to kill and inhibit pathogens. By 1874 Abraham Groves (1847–1935), had introduced the practice of sterilising surgical instruments and wearing rubber gloves. Anaesthesia, although practised for centuries in the form of alcohol as an analgesic, became more of a science at this period. William Morton, an American dentist, coined the word 'anaesthesia' in 1846, when he adopted the use of rectified sulphuric ether.

▲ *Joseph Lister, the first pioneer of antiseptics and anaesthetics in surgery.*

1877   THE PHONOGRAPH

HAVING invented the telephone, a way for recording audible messages was sought. In 1877 the famous American inventor, Thomas Edison (1847–1931), made the first demonstration of a machine which he called the phonograph. It comprised a tin-foil cylinder held on a rotating drum. Sound was converted, via a vibrating needle touching the tinfoil, into a spiralling sound track or line on the surface. When the machine was operated in reverse, a needle would pick up the characteristics of the scribed line and an amplifier transmitted the sound. The gramophone record, a horizontal disc, as opposed to Edison's drum, was invented by Emile Berliner (1851–1929) in 1887.

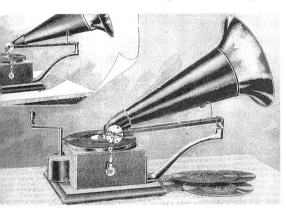

▲ *Emile Berliner's gramophone.*

The first gramophone records were made from shellac, a hard resinous substance derived from the lac insect.

1888   RADIO WAVES

BOTH the telegraph and telephone relied on a physical wire link to be able to convey messages. This had obvious limitations as it could be cut, although the first submarine cable was successfully laid across the Atlantic in 1857. Twelve years after the invention of the telephone, in 1888, a German scientist named Heinrich Hertz (1854–94) discovered the existence of radio waves. This led the brilliant Guglielmo Marconi (1874–1937) to make the first successful transmission using radio waves, which he quickly demonstrated could be sent without the receiver being visible. In 1901 the first radio transmission all the way across the Atlantic was made, and the domestic 'wireless' was only a few years away. Marconi's invention had an immediate impact on world communications, particularly early on with shipping, because the telegraph and telephone could not be used.

1895   RADIOACTIVITY AND X-RAYS

WHILE experimenting with a cathode ray tube in 1895, which would later be developed into the television, Wilhelm Rontgen (1845–1923) noticed a new phenomenon. Invisible rays being emitted by the device, which he dubbed X-rays, were causing various chemicals to glow. He then discovered that the rays, although invisible to the eye, would affect a photographic plate. What was more, the X-rays had the ability to travel through some solid materials and not others, which meant that they could be used to see inside the body and look for breaks in bones, or bits of metal such as bullets or bits of shrapnel. X-rays are high-frequency electromagnetic radiation waves. Rπntgen's discovery made an enormous contribution to medical diagnosis, which had previously relied on a great deal of guesswork and painful manipulation of the patient.

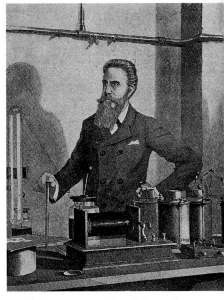

▲ *Wilhelm Rontgen won the Nobel Prize for his discovery of X-rays.*

Religions, Belief and Thought

1800s   AMERICAN TRANSCENDENTALISM

RALPH Waldo Emerson (1803–82) and Henry David Thoreau (1817–62), initiated a philosophical and literary movement, known as American Transcendentalism, which drew upon the teachings of the *Bhagavad Gita* and other Eastern texts to provide a basis for experiencing the divine in the natural world. Despite its somewhat exotic origins, the movement's values, such as self-reliance and simple living, fitted well with American society and have inspired many significant events from the first World Parliament of Religions in Chicago to the conservation movement and the creation of national parks.

1830   JOSEPH SMITH AND THE MORMON CHURCH

THE Church of Jesus Christ of Latter Day Saints was founded by an American Christian, Joseph Smith (1805–44), following a vision in 1820 in which he was visited by Jesus Christ and God the Father. In 1823, the angel Moroni appeared to him and told him about the *Book of Mormon,* a record of the early inhabitants of the Americas and their prophets. In 1827, Joseph Smith received the Book of Mormon, which was written on plates of gold, and he translated it into English in 1829. This book supports and verifies the Bible and contains witnesses of Jesus Christ from ancient America. For this reason it is called the Book of Mormon: Another Testament of Jesus Christ. Joseph Smith organized the Church with himself as the prophet in 1830. Opponents drove him and his supporters out of several states and in 1844 Joseph Smith was killed in Carthage, Illinois. Most of the remaining members of the Church moved to Utah and founded Salt Lake City under the leadership of Brigham Young.

1836   FOUNDATIONS OF COMMUNISM

KARL Marx, a middle-class German Jew, studied philosophy at the University of Berlin from 1836 before editing a radical newspaper. After the failed 1848 revolt in Germany, he fled to England, where he wrote *The Communist Manifesto* and *Das Kapital*. In these, he attempts to provide a scientific foundation for socialism (countering the utopian socialism of Proudhon and Bakunin). Like the English economists, he sees production as based on land, labour and capital, but he points out that whoever controls the mode of production controls the economics and politics of the country. Control by landowners causes feudalism, control by investors causes capitalism and control by labourers causes socialism. Public ownership of the means of the production was seen as the necessary basis for fair and meaningful work.

▲ *Karl Marx, the first exponent of Communist ideals.*

1836   THE BIRTH OF RAMAKRISHNA

RAMAKRISHNA was a Hindu mystic from Bengal. As a priest he practised *bhakti*, devotional prayer to the god Kali. He then experimented with prayer, meditation and worship in several of the major religions, including Islam and Christianity, having ecstatic visions as a result of each of these and he is chiefly remembered for teaching that there is one God common to all religions. His life is commemorated in the work of the Ramakrishna Mission, created by his disciple, Swami Vivekananda (1863–1902).

1840s REFORM AND CONSERVATIVE JUDAISM

THE 1840s marked the emergence of several distinct movements in Judaism that split from traditional Orthodoxy. These were rooted in recognition by Jews that they were citizens of their host nations and not a nation within a nation. Reform Judaism, which developed amongst immigrants to the United States, was an attempt to adapt Judaism to Western society by distinguishing between the unchangeable and universal teachings of Judaism and those that were merely cultural traditions. Conservative Judaism made a similar distinction but treated far more of the teachings as unchangeable. This approach was opposed by the Zionists, who saw themselves primarily as citizens of the future nation of Israel – a stance that brought them into conflict with the societies they lived in.

1859 EVOLUTION AND SOCIAL DARWINISM

THE Origin of Species by Means of Natural Selection, by English biologist Charles Darwin, was published in 1859. Alfred Russel Wallace independently reached similar conclusions about the nature and process of evolution. The idea that species developed over time, and that humans had developed from apes, shook

the intellectual world and Christianity. Other scientists, using his idea of the 'survival of the fittest', concluded that Europeans had conquered the world because they were more evolved (although Darwin did not say this). Social Darwinists believe that life is an endless struggle and that only the most assertive and aggressive people, businesses and nations survive. Peter Kropotkin, in his *Mutual Aid,* countered this argument by pointing out that the ability to co-operate was a form of fitness that encouraged survival.

◀ *Charles Darwin.*

1893   GANDHI'S CAMPAIGN BEGINS

MOHANDAS Karamchand Gandhi is revered today as the father of the Indian nation. Born near Bombay in 1869, he studied law in England then, as a barrister, moved to South Africa. He first experienced the apartheid policy when he was thrown out of a first-class railway carriage at Pietermaritzburg in 1893. From then on he campaigned for justice using non-violence (*ahimsa*) or what he called *satyagraha* ('truth force'). In 1909, he established Tolstoy Farm, a self-sufficient vegetarian community for his satyagrahis. On returning to India in 1914 he dedicated himself to obtaining Indian independence from the British Empire through non-violent action. With independence, the country underwent partition into Muslim Pakistan and largely Hindu India and over one mil-

▲ *Mahatma Gandhi.*

lion died in religious conflict. Gandhi promoted religious harmony, however. Hindu extremists, angered at this policy, assassinated him in 1948.

1893   SWAMI VIVEKANANDA AND THE REDISCOVERY OF HINDUISM

SWAMI Vivekananda (1863–1902) was a disciple of Ramakrishna and the most important recent systematiser of Hindu thought. In developing a philosophy that brought together all the main strands of the Hindu tradition from *advaita* ('meditation') to *bhakti* ('devotion') he virtually created modern Hinduism. The central teaching is that God is beyond all concepts and images and can be known directly through meditation, but that God also takes many forms and so devotional worship is also a true form of religion. As well as providing a means to unite Hinduism, it provided a means to bring harmony between all faiths, and this resulted in worldwide attention when he spoke at the 1893 World Parliament of Religions.

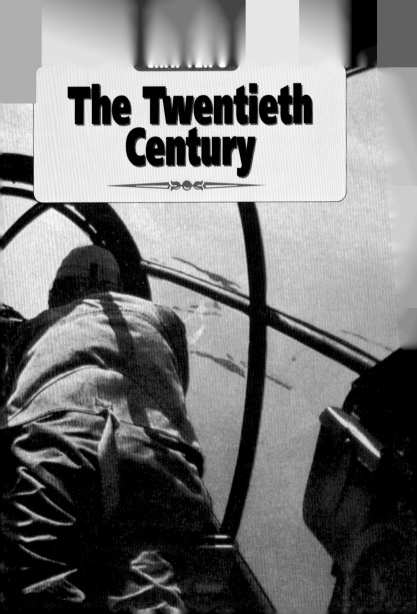

The Twentieth Century

Power and Politics

1904   THE ENTENTE CORDIALE

THROUGHOUT the second half of the nineteenth century, Britain had avoided any long-term European commitments. British politicians took part in conferences and agreements, but undertook no treaty obligations. In 1902, however, Britain signed a treaty with Japan and in 1904 signed the much more important Entente Cordiale with France. These treaties brought to an

▲ *The assassination of Archduke Franz Ferdinand and his wife.*

end the period of 'Splendid Isolation' in British foreign policy. Three years later in 1904, Britain signed an entente with Russia, so creating the Triple Entente. This effectively meant that Europe was now divided into two armed camps, each made up of three powers and each with a series of built-in clauses, which involved automatic and immediate military action. The stage was now set for a showdown.

1914   SARAJEVO

ON 28 June 1914 the Archduke Franz Ferdinand, heir to the Austrian throne, and his wife were shot dead by a Serbian terrorist Gavrilo Princip. Under normal circumstances this incident would have passed without major repercussions, but the build-up of alliances and the consequent heightening of tensions turned what was a political matter into an international tragedy. The Austrian government had been looking for an excuse to crush Serbia, which stood in their way in the Balkans. When Russia mobilised in support of the Serbs, Germany automatically became involved and this brought in France. By 12 August the major European powers were involved in a catastrophic slogging match, that would last for more than four years.

1917   THE OCTOBER REVOLUTION

FROM March to October 1917 Russia was ruled by the Provisional Government. This had no legal standing, but was intended to govern until a general election could be held, this being planned for November. The

▲ *Bolshevik leader Leon Trotsky*

Provisional Government gradually became more and more unpopular, partly because it decided to continue the war against Germany, but also because food shortages and inflation grew even worse. On 24–25 October the Bolsheviks overthrew the Provisional Government in a coup planned and led by Leon Trotsky, Lenin's second in command. A month later the general election was held. This was won by the Socialist-Revolutionary Party, but when the Assembly met in January Lenin dissolved it by force and began to rule as a dictator.

1919   THE RISE OF FASCISM

FASCISM developed in Italy after the First World War. The term came from the Roman word 'fasces', a bundle of rods and an axe, that was carried before a Roman magistrate. They represented the power of a magistrate to order corporal punishment and capital punishment. The fasces became the symbol of the Fascist Party. Fascists believed in a strong central government headed by a dictator. They thought that ordinary people should be prepared to sacrifice their own personal liberty for the good of the state. For example they believed that men and women had different roles in society. They opposed foreign influences and instead wanted Italy to be self-sufficient. They described this economic system as 'Autarky'.

1920s   THE WARLORDS

IN the 1920s central government in China broke down and power fell into the hands of local rulers who became known as the 'Warlords'. Although

some, such as Yen Hsi-shan of Shansi, ruled efficiently, most were simply local dictators taking advantage of the situation. The Warlords were crushed by military campaigns by Jiang-Jieshi, which gave him even more power within the Kuomintang and led to a split in 1927 between the Nationalist members on one side and the Radicals and Communists on the other. The Communists, led by Mao Zedong, set up a commune in Kiangsi where they lived until 1934. They were then forced to leave by attacks from the Kuomintang and set out on the Long March to the province of Shensi. This became part of Chinese Communist mythology.

▲ *Prince Yuan Shi-k'ai of China.*

1922   MUSSOLINI

BENITO Mussolini was the leader of the Fascist Party. He had fought in the First World War and had been very angry at the treatment Italy had received at the Treaty of Versailles. From 1919 to 1922 he organised a propaganda campaign through his paper *Il Popolo d'Italia*. He made himself out to be a strong man who could solve Italy's problems. His supporters, known as the Blackshirts, were organised into Fascio di Combattimento. In some parts of Italy, Bologna for example, they were the main source of law and order. They punished criminals, broke up strikes and attacked Mussolini's opponents. In October 1922 Mussolini organised a 'March on Rome' by his Blackshirts. This was intended to put pressure on the government, in fact it led to Mussolini being appointed prime minister of Italy. He became the first dictator in western Europe.

▲ *An Italian magazine depicting Facsist leader Benito Mussolini.*

1928   THE FIVE-YEAR PLANS

IN 1928 Stalin announced the First Five-Year Plan. This was an attempt to develop Soviet industry, which Stalin believed was 100 years behind the West. Every factory, coalmine and industrial plant in the Soviet Union was set a series of targets for the next five years, which it had to meet. The targets were worked out in Moscow by the state-planning agency, Gosplan. The First Five-Year Plan also included the collectivisation of all the farms in the Soviet Union. Farmers and peasants were forced to amalgamate their farms into large state farms. Second and Third Five-Year Plans followed in the 1930s. Overall, industrial production increased by about 400 per cent, but the plans encouraged quantity not quality. Fifty per cent of tractors broke down and could not be repaired.

1933   HITLER IN POWER

HITLER became Chancellor of Germany in January 1933 and was given total power when the Enabling Act was passed in March. This allowed him to govern without the Reichstag, the German Parliament, for the next four years. By then Germany had been changed completely. All political parties and trade unions had been banned. Children were indoctrinated in Nazi ideas by schools and youth organisations, such as the Hitler Youth. Almost all married women had been forced to give up work and were encouraged to have at least four babies. Newspapers, the cinema, books, the arts, music and radio were all controlled by the Nazis and their laws were enforced by the secret state police, the Gestapo. A total dictatorship had been set up in Germany.

1936   THE SPANISH CIVIL WAR

THE Spanish Civil War broke out in the summer of 1936. It was fought between the forces of the Popular Front, the elected government of Spain and the rebel Falangists, led by General Francisco Franco. The Falangists wanted to overthrow the Popular Front Republicans who had begun to undermine the power of the Church and the position of the landowners. Because Franco was a Fascist, he received aid from both Mussolini, who sent 70,000 men and Hitler, who sent the Condor Legion of 10,000 men. Hitler used the war as an opportunity to try out the strength of his new armed forces and to practise 'Blitzkrieg', the strategy of mobile warfare that he was to use at the beginning of the Second World War.

▲ *Spanish dictator and soldier General Francisco Franco.*

1945   THE IMPACT OF THE SECOND WORLD WAR

DURING the Second World War, Gandhi organised the 'Quit India' campaign. This was a response to the British government's decision to announce that India had declared war on Germany without consulting Indians. Gandhi's campaign increased the influence of the Muslim League, led by M. A. Jinnah. When the war ended in 1945, Jinnah demanded a separate Muslim state, Pakistan. For the first time there was widespread violence between Hindus and Muslims, especially in Calcutta in August 1946, when Jinnah attempted to put pressure on the British to allow 'partition'. It became increasingly obvious that the two religions could not coexist.

1945   HIROSHIMA

▲ *US president Harry S. Truman in 1945.*

ON 12 April 1945, Harry S. Truman became President of the USA on the death of Franklin Roosevelt. On his desk he put the notice; 'The Buck Stops Here'. Just over three months later he had to take one of the momentous decisions ever taken. While at the Potsdam Conference he was told that the Atomic Bomb was ready to be used on Japan. After lengthy discussion, Truman decided to use the bomb. He was told by his chiefs of staff that one million casualties would be caused if Japan were to be invaded. The bomb was dropped on 6 August 1945 on the city of Hiroshima, some 70,000 people were killed. The bomb not only marked the beginning of a new period in the history of mankind, but also increased the hostility between Truman and the Soviet leader Stalin, who had not been told about the bomb in advance. It became a factor in the development of the Cold War.

1945   THE HOLOCAUST

THE Holocaust is the name given to the mass slaughter of Jews and other groups by the Nazis preceding and during the Second World War. Hitler blamed the Jews for causing the defeat of Germany during the First World War and believed that he could purify the German race by ridding it of all foreign groups. This included gypsies, Slavs, cripples and the mentally ill as well as Jews. At first the Nazis tried to force the Jews to leave Germany by banning them from the professions, preventing them from voting and making it more and more difficult for them to earn a living. Jews were attacked on the street and their property was smashed. But after the outbreak of war Hitler began to force Jews to live in Ghettos, and then, from January 1942, began mass murder in extermination camps using poison gas. By the end of the war in 1945 about six million people had been killed.

▲ *Adolf Hitler organised mass-extermination of the Jews in what he called the 'Final Solution'.*

1946   THE IRON CURTAIN

IN 1945 and 1946 Stalin built the Iron Curtain across Europe. It was a barrier, that ran for a thousand miles from the Baltic to the Adriatic cutting Europe in two. Its purpose was simple, to prevent any western influence from reaching the eastern European countries controlled by Stalin. In particular, it cut Germany into two sections, the Soviet zone and the three western zones. The Iron Curtain received a very hostile reception in the West, which surprised Stalin. At Yalta and Potsdam he had agreed that the West could do as it

liked in western
Europe and he
assumed that, there-
fore, he could do as
he liked in the East.
As always, Stalin's
main preoccupation
was security, and the
Iron Curtain seemed
to him a natural step.
To the West it cor-
rectly suggested the
beginning of another
form of dictatorship.

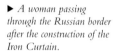

▶ *A woman passing
through the Russian border
after the construction of the
Iron Curtain.*

1949   THE COMMUNIST REVOLUTION

IN 1949, after years of fighting, the Chinese Communist Party seized power
and the Kuomintang, led by Jiang-Jieshi, fled to the island of Formosa, eventually establishing the state of Taiwan. Mao Zedong set up a programme of
industrial development based on Five-Year Plans; however, his distrust of
intellectuals and technical experts held back progress. Much of the work in
building dams and other large-scale enterprises was done by manual labour.
In 1957 the 'Great Leap Forward', in which people throughout China were
asked to set up blast furnaces in their back gardens was a disaster. All over
China the harvest was left to rot and there was widespread famine.

1950s   EUROPEAN UNION

THE first moves towards European union took place in the years after the Second World War. In March 1948 the Brussels Treaty was signed by Britain, France, Belgium, the Netherlands and Luxembourg. This included plans for economic, social and military co-operation. In May 1948 a Congress of Europe to discuss plans for European union was held, and in May 1949 the Council of Europe was set up, with headquarters at Strasbourg. In May 1952 a European Defence Community was set up by Italy, France, the Netherlands, West Germany, Belgium and Luxembourg. This could have led to an integrated European army, but it collapsed when the French Parliament rejected the treaty in 1954. This was the first sign that national politics could make integration increasingly difficult.

▲ *Western powers signing the Brussels Pact, in one of the first steps towards European union.*

1955   NATO AND THE WARSAW PACT

NATO was set up in 1949 after the Berlin Blockade. It was a military alliance involving countries on either side of the North Atlantic. It changed relations between East and West by uniting the countries of the West, which led to the stationing of US forces in western Europe for the first time. The most important clause in the NATO treaty was that an attack on one country was considered to be an attack on all of them. In other words, the East could not pick off democratic countries without the risk of a war with NATO. The Soviet Union did not react to NATO until West Germany was admitted as a member in 1955. After this it set up the Warsaw Pact, a military alliance between the Communist countries of eastern Europe.

▲ *The opening of the European Parliament in Strasbourg, 7 July 1979.*

1960s   THE EEC

THE EEC developed three main organisations. The Commission, in Brussels, was made up of representatives from all of the member countries, who were appointed by their governments. Each 'Commissioner' was responsible for an area of policy. The role of the Commission was to carry the policies of the EEC. Policies were decided by the Council of Ministers, which was made up of politicians from each of the member states. This could meet anywhere. At important meetings the prime ministers would attend, on other occasions it would be the minister responsible for the area of policy to be discussed, such as farming for example. Finally there was a European Parliament in Strasbourg, which contained elected representatives from each member country. The Parliament could discuss, argue and even question Commissioners, but it had no legislative power.

1961   THE BERLIN WALL

▲ *Between the walls that divided East and West Germany in Berlin.*

THE Berlin Wall was built in August 1961. It separated families from one another and trapped people who had crossed into the other side of Berlin. For 12 years people had been escaping from East Berlin to West Berlin and in 1961 the number reached thousands every week. Most of the people who escaped were skilled workers, doctors or engineers. The Wall was an attempt to stop the drain of people from East to West. It was very effective, but it did not stop people trying to escape. The Wall also increased tension between the superpowers. The US President Kennedy visited West Berlin to show his support for its citizens.

1961   BAY OF PIGS INVASION

UNTIL 1959 Cuba was governed by a pro-American dictator Batista. But in 1959 he was overthrown by a group of rebels led by Fidel Castro. The USA cut off all aid to Cuba, and Castro in turn nationalised all US assets and property in Cuba. Khrushchev took advantage of the situation by agreeing to buy one million tonnes of Cuban sugar every year at inflated prices. This brought Cuba Soviet influence and Castro set up a Communist regime. Many US citizens were horrified. Communism now existed only, 70 miles off the coast of Florida. Eisenhower, the US president, authorised an attempt to overthrow Castro by landing a force of Cuban exiles at the Bay of Pigs. The landing actually took place in April 1961, after Eisenhower had left office, and turned out to be a disaster. The 1,500-strong force of Cubans were all killed or captured.

1972   SALT

IN 1969 the superpowers began Strategic Arms Limitation Talks. These were aimed at limiting the number of the very biggest nuclear weapons. The first treaty, known as SALT 1, was signed in 1972. Its most important clause was a five-year moratorium on the building of strategic weapons. This agreement did not lessen the risk of nuclear war, the superpowers had more than enough weapons already, and it did not affect intermediate or tactical weapons, but it was the first agreement of its kind. SALT 2 was agreed in 1979. This was a much more

▲ *Prisoners from the Bay of Pigs invasion being returned to the United States.*

important treaty as it limited the number of strategic weapons that the 2 superpowers could build. Each would have no more than 2,500. However, the treaty was never ratified by the US Congress, because of the Soviet invasion of Afghanistan in December 1979.

1980s   THE EVIL EMPIRE

IN 1981 Ronald Reagan became President of the USA. He was a fierce opponent of Communism and relations between the superpowers deteriorated. In 1980 the USA had boycotted the Olympic Games in Moscow and in 1984 the USSR boycotted the Games in Los Angeles. Disarmament talks made no progress for years. The situation was made worse by internal politics in the USSR. Leonid Brezhnev, who had been president since 1964, was very ill and corruption was widespread. When he died in 1982, Yuri Andropov replaced him, but he also soon fell ill and died in 1984. His successor, Konstantin Chernenko died in 1985. For five years there had been little prospect of real change, either internally or externally.

▼ *The funeral of Soviet president Leonid Brezhnev, whose death marked the start of years of stagnation in the USSR.*

1985   GORBACHEV

IN 1985 Mikhail Gorbachev became the
President of the Soviet Union and
announced his policies of *Perestroika* and
Glasnost. Perestroika involved the restructuring of the Soviet economy and *Glasnost*
meant openness. This applied both internally and externally. Gorbachev was aware
that the Soviet Union was bankrupt and
that he had to find ways of saving money
as quickly as possible, so he immediately
restarted disarmament talks with the USA
and became very well known and very
popular in the West. He was able to develop a close friendship with the western
leaders, which enabled a number of
treaties to be signed in the years from
1986 to 1991. In 1989 Gorbachev and
President Bush of the USA were able to
announce that the Cold War was over.

▶ *Soviet president Mikhail Gorbachev developed a
close relationship with Western leaders.*

1989   THE WALL COMES DOWN

SINCE 1945 the Soviet Union had kept military forces in the countries of
eastern Europe. Those countries had been cut off from the West by the Iron
Curtain, that Stalin had built in 1945–46. The most famous example of the
Iron Curtain was the Berlin Wall, which had been built on Khrushchev's
orders in 1961. These actions had been very expensive. In 1989 Mikhail
Gorbachev, the Soviet President, began to withdraw forces from eastern

▲ *Crowds in the Postdamer Platz in Berlin begin to break down the Wall.*

Europe in an effort to save money. The West German government paid the expenses of the forces, which left East Germany. As Soviet troops left, country after country withdrew from the Warsaw Pact and threw off Communism, finally, in November 1989; crowds in Berlin began to knock chunks from the Berlin Wall. By the end of the year pieces were being sold as souvenirs.

1990s   POLITICAL UNITY

THE EEC became the European Community in the 1970s and then became known as the European Union in the 1990s. This was a sign that the Community was changing significantly. In particular a much higher level of integration was taking place. Taxes and laws were being brought into line. In 1992 the Single Market was set up, all goods and people could now travel freely throughout the member countries. Work permits were not required. Terms for a single currency were agreed in 1997, to come into effect in 1999. Co-operation between police and armed forces increased and the Community, in addition, began to be seen as a political force. It attempted to intervene in the Balkans and made common representations on world-wide issues.

War and Peace

1900   DREADNOUGHT

THE development of steel manufacturing allowed enormous steps to be made in the production of ships from 1870 on. By 1900, the thin steel battleships, with a displacement of 15,000 tons and a speed of 18 knots were fast becoming the norm. Britain had intensified the fleet build-up in 1899, concerned that the joint fleets of France and Russia rivalled her own. The first Dreadnought was laid down in 1904, it was a significant improvement on anything produced elsewhere in the world. This British vessel, with a speed of between 18–25 knots boasted ten 12-in guns and would become the model for capital ships until the Second World War. Britain and Germany now dominated the seas around Europe.

▲ *A cigarette card depicting a Dreadnought battleship.*

1901   AFTER PRETORIA

NO sooner had the British begun to reduce the number of troops in South Africa than Boer leaders, among them such soldiers and future statesmen as Louis Botha and Jan Christiaan Smuts, launched extensive and well-planned guerrilla warfare against the occupying British troops. The fighting continued for the next year and was finally only quelled through the severe tactics of the new British commander-in-chief, Kitchener. He exhausted the Boers by devastating the Afrikaner farms that sustained and sheltered the guerrillas, placing black African and Afrikaner women and children in concentration camps, and building a strategic chain of formidable iron blockhouses for his troops. British losses totalled about 28,000 men. Afrikaner losses were about 4,000 men, plus more than 20,000 civilians who died from disease in the concentration camps.

1914   THE WAR IN THE EAST

THE Eastern War began on 17 August 1914, when the Russians invaded eastern Prussia in a full-scale offensive. Two days later, General Alexander Samsonov's Second Army attacked around the right flank of the German Eighth Army commanded by General Friedrich von Prittwitz . Prittwitz proposed abandoning most of East Prussia including Konigsberg. He was immediately replaced by Field Marshall Paul von Hindenburg and his new chief-of-staff, Erich von Ludendorff. By 27 August they had fallen on Samsonov's Army, taking it in both flanks in a near-perfect double envelopment. The Battle of Tannenberg was over by 30 August when Samsonov's command disintegrated at a cost of 92,000 captured. By 5 September German forces under General August Mackensen then defeated Rennenkampf at the Battle of Masurian Lakes, where the Russians suffered over 100,000 casualties.

1916   THE SOMME OFFENSIVE

ON 1 July 1916 the British and French launched the Somme offensive. This offensive was launched against some of the heaviest German fortifications on the entire western front. The British General Haig resisted the idea, but French Commander Joffre won the argument and the campaign began. The Somme saw the first use of tanks, and was preceded by the war's greatest

▲ *Bombardment in the Valley of the Somme.*

artillery barrage. Despite these advantages, the general slaughter of allied troops that occurred was infamous, with the British suffering 65,000 casualties on the first day alone. When the October rains finally put an end to the prolonged carnage, 400,000 British, 200,000 French and 450,000 Germans had become casualties. The Allies only captured a few miles of ground, but the Germans responded by withdrawing to their new Hindenburg line in early 1917.

1916   THE VERDUN BULGE

IN 1916 the German Commander in Chief, Erich von Falkenhayn, put into action his idea for 'bleeding white' the French Army. His plan was to attack a point that the French would not allow to fall, and assure that the point was well covered by artillery. His target was the 'Verdun Bulge', which his troops first assaulted on 21 February, after the most concentrated bombardment of the war. The campaign carried on for four terrible months, during which 300,000 Germans and 460,000 French became casualties. This series of battles, one of the greatest slaughters in history until this time, only

L'HÉROÏQUE DÉFENSE DU FORT DE VAUX

▶ *French magazine depicting the French defence at Verdun.*

marginally achieved the original German goals. The French were indeed 'bled white', but not as severely as had been hoped.

1918   THE YANKS ARE COMING

THE British attacked at Arras on 9 April suffering 84,000 casualties but achieved no breakthrough. Before this battle had ended, the new French commander, Nivelle, launched his own offensive from Soissons to Rheims. This offensive ground to a halt on its first day, and by the time the assault finished the French had suffered 220,000 casualties, and many French soldiers mutinied. In November, the British launched an attack toward Cambrai using hundreds of tanks. All three German lines were broken, but within days, German counter-attacks drove the British back to their starting positions. The last great German offensive was launched on 21 March 1918, with a 6,000-gun barrage and a heavy gas attack. The Allies suffered 350,000 casualties, but more troops were rushed in from across the Channel, and American soldiers began arriving.

▼ *Spanish troops during the Civil War.*

1936   THE SPANISH CIVIL WAR

DURING its first months, the Spanish Civil War acquired international political and ideological significance. Within less than a year from the conflict's onset, Fascist Italy sent about 70,000 ground troops to aid the Nationalists, and Nazi Germany provided planes, pilots, arms and technicians. The USSR sent weapons and advisors to the Republicans; the Comintern organised thousands of liberals and leftists from 53 foreign countries into volunteer International Brigades formed to fight fascism. Both sides engaged in mass arrests and executions in the name of anti-communism or anti-fascism. Serving as a battleground for conflicting nations and as a proving ground for new weapons, the Civil War later became known as a dress rehearsal for the Second World War.

◀ *German planes during the Second World War.*

1939   BLITZKRIEG

ON the morning of 1 September 1939 waves of German bombers hit the railways and hopelessly snarled the Polish mobilisation. In four more days, two army groups, one on the north from East Prussia, the other on the south from Silesia, had broken through on relatively narrow fronts and were sending armoured spearheads on fast drives toward Warsaw and Brêst. This was blitzkrieg ('lightning war'); the use of armour, air power and mobile infantry in a pincers movement to encircle the enemy. On 17 September a second, deeper encirclement closed 160 km (100 miles) east, near Brêst Litovsk. By 20 September practically the whole country was in German or Soviet hands, and only isolated pockets continued to resist until 6 October.

1940   THE BATTLE OF BRITAIN

FOLLOWING the fall of France, Hitler hoped that Britain would accept

German control of the Continent and seek peace. But Britain shunned the Chancellor's overtures of July 1940, and, in August, the German Luftwaffe of Hermann Goering began an all-out attack on British ports, airfields and industrial centres and, finally, on London. The goal was to crush British morale and wipe out the RAF in preparation for Operation Sea Lion, an invasion of England. The Battle of Britain was the first great air battle in history. For 57 nights, an average force of 160 bombers attacked London. The outnumbered RAF, employing the effective Spitfire fighter and aided by radar, destroyed 1,733 aircraft while losing 915 fighters.

▲ *Air attacks, made seriously for the first time during the Second World War, began a new age to warfare.*

1941   THE DESERT FOX

ITALY managed to overrun British Somaliland, defended only by a small garrison, in August 1940. But Mussolini's triumph was short-lived, for by the next summer the British had not only recaptured that territory but had driven the Italians from their East African possessions. In September 1940, Mussolini moved a second army of Italians and North African troops across the Libyan border to establish themselves about 100 km (60 miles) inside Egypt. The British struck back in December in a surprise attack that carried them halfway across Libya by early February 1941. In March 1941 Germany's Afrika Korps, commanded by General Erwin Rommel, arrived at Tripoli. By mid-April, Rommel had reconquered all of Libya except Tobruk; his exploits earned him the nickname 'the Desert Fox'.

1941   PEARL HARBOR

IN late 1941 more than 75 US warships were based at this 'Gibraltar of the Pacific'. All US aircraft carriers were elsewhere. On 26 November a Japanese task force departed in secret from the Kuril Islands. Observing radio silence, it reached a launching point on 7 December. At 7:50 a.m., the first wave of Japanese planes struck Pearl Harbor, bombarding airfields and battleships moored at the concrete quays. A second wave followed. Eighteen US ships were hit, and more than 200 aircraft destroyed or damaged. The attack was, however, a colossal political and psychological blunder, for it mobilised US public opinion against the Japanese and served as the catalyst that brought the United States into the war.

▼ *Japanese air attack on Pearl Harbor.*

Il Giappone in guerra. Un attacco in massa di aeroplani nipponici sopra una base americana nell'Oceano Pacifico: una nave da battaglia degli Stati Uniti viene colpita e incendiata.

1943   TANK WARFARE

ON the eastern front, since Stalingrad, the Germans had shortened their lines, while the Soviet troops were stretched over a massive front with a bulge westward around Kursk. On 5 July 1943, the Germans, using their new Tiger and Panther tanks, struck at this

▲ *Tank warfare played a major part in offensives from both sides during the Second World War.*

Soviet salient. Hitler committed more than 1,000 planes against the Red Army's enormous concentration of troops, artillery pieces and tanks. The encounter developed into one of the largest and most vicious armour battles ever fought. More than 3,000 tanks were engaged on the grasslands. On 12 July 1943 the Soviets moved in fresh tank divisions, and the advantage finally swung to the Russians. Manstein, having lost 70,000 men, half his tanks, and more than 1,000 planes, was forced to withdraw.

1944   D-DAY

ON 6 June 1944 waves of Allied troops moved ashore between Cherbourg and Le Havre in history's largest amphibious operation, involving approximately 5,000 ships of all kinds. About 11,000 Allied aircraft operated over the invasion area. More than 150,000 troops disembarked at Normandy on D-Day. The Germans struck back vigorously. For more than a month they resisted while Allied forces were being built up on the crowded beaches. On 15 August 1944 a fleet of Allied warships appeared off the French Mediterranean coast between Toulon and Cannes. Following a heavy bombardment they unloaded an army of US and French troops. Speedily taking Marseilles and Nice, the Allies headed northward along the Rhone River. German troops in western France were now threatened with isolation.

▲ Allied troops landing in Normandy on D-Day.

1945   THE ORIGINS OF THE VIETNAM WAR

FRENCH Indochina, which included Vietnam, Cambodia (Kampuchea) and Laos, was occupied by Japanese forces during the Second World War. Communist leader Ho Chi Minh and his Viet declared Vietnam an independent republic in 1945. The United States supported the restoration of French rule. When fighting erupted between France and the Viet Minh in 1947, the Americans aided the French and backed Emperor Bao Dai. By 1953 they were providing 80 per cent of the cost of France's war effort. In 1954 the French, hoping to win a decisive victory, lured the Viet Minh into a set-piece battle at Dien Bien Phu but were in turn besieged there. Defeat at Dien Bien Phu made France decide to withdraw from Indochina.

1950   INVASION

THE Korean War began between North Korea (supported by China) and South Korea, aided by the United Nations (although the bulk of the troops were provided by the USA). North Korean forces invaded the South on 25 June 1950. The Security Council of the United Nations, owing to a walk-out by the USSR, voted to oppose them. By September 1950 the North Koreans had overrun most of the South, with the UN forces holding a small area, the Pusan perimeter, in the south-east. The course of the war changed after the surprise landing of US troops later the same month at Inchon on South Korea's north-west coast. This dramatic counter-attack caught the North Koreans off guard and it was their turn to retreat in confusion.

▲ *Memorial to the Korean War in Washington, DC.*

1954   GENEVA AND BEYOND

FOLLOWING the Geneva agreement of 1954, there were five years of relative calm until, in 1959, relations between North and South Vietnam again became critical. The Ngo Dinh Diem regime in Saigon tried to eliminate the remaining Communists in the south, and the Communist government of Ho Chi Minh in Hanoi decided to assist a new rebellion south of the 17th parallel. By the end of 1960 the anti-Diem forces in the south had formed a national-liberation front under the leadership of the southern Communists and during 1961 Diem, who had depended on US aid since 1954, sought additional protection. When Kennedy died (1963), there were about 16,700 US troops in South Vietnam, but the situation was still far from under control.

1964   TONKIN GULF INCIDENT

AFTER the Tonkin Gulf Incident in August 1964, in which the US navy claimed that two of its ships were attacked by North Vietnamese patrol boats, US Congress passed a resolution to take unlimited action to resolve the crisis in South East Asia. An attack on a US base at Pleiku in February 1965 was used as the justification for starting air attacks on the North, which were to be a daily feature of the war until 1968. The US began sending in combat troops to Vietnam (April 1965), increasing steadily until March 1968. The political crisis in Saigon was eased with the emergence of Nguyen Cao Ky as prime minister (1965–67), and the establishment of a new constitution in 1966 and the election of Nguyen Van Thieu as president in 1967.

1969   CAMBODIA

THE war continued through-out 1969–71 and spread across the region. The US brought Cambodia into the war, securing the removal of Sihanouk's neutral regime in Phnom Penh. Heavy bombing of Cambodia drew that country into the conflict and ultimately resulted in the Khmer Rouge govern-ment. Anxious to break the stalemate, North Vietnam launched a new and much heavier offensive against the South Vietnamese army in

▲ *Soldiers in Pleiku, South Vietnam, where an attack on the US base initiated retaliatory action in the North.*

the Quang Tri province and in the region of An Loc (north of Saigon) in the spring of 1972. There were now fewer than 100,000 US troops in Vietnam and so the Americans responded with intense bombing of the north, the mining of Haiphong harbour, and unlimited air support for South Vietnamese ground troops.

▲ *US helicopters in Vietnam.*

1972   THE PARIS TREATY AND AFTER ...

CONTACTS between Hanoi and Washington during 1972 led eventually to the signing of the Paris Treaty in January 1973. US forces finally left South Vietnam in March 1973, and for two years the South Vietnamese government of Nguyen Van Thieu sought to continue the US policy of pacification. But the Viet Cong provisional revolutionary government of South Vietnam was making substantial political gains in the countryside and in late 1974 North Vietnam breached the cease-fire with a final offensive against the

▲ *US troops in Saigon in 1972.*

South. By March 1975 South Vietnamese morale had collapsed, and in April the communist forces took Saigon with only a limited amount of fighting. The war was over and Vietnam was reunited as the Socialist Republic of Vietnam in July 1976.

1973   YOM KIPPUR WAR

ON 6 October 1973 Egypt and Syria, frustrated by Israel's refusal to give up Arab territory, joined to launch a surprise attack on Israeli occupation forces. The Syrians, aided by troops from Jordan and Iraq, initially made some gains in the north, but by 11 October they had been turned back, and the Israelis advanced into Syria. In the south, the Egyptians crossed the Suez Canal and penetrated about 10 km (6 miles) into Israeli-occupied Sinai before they were stalled. On 16 October the Israelis counter-attacked and invaded Egypt itself. A cease-fire took effect on the Syrian front on 22 October and in Egypt two days later. Although militarily won by Israel, Egypt, by the initial performance of its army, managed to turn the war into a psychological victory.

1979   THE RUSSIAN INVASION OF AFGHANISTAN

ON 25 December 1979 Soviet forces invaded Afghanistan. They quickly won control of Kabul. But the government, dependent on Soviet military forces, was unpopular, and the rebellion intensified. During the next few years about three million war refugees fled to Pakistan and 1.5 million fled to Iran. The anti-government guerrilla forces included dozens of factions. They operated from bases around Peshawar, Pakistan and Iran. Weapons and money from the United States, Saudi Arabia, Iran and China sustained them. During the 1980s Soviet forces increasingly bore the brunt of the fighting. By 1986 about 118,000 Soviet troops and 50,000 Afghan government troops were facing perhaps 130,000 guerrillas. Estimates of combat fatalities range between 700,000 and 1.3 million people. The Soviets completed their with-drawal in 1989.

1982   THE FALKLANDS WAR

NEGOTIATIONS to settle the sovereignty dispute between Argentina and Great Britain over the Falkland Islands began in the mid-1960s at the United Nations. The talks were still in progress in April 1982, when Argentine forces invaded and occupied the islands for about 10 weeks in an attempt to settle the issue by force. They were defeated by a British task force and formally surrendered on 14 June. Although numerically superior, the Argentines were out-fought and out-commanded by the British. Casualties were comparative-ly light, despite the use of modern weaponry. Argentina continued to claim the islands; the British government refused to participate in further negotia-tions, but the two nations resumed diplomatic relations in 1990.

1991   THE BREAK-UP OF YUGOSLAVIA

THE wars in Yugoslavia began in the summer of 1991 after Slovenia and Croatia declared their independence. In July of that year, the Yugoslav People's Army (JNA), which consisted mainly of Serbs, intervened in Slovenia with the intention of removing the Slovenian government and

▲ *Royal Marines in training during the Falklands War in 1982; the British were forced to fight when Argentine troops invaded the islands, trying to settle the sovereignty dispute.*

disarming its defence forces; Slovenian troops repelled the Yugoslav forces after 10 days. The war in Bosnia began in the spring of 1992, when the new government declared independence from Yugoslavia. Serbian nationalists within Bosnia violently occupied more than 60 per cent of Bosnian territory; thousands of Muslims and Croats were murdered or expelled from their homes. The tribunal for massacring civilians during the war indicted more than 50 Bosnians, the majority of whom were Serbs. They included Bosnian Serb leader Radovan Karadzic and military commander Ratko Mladic.

1991   THE GULF WAR

THE crisis began in August 1990, when Iraq, led by President Saddam Hussein, invaded and annexed Kuwait. Between August and November the United Nations Security Council passed a series of resolutions that culminated in the demand that Iraq withdraw unconditionally from Kuwait by 15 January 1991. By that time, some 500,000 allied ground, air and naval forces – chiefly from the United States, Saudi Arabia, Great Britain, Egypt, Syria and France – were arrayed against an Iraqi army, estimated at that time to number 540,000. The land offensive, Desert Storm, was launched and within 100 hours, the city of Kuwait had been liberated, and tens of thousands of Iraqi troops had deserted, surrendered, or been captured or killed.

▲ *Kuwaiti soldiers; tension between Iraq under the leadership of Saddam Hussein and Kuwait continued throughout the 1990s.*

Society and Culture

1900 REPRESSION RULES

REPRESSION remained the reaction of authority under challenge even while humanitarians gained ground elsewhere. In 1900, the Boxer Rebellion of Chinese opposed to the powerful influence of foreigners in China was put down with great ferocity. Captured Boxers were beheaded and their executioners posed for photographs with the dismembered bodies. In Russia, protests against Tsarist rule in 1901, 1902 and 1905 were put down no less forcefully. However, Russia could no longer afford this kind of response. Millions of peasants lived in appalling poverty and deprivation, and anarchists were willing to murder and terrorise to get what they wanted. Eventually, the Russian tsar, Nicholas II (1868–1918) and his family faced the ultimate terror – their capture and slaughter by the Bolsheviks in 1918.

▲ *The Chinese Boxer Rebellion of 1900.*

1903   VOTES FOR WOMEN

WOMEN sought the vote as early as 1880 but their polite requests got nowhere. After 1903, when Emmeline Pankhurst (1858–1928) founded the Women's Social and Political Union, her suffragism was more militant. Suffragettes chained themselves to railings, smashed windows, set fire to pillar boxes and one, Emily Davison, committed suicide by throwing herself in front of King George V's horse during a race in 1913. Violence was matched by violence, notably the force-feeding of suffragettes, which so damaged Mrs. Pankhurst that it contributed to her death. Her efforts, however, made such a

▲ *Emmeline Pankhurst, founder of the Women's Social and Political Union, with her daughter Christabel.*

prominent issue of votes for women that after they had undertaken men's jobs during the First World War some were enfranchised in 1918. All adult women in Britain were allowed to vote after 1928.

1914   THE WAR TO END ALL WARS

THE declaration of war on 4 August 1914 was greeted, in Britain, France and Germany, in the traditional way: by cheering crowds, excitement and patriotic flag-waving. Only three months later, this jubilant mood was replaced by disillusionment as lethal modern weapons forced the combatants in France to retire into trenches and largely remain there, among the mud, sludge, filth, corpses and rats, as long as the fighting lasted. Shock and rage increased when in 1915, German zeppelin air raids over Britain made dangerous the one place – the home – where people had always presumed themselves to be safe. Even among the victors, the end of the war on 11 November 1918 was greeted sombrely, with heartfelt relief.

1916 DIVIDE AND RULE

IN 1916, when the British encouraged the Arabs in Palestine to revolt against their Ottoman Turkish masters – a revolt which succeeded brilliantly – they came to believe that a measure of independence would be their reward. In 1917, in the Balfour Declaration, the British gave a broad hint to the Jews that Palestine, their ancient ancestral home, would be theirs. The result was that Palestine, which became a British mandate from the League of Nations after the War, was the scene of vicious rivalry and hatred, outbreaks of fighting and raiding that the British tried, but ultimately failed, to bring under control. Worse still, both Jew and Arab came to believe that the British were favouring the opposing side.

1920s NO HOME FIT FOR HEROES

THE 'home fit for heroes' promised by British Prime Minister David Lloyd George (1863–1945) proved a myth. Many 'heroes' returned home to unemployment. Some sold matches in the streets, displaying their medals to encourage custom. Domestic servants who had hoped to escape it, were forced back into service. In defeated Germany, rampant inflation and crippling reparations imposed by the victors led to mass poverty and destitution. The rescue promised by the Nazi Führer Adolf Hitler, who came to power in 1933, seemed a tempting way out, with assurances of full employment and socialist benefits. Too late, the Germans realised the price: total submission to Nazi rule and for some – liberals, homosexuals, Jews, gypsies – imprisonment or death.

▲ *British prime minister David Lloyd George, with his wife and daughter.*

▲ *Typical twenties costumes; women like this were known as 'flappers'.*

1920s   THE ROARING TWENTIES

AFTER the War, some young men and women blanked out their grief for lost friends and relatives with thrills and pleasure. There were wild parties and new, provocative dances like the 'Black Bottom'. Cars crammed with noisy young people headed for night clubs, from which many did not emerge until dawn. Young women in particular claimed new freedoms – they cut their hair short, wore 'indecently' short skirts – above the knee in 1926 – or drank and smoked, things which would never have been permitted them only a short while before. The so-called 'Roaring Twenties' was a crazy time, but not one in which the mass of people could share; their reaction to the war was despair.

1929   THE WALL STREET CRASH

THE early post-war period was boom time in the USA. War industries, turning over to civilian production, poured out goods for an eager consumer market. Rich dividends were promised to investors, some of whom, the smaller ones, invested their entire savings in stocks and shares. They felt certain of making a profit. Instead, they faced ruin. The boom was a bubble that

▶ *Despair on the streets of America after the Wall Street Crash.*

had to burst. Signs that the US economy was not as healthy as investors believed began to appear. Stock values began to fall. Then, on 24 October 1929, the pressure became so great that the New York stock exchange crashed. Investors besieged banks clamouring to withdraw their money, but for many, it was too late. They had lost everything.

1930s   HOLOCAUST

PREJUDICE, persecution and pogroms had stalked Jews for many centuries, but nothing compared to the Nazis' systematic attempt to exterminate them as a race during the Second World War. All over occupied Europe, Jews were rounded up, crammed into cattle trucks and transported to the extermination camps the Nazis had set up in Poland and Germany. The Nazis had also constructed gas chambers where the Jews were taken, supposedly to take showers, but were then shut in and gassed to death *en masse*. Later, their bodies were burned in ovens. Some six million were wiped out in this horrific fashion. Jews, however, were not the only victims of Nazi 'ethnic cleansing': gypsies, also regarded by the Nazis as a blight on society, received the same sadistic treatment and four million died.

1940   CONQUERORS AND CONQUERED

BETWEEN April and June 1940, Nazi Germany overran Norway, Denmark, France, Belgium and the Netherlands and in 1941, parts of Russia. Poland had already been conquered in 1939. These countries were now forced to live under foreign, and often retributive, domination as the Nazi conquest brought curfews, shortages and savage punishments for disobedience. This produced several reactions. Most people simply tried to survive as best they could and keep out of trouble. Others risked everything to form resistance movements, and were not always helped by their compatriots who thought it best to keep their heads down. Some collaborated with the Germans, seeking safety by fraternising with the winning side. Their punishment after the War was savage.

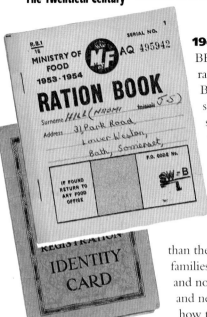

▲ Ration books were issued in 1940.

1940 RATIONING

BECAUSE of its island location, rationing was essential in wartime Britain. Luxuries, and certain food-stuffs, especially from distant countries such as oranges and bananas, and for a time, chocolate, were unobtainable. Essentials – butter, eggs, meat, fish, clothing – were strictly apportioned out through ration books containing coupons. It was a well-considered system and in fact provided some Britons with better nutrition than they had had in peacetime, when poor families relied too much on carbohydrates and not enough on vital proteins. The radio and newspapers carried regular hints on how to make the most of the rations, but there were, of course, black marketeers and many who were willing to buy from them. Others, who told the police about blackmarketing activities, could be ostracised.

1941 RESISTING THE NAZIS

IN the Nazi-occupied countries, those who chose resistance not only risked their lives every day, but assumed the tremendous nervous strain of a clandestine existence. Some were simply patriots, determined to eject the hated invader from their land. Others had their own agendas, such as the Communists in Yugoslavia or the supporters of the 'Free French' General Charles de Gaulle (1890–1970), who hoped for political power after the War. Whatever their motivations, resistance fighters lived a life of constant suspense, constant watchfulness and always the danger of betrayal. They knew what capture could mean – torture, imprisonment and death – and that all their willpower would be needed not to yield the information that the Nazis tried to force out of them.

▲ *French citizens queuing to join the Resistance movement.*

1947   ORIGINS OF COLONIAL INDEPENDENCE

THE effects of independence in many former colonial territories laid bare the effects of imperialism. Native cultures had necessarily been suppressed during the long decades of colonial rule. When independence revived them, the spectacle was sometimes alarming. For instance, in Africa, where Ghana (the former Gold Coast) was the first imperial possession to be granted independence, in 1957, the leaders of countries accepted Britain's 'gift' of a demo-cratic, parliamentary system. Before long, however, their tendency towards rule by one 'strong man', a characteristic of their pre-colonial days, reasserted itself. Tribalism was also now expressed in damaging civil wars. This greatly exacerbated the basic poverty of newly independent countries and sank them in a slough from which many have not yet recovered.

1947   THE SEEDS OF FREEDOM

THE quest for freedom seemed to be in the air once the Second World War was over. As imperial powers, the French and the Dutch had suffered severe loss of face during the War, and Britain, though a major victor, had been impoverished by its efforts. The new Labour Government elected in Britain in 1945 believed, too, that colonial rule should come to an end, and in 1947, with the independence of India and the creation of Pakistan for the Muslims, a long process of de-colonisation began. Other lessons had gone home elsewhere. During the War, Black Americans had made their own considerable contribution, and suffered their own losses. The segregated regiments in which army GIs had served now seemed iniquitous, and Black Americans baulked at returning to their previous, downtrodden status.

▲ *Nelson Mandela, whose campaigns eventually overthrew the apartheid regime in South Africa.*

1948   APARTHEID

SOUTH Africa imposed apartheid – the separation of the black and white races – in 1948, but this was merely official sanction on a situation that had long existed. The Boers, the white South Africans of Dutch descent, believed Blacks to be inferior and had, in fact, found justification for that in the Bible. Their thinking, of course, ran counter to the more liberal ways of thought gaining ground in the West during the 1960s, but South Africa's comparative isolation enabled them to sustain it. The liberalising influences put pressure on South Africa nonetheless. In the West, a campaign of sanctions and censure began to make apartheid untenable. Over 30 years passed and much suffering took place before it succeeded.

1949　　THE STATE OF ISRAEL

IN 1944 and 1945, as the Allied forces closed in on Nazi Germany, the ghastly revelations of the liberated camps, with their skeletal, dehumanised survivors, shocked and appalled the world. This gave a powerful impetus to the aspirations of Jews in Palestine who believed that, without a country of their own, this 'Holocaust'could happen again. Once the British, exasperated by the savage Arab-Jewish rivalries, returned the Palestine mandate to the new United Nations, a vote was taken there in 1947 to create the State of Israel. The new state was immediately challenged by the surrounding Arab countries and a bitter war ensued. By 1949, after nine months, Israel prevailed, but Arab-Israeli hatred survived and has scarred the region ever since.

▲ *Victims of the 'Final Solution', Jews from the concentration camp Bergen-Belsen.*

1954   THE WORLD OPENS UP

TELEVISION, invented in 1925, was the first medium to open up a window on the world after it became widely available by about 1954. Through television, life can be observed going on in distant places, even beneath the sea. Jumbo

jets can carry 300 people or more to the other side of the world in a few hours. Computer users can make instant links, letters that would take days or weeks to travel by post, appear instantly as faxes. E-mails flash on to computer screens at the touch of a mouse arrow. These capabilities are so familiar on the brink of the millennium that they have lost much of their wonder, yet barely 40 years ago they were not yet possible.

◄ *Advertisement for television in the 1950s.*

1960s   AGAINST WAR

IT had always been the fate of young men to fight and die in society's wars. This principle could be maintained as long as war was considered glorious and patriotic, but the young generation, born during or just after the Second World War, sought to break what they saw as a pernicious mould. Pacifism was nothing new at this time, but the scale of it was. The Korean War (1950–53) and the fighting in French Indochina, Greece and Malaya suggested that nothing had changed. However, vociferous, often violent, protests and demonstrations took place as the young challenged the Establishment's presumption that yet another generation would let itself be decimated by war. With this, other Establishment values came under equally heavy fire.

1960s   GIVE PEACE A CHANCE

THE mass social revolt of the young, which left their elders feeling thoroughly beleaguered, seemed to involve everything pugnaciously different from the principles of existing society. Young men grew their hair long. Young women wore revealing miniskirts. They lived together before marriage, experimented with drugs, embraced mystical religions such as Zen Buddhism, and gathered at rock festivals to listen to their own brand of popular music. Some, such as the Flower Children, went so far as to create an 'alternative society' with some of the same elements. It included a philosophy which sprang from their idea that if only everyone would 'give peace a chance' as one of their songs went, then the world would be a wonderful place.

1960s   SPURNING THE GLOBAL VILLAGE

THE materialistic life, with its emphasis on consumerism, is spurned by the unconventional 'hippies' who adhere to their principles even though the 1960s, which gave rise to them, are long past. A great deal about the 1960s still lives through them – the hallucinogenic drugs, the long hair, the transcendental meditation, but also a strong sense of community, the desire for peaceful co-existence and a belief in love as the magic elixir for a good and happy life. Realising, even so, that most of the world does not seek to run on these lines, hippies tend to live in tight, sometimes remote communities or, in their more recent 'New Age Traveller' persona, they move from place to place like gypsies.

▶ *'Hippies' during the 1960s.*

1960s   BAN THE BOMB!

PROTEST soon became the virtual symbol of the 1960s, with rallies, marches, demonstrations and clashes with the police. The Nuclear Age that followed the atomic bombing of Japan in 1945, produced rowdy, vociferous demonstrations in Britain, France and Germany demanding that the government eschew atomic weapons. The war in Vietnam, too, roused fury at what young Americans, British and French saw as an immoral conflict. Some Americans went to Canada to avoid being drafted and were dubbed cowards by some, but heroes by others. In America, too, Martin Luther King (1929–68) used peaceful, but determined, methods to promote black equality. Malcolm Little (Malcolm X) (1926–65) preferred more violent ways to achieve the same object. Both were assassinated.

▲ *Martin Luther King, who advocated peaceful methods in the fight for black equality.*

1960s   WOMEN'S LIBERATION

THE centuries-old subordination of women to men could basically be regarded in two ways: women were either nurturers of children, performing society's most vital single task, or victims of male oppression, which denied them their ambitions and talents. The women's liberation movement took the latter view, and the clamour began for equality with men, abortion 'on demand', access to education and training, as well as to jobs formerly reserved for men, even access to men's clubs and other 'bastions' of male domination. There was, naturally enough, resistance – and not just from men, either. Concerns were voiced that if women abandoned their traditional role, or even supplemented it with the new roles they demanded, the fabric of society could suffer.

1969   SPACE EXPLORATION AND ITS BENEFITS

FOR centuries mankind had been struggling to unravel the mysteries of space. The first moon landing in 1969 was one of the greatest breakthoughs in space exploration. Space is not simply a playground for scientists or the source of exciting television transmissions. Benefits for humanity can come from space exploration. Medical research could gain much from the germ-free conditions to be found in space. Minerals brought back from the Moon could lead to new drugs. The experiences of astronauts, in particular weightlessness, may lead to new understandings of the human body and its capabilities. The Hubble Space Telescope, launched in 1990, is able to make its observations without the interference from the atmosphere that sometimes complicates the work of Earth-based

◄ *An astronaut from the shuttle* Challenger *'walks' in space.*

astronomers. This makes possible closer observations of the stars, including the Sun and greater understanding of their functions and of the Sun's effects on Earth and its life.

1970s   ISLAM VS THE WEST

ISLAM and Christianity were rivals, often savage rivals, almost from the moment Islam was founded in AD 624. The Western world, which was largely the product of Christianity, has now taken over as Islam's modern challenger, and one which fundamentalist Muslims in particular regard as an evil to be expunged. Several Muslim countries, such as Iran and Algeria, have sought to close themselves off from 'pernicious' Western influences, though still dealing with the West for political or trade purposes. Their rivalry is, however, a fruitful ground for Muslim terrorist groups who have used modern weaponry, especially bombs, to make their presence known. This has often resulted in scenes of destruction and carnage, made all the more impactive by graphic television coverage. Since the 1970s terrorism has been widespread in many countries, and has become a characteristic of modern religious conflict.

1990s   REMAINING PROBLEMS

ON the brink of the third millennium, the world is not without its serious problems – war, urban crime, economic difficulties, poverty, family break-down. There is, however, a distinct internationalism at work in the search for some solutions. Scientists and governments have come together to tackle AIDS, HIV and drug abuse, all of them international problems. International aid has many times gone to the rescue of famine sufferers in Ethiopia, the Sudan and many other places. Multinational forces have policed trouble spots such as the civil war-torn former Yugoslavia. Environmentalists fight to pre-serve Earth and its life, activists to save endangered species. Among ordinary people, television no sooner shows terrible scenes of suffering and depriva-tion from anywhere in the world than donations flow in to mitigate them.

Exploration and Empires

1909   REACHING THE NORTH POLE

NORWEGIAN scientist Fridtjof Nansen (1861–1930) was a principal polar explorer who completed the first expedition to the Greenland ice cap (1888–89). He then designed a ship capable of withstanding the pressure exerted by ice and embarked on an expedition across the Arctic basin in 1893 by drifting with the ice instead of ramming it. After realising that the ship was not drifting towards the North Pole he set off with a companion to reach it on specially designed sledges but was forced to turn back 370 km (230 miles) from their objective. In 1909 American Robert Peary (1856–1920) claimed to have reached the North Pole with eskimos on sledges. The Japanese adventurer Naomi Uemura made the first solo trek to the North Pole (1978).

▲ *Norwegian explorer and scientist Fridtjof Nansen.*

1910 THE SOUTH POLE

ANTARCTICA was the last continent to be explored. In 1908 Ernest Shackleton's (1874–1922) British expedition set out on a 1,300-km (800-mile) trek to the South Pole but food shortages forced them to turn back 160 km (100 miles) from their objective. The 'race' to the South Pole began in 1910 between a Norwegian team led by Roald Amundsen and a British one led by Robert Scott (1868–1912). Using Inuit survival skills, dog sledges and fur clothing, the Norwegians advanced faster than the mixture of horses, dogs and motor-sledges used by Scott. Amundsen took seven weeks to reach the pole in December 1911. Scott's team arrived in January 1912 but the entire team perished on the return journey.

◀ *Irish Antarctic explorer Ernest Henry Shackleton.*

1919   INTER-WAR UNREST: AMRITSAR

DURING the First World War the imperial empires maintained the co-operation of their colonial subjects but the inter-war period exposed the fragility of their imperial control. Efforts to satisfy Arab aspirations in the Middle East led to Britain establishing the kingdoms of Iraq (declared independent in 1932) and Transjordan. Similar promises made to the Jews for a 'National Home' in Palestine created more complications and violence. The Indian independence movement proved a serious threat to British rule with growing

demands for Indian representation in central government. The 1919 Amritsar massacre of 400 Indians hardened nationalist campaigners and emergency powers were subsequently introduced to repress protests amid growing violence.

▲ *The Amritsar Massacre, in which 400 Indians were killed and a further 1,200 wounded.*

1920s ANTARCTIC EXPLORATION

ERNEST Shackleton led a voyage across the continent (1915–17) after drifting in ice for nine months. The crew were forced into lifeboats after the ship began to be crushed by ice. A small party finally reached their base camp on foot, and all were eventually saved. In 1929 Richard Byrd flew over the South Pole, Amundsen became the first man to reach both poles after flying over the North Pole in 1926, and American Lincoln Ellsworth (1880–1951) made the first flight across Antarctica (1935). Many nations have laid claims to Antarctica but conflict has been averted by international treaties that encourage conservation and co-operation in research. The potential to extract minerals from Antarctica may still generate rivalry over the continent.

1930s THE GREATER EAST ASIA CO-PROSPERITY SPHERE

JAPAN'S invasions were initially perceived as liberating nations from European colonists. Semi-independent governments were appointed except in the 'inferior' South-East Asia region. Often Japan failed to mobilise occupied areas and faced disorder and hostility instead of co-operation. Local nationalists were often given responsibilities but they used this collaboration to bolster their movements. Japanese barbarity was commonplace with forced labour, massacres and human-rights violations. This was first displayed during the Manchuria invasion (1931) and the invasion of China (1937) where 250,000 people died in Nanking alone. China responded by bitterly resisting Japan and 15 million Chinese died from fighting and appalling conditions.

1930s   GANDHI AND THE INDIAN STRUGGLE

THE 1935 Government of India Act granted limited self-government and progressively pledged to transfer power. Such vague promises failed to satisfy the Indian National Congress. Nationalist leader M. K. Gandhi (1869–1948) led a campaign of satyagraha: passive civil disobedience and the boycotting of European goods. In 1931 the British imprisoned Gandhi but failed to suppress the momentum for change. In the immediate post-war period, war-weary imperial powers were often unable fully to restore colonial control. Civil unrest in India and a naval mutiny (1946) forced Britain to accelerate moves towards independence. In elections Indian Muslims in the north voted overwhelmingly for the Muslim League, which demanded a separate state. In August 1947 the country was partitioned into independent India (mainly Hindu) and the newly created Pakistan (mainly Muslim).

1935   THE 'NEW ROME'

ITALY'S empire, forged by the infamous Benito Mussolini, was a small and short-lived creation. It began with the invasion of Ethiopia in 1935, followed by Albania in 1939 and British Somaliland in 1940. Sections of France, Yugoslavia and Greece also came under her control. Italy, however, lacked the capability and the commitment to retain her conquests. Britain repulsed her attack on Egypt (1940–41)

▲ *Italian dictator Benito Mussolini.*

then recaptured East Africa (1941). Public support for fascist imperialism – and the war–was short-lived. Before Mussolini fell from power (1943) the empire was already strained by deteriorating relations with Germany in the occupied regions they shared, especially over the treatment of Jews.

1936 MILITARISM IN JAPAN

JAPAN had seen the rise of militaristic and imperialistic movements since 1918. Since Japan's emergence from isolationism in the nineteenth century to become modern and industrialised, the nation had developed into a leading military and economic force within Asia. It had already gained territory from China (1894–95) and Russia (1899–1902) through military conquests. After the First World War it gained former

▲ *Officials proclaim the New State of Manchuria.*

German islands and Chinese outposts. Overseas expansion became a key policy in the inter-war period with Japan invading Manchuria (1931). After the military took power (1936) they began attacking China (1937). Japan's aim was for a 'Greater East Asia Co-Prosperity Sphere', in theory a mutually beneficial trading network; in reality a framework to secure raw materials for Japan and markets for her exports.

1939 OCCUPIED POPULATIONS

THE effects upon Nazi-occupied populations were traumatic. Intellectual freedoms were constrained by Nazi doctrine, cultural and religious expression was replaced by the Nazi identity, politics was repressed by propaganda, information was censored and freedom of movement limited. Economic dislocation impoverished populations and food production was directed to Germany. As conditions deteriorated and transport systems faltered the rationing of populations reached critical levels. One of the most terrifying manifestations of the New Order was the Nazi attempt to achieve racial supremacy. The Nazis aimed to create a demographic transformation in Europe by gathering the German race. This involved enslaving the Slavs and destroying the Jews. Unlike the barbarism of former conquerors, Nazi violence was not random, but systematic, and millions were killed with bureaucratic efficiency.

▲ *Vidkum Quisling, whose war crimes included the mass-execution of Norwegian citizens.*

1940s   THE NAZIS PLUNDER EUROPE

GERMANY had anticipated a rapid victory and economic planning focused upon restructuring her empire for the post-war era. The prolonged war, however, presented Germany with pressing needs. Economic squads swarmed into conquered lands to seize raw materials, gold and machinery. Germany assumed control of fuel, materials, currency and prices. Occupation costs were imposed on countries with France paying 10.9 per cent of her national income in 1940 and 36.6 per cent by 1943. German labour shortages were relieved by prisoners-of-war, and 'voluntary' or forced foreign workers were compelled to work in Germany. By 1944, some 2 million prisoners-of-war and 7.5 million adults and children from across German-occupied Europe were working in Germany.

▲ *German prisoners after the Battle of Stalingrad in 1943.*

1945 BEYOND THE SECOND WORLD WAR

THE fascist empires of Germany and Italy had collapsed by 1945 at the end of the Second World War. A total of 60 million people had died during this time. The human and material cost of these regimes was unprecedented, and they opened the eyes of the world to the dangers of such political cults. Their rise, domination and collapse had far-reaching repercussions for the shape of the post-war world, the pre-war colonial powers and the ascendancy of new power blocs. In this short period, the world view of persecution, basic human rights and warfare itself had changed forever.

1946 OPERATION HIGHJUMP

IN 1946, Admiral Richard Byrd (1888–1957) returned to Antarctica to lead the largest expedition ever mounted to that inhospitable continent. Operation Highjump involved a fleet of 13 ships and 4,700 men. Highjump charted a large extent of the coastline of the ice pack covering the pole. Expeditions such as these were considered highly prestigious in the ideological war between the United States and the Soviet Union. The scientists involved, however, preferred activities such as the International Geophysical

Year (1957–58). Some 12 nations participated in this, involved in projects such as the causes of earthquakes, oceanography, meteorology and the crossing of the Antarctic.

1947 THE DIVISION OF EUROPE

THE Soviet leader, Joseph Stalin (1879–1953), feared American military power, especially the American monopoly of atomic weapons. When Winston Churchill (1874–1965), made his notorious 'Iron Curtain' speech in February 1946, the suspicious Stalin denounced it as 'a dangerous act'. In 1947–48 the Communists seized power in eastern Europe under the domination of the Soviet Union. At the same time the Soviets gave considerable financial support to the Communist parties of France and Italy. In that year, the United States launched the Marshall Plan, giving financial aid to the governments of Western Europe. This aid, and other assistance to pro-capitalist parties helped defeat the Communists in elections in 1948.

▲ *Cartoon depicting the Soviet leader Joseph Stalin.*

1948 COLLAPSING EMPIRES

THE Second World War saw the first steps towards the collapse of colonial rule, as European powers became embroiled in a global conflict that exposed deep cracks in the foundations of imperialism. The omnipotence of colonial powers was shattered by the conquests of their homelands or colonies. Bargaining for support, Britain offered India post-war independence in return for Indian help during the war. The Indian National Congress demanded independence immediately and in an about-turn an Indian National Army even fought with the Japanese against Britain. Resistance groups who campaigned against occupation planned to fight both the Axis powers and the imperialists.

1948 GLOBAL COLD WAR

THE beginning of the Cold War is normally associated with the Berlin Blockade of 1948. At the beginning of 1949, the Communists triumphed in a civil war in China, while in August, the Soviet Union detonated an atomic bomb. Suddenly, the Communist bloc had been transformed into a genuine global rival to the United States. In 1950, the Communists of North Korea invaded the American-backed South Korea. The United Nations,

▲ *Troops in Berlin at the beginning of the Cold War in 1948.*

founded to end such conflicts, intervened when the Soviet Union boycotted a crucial Security Council meeting, and so was not able to use its veto against an American proposal to name North Korea as the aggressor. Hundreds of thousands of American and allied troops now invaded Korea under the flag of the United Nations, and the war lasted until 1953.

1950s   THE DOMINO ERA

COMMUNISTS were frequently involved in the highest councils of independence movements, which therefore became suspect in the eyes of the United States. The worst offenders from this perspective were the Indochinese Communists led by Ho Chi Minh (1890–1969). When the French finally agreed to the independence of Indochina, the United States supported an anti-Communist régime in its own state in the south. The war continued because political leaders in the United States had adopted a strategy of containment. Friendly governments were established in states bordering the Communist bloc, and linked by means of military alliances such as the Baghdad Pact of 1955 between Turkey, Iraq, Iran and Pakistan. The strategy was publicised under the less aggressive name of the 'Domino theory'.

1956   THE SUEZ CRISIS

WITH little colonial reform in Africa, independence campaigns arose. The first major incident which exposed imperial vulnerability was the Kenyan Mau-Mau guerrilla war (1952–56). Nations like Britain became increasingly aware that decolonisation would not disrupt overseas economic interests, but would relieve them of imperial defence and administration. The 1956 Suez Crisis, where France and Britain had to make a humiliating withdrawal from Egypt under US pressure, undermined the credibility of the colonial powers and revealed their declining global status. A major review of Britain's imperial position resulted in Ghana becoming the first independent 'black' nation

▲ *The President of North Vietnam Ho Chi Minh with the Yugoslav President Marshal Tito.*

in Africa (1957). By 1964 British prime minister Harold Macmillan (1894–1986) spoke of a 'wind of change' as decolonisation spread through Africa and the Caribbean.

1956　　FIGHTING AND FREEDOM IN AFRICA

IN 1956 France left Morocco and Tunisia, but Algerian independence was

opposed by the one million Algerians of French descent (colons) who rejected the idea of an Arab Muslim state. In 1954 a nationalist Arab rebellion sparked a bitter civil conflict. To halt any withdrawal French army officers sympathetic to the colons revolted (1958) and a new premier, Charles de Gaulle (1890–1970), was appointed. De Gaulle withdrew from the colonies of Guinea (1958), Cameroon, Congo, Gabon, Chad and the Central African Republic (1960). Algeria

▲ *French premier Charles de Gaulle, who ordered the withdrawal of troops from Africa.*

finally gained independence in 1962. The ruling white minority in Southern Rhodesia declared independence in 1965 and excluded Blacks from power. White-dominated South Africa adopted a racist apartheid policy in 1948 and amid opposition from the British Commonwealth became a republic (1948).

1957   THE HIGH WATERMARK OF COMMUNISM

IN October 1957 the Soviet Union's considerable investment of resources into rocket technology paid off with the launch of an unmanned satellite, called Sputnik, into space.

Politicians and military leaders in the United States were alarmed. The United States had, in 1955, openly declared its intention of launching a space satellite in 1958 as part of International Geophysical Year. The Soviets had kept quiet, and beaten the United States to it. The advantage the Soviets had in rocket technology enabled them to repeat the feat of beating the United States in what had been christened 'the Space Race'. In 1959 a Cuban civil war ended with the victory of Fidel Castro (b. 1927), a man who openly welcomed the support of Cuba's Communists to his regime.

▲ *Revolutionary Fidel Castro, who ousted Cuban dictator Batista in 1958 and introduced a programme of Marxist-Leninist reforms.*

1960s   THE SPACE AGE

ENTERING space required a rocket capable of breaking through Earth's gravity. This was first achieved by American Robert Goddard's (1882–1945) liquid-fuel rocket (1926). In 1957 the first satellite was launched by the Soviet Union. The first manned space flight carried Russian Yuri Gagarin (1934–1968) in 1961. John Glenn became the first American to orbit the Earth in 1962. Russian Valentina Tereshkova (b. 1937) became the first woman astronaut (1963) and Russian Alexei Leonov made the first space walk (1965). Space exploration became entangled with superpower rivalry and became a showpiece for displaying technical superiority with obvious military implications. One of the greatest missions was the 'race' to the Moon. In July 1969 the United States won when Neil Armstrong

▲ *Russian astronaut Yuri Gagarin, who became the first man in space in 1961.*

(b. 1930), Buzz Aldrin (b. 1930) and Michael Collins (b. 1930) landed on lunar soil. The first space station was launched by the Soviet Union in 1974.

1960   THE SUBMERSIBLE RECORD

IN 1930 the Swiss inventor William Beebe designed a spherical diving machine capable of withstanding water pressure at deep levels and in 1948 Swiss scientist Auguste Piccard (1884–1962) designed a submersible that could dive and surface without assistance from a ship. In 1960 a submersible made a record-breaking descent 11 km (7 miles) to Mariana Trench in the Pacific Ocean, the world's deepest recorded place. In 1943 Frenchmen Jacques Cousteau and Emile Gaynon designed the first aqualung: cylinders containing compressed air fed to divers through a mouthpiece. This invention opened a new era in exploration as divers could now descend to 60 m (200 ft) without being constrained by heavy suits or air cables.

1975   THE UNITED STATES AND THE SOVIET UNION

SO much of the Soviet Union's resources were devoted to military expenditure that it was distorting economic development. After the victory of North Vietnam in 1975, the United States began to reject Soviet overtures to reduce tension between the superpowers. In 1979 when an internal political dispute threatened the stability of a Soviet-sponsored regime in Afghanistan, the Red Army invaded. This intervention allowed the United States to sponsor a guerrilla movement of Islamic militants. By 1985, when Mikhail Gorbachev (b. 1931) emerged as party leader, it signalled an end to old policies. Once

▲ *Peacekeeping troops in Afghanistan in 1992.*

the threat of military intervention was lifted, the Communist bloc fell apart. Non-Communists formed a government in Poland in 1989, and in 1991, the Soviet Union itself disintegrated.

1977   SPACE EXPLORATION: US *VOYAGERS*

HUMAN space travel still involves considerable obstacles. Prolonged weightlessness causes physical problems. Protective clothing must be worn at all times outside the aircraft because of extreme temperatures and radioactivity. Space debris from previous explorations is now posing a threat as a collision

with fast-moving fragments can damage craft and cause depressurisation. Space probes capable of breaking fee of gravity are a major part of exploration. They have the capability to send back pictures and signals from distant destinations that would be too hazardous and costly for manned flights. US *Voyager 1* and *2*, launched in 1977, have made some spectacular discoveries during flights to Jupiter, Saturn, Uranus and Neptune.

◄ *The launch of the space shuttle* Columbia *in 1982.*

1990s   THE EMPIRE OF MONEY?

DURING the 1990s, the old-style imperialism of military conquest and occupation vanished. Computer technology plays an important part in the global economy. By the late 1990s it had become so integrated that it was possible to order something from Japan via the Internet and have it arrive in Europe by airmail within a couple of days. Exploration in search of resources to exploit has been superseded by space satellites that can help create resource maps of the whole world. Imperial power in the 1990s resides in the flow of money that can, in a matter of hours, devastate a major economy, as happened in Britain in 1992, in Mexico in 1994–95 and in Russia in 1998.

Trade and Industry

1903   THE MOTOR-VEHICLE INDUSTRY

THE motor-vehicle industry is the world's largest industry, employing about one-tenth of all manufacturing workers. Vehicle manufacture began in France, in about 1890, at first in small workshops producing one car at a time. About 10 years later vehicle factories appeared in the United States.

▼ *The Ford Model T, the first car made on an assembly line.*

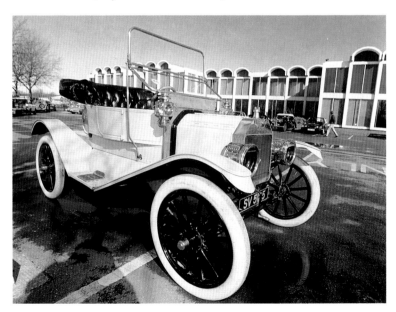

In the early days the European makers built all the necessary parts themselves whereas the Americans assembled parts they bought in from other firms. Henry Ford founded the Ford Motor Company in 1903 and five years later invented the famous Model T Ford, which was made on an assembly line using standard, mass-produced parts. In the same year (1908) William Durant founded the General Motors Corporation in Detroit, as was Ford.

1914 THE INVENTION OF INVENTION

THE process of invention underwent an important change from 1914 onwards. Before then most inventions had been made by individuals working to their own brief and from their own passion or inspiration. The inventors often had heart-wrenching difficulty in persuading others of the value of their work, let alone in getting the invention put into production.

▲ *Motoring pioneer Henry Ford, one of the first producers of mass-produced cars.*

The First World War changed this. From then on, manufacturers and managers analysed where there were bottlenecks or inefficiencies, identified what kinds of machine or weapon or process were needed and then commissioned experts to come up with ideas that met the specifications. Invention was thus deliberate rather than accidental, and was controlled by technological advance. The rate of invention accelerated enormously and the link between theory and practice became infinitely more direct.

1918 JAPANESE INDUSTRIAL ETHOS AND DEVELOPMENT

AFTER the First World War, when Japan was keen to industrialise in order to become militarily strong, cheap labour, efficient new machinery and active government participation brought striking success. Japanese samurai traditions persisted, with minor adaptations. Profit was never an end in itself but was secondary to honour and prestige. The old warrior virtues of courage, endurance and loyalty translated smoothly into managerial skills. The relationships between samurai and peasant also carried over into the workplace: managers commanded, workers obeyed and, in return for absolute loyalty, were looked after lifelong. Similarly, the practice of 'putting out' – hiring outworkers and purchasing their finished products at decent prices – was a system of benevolent patronage. The economic miracle in Japan was not therefore the product of modern, democratic ideas.

▲ *Samurai traditions continued in Japan into the twentieth century.*

1920s HYPERINFLATION IN GERMANY

INFLATION is the rate of increase of prices. Inflation makes people's savings worth less and makes the whole economy less efficient. To keep inflation under control, governments now work with trade unions and businesses to limit wage and price rises. Extremely high inflation, normally interpreted as more than 1,000 per cent a year, is called hyperinflation. This happened in Germany in 1922–23. Workers had to be paid twice a day! In Europe in the sixteenth century, prices rose about 400 per cent after silver discovered in

Peru brought an abundance of bullion to Europe. Later, inflation hit developing countries badly, partly because of the dramatic oil-price increase of 1973–74 and poor harvests worldwide.

1930s   THE GREAT DEPRESSION

THE Great Depression was a worldwide economic slump that began in 1929 with the Wall Street Crash. The Crash was caused by excessive investment in the domestic US market that pushed prices up to unsustainable levels, whereupon shareholders switched to selling and prices plummeted. On 'Black Tuesday', 29 October, alone, 16 million shares were traded and $10 billion wiped off share values. The Crash caused large-scale bankruptcies and unemployment rose by nearly two million within six months. Elsewhere in the world, too, banks, unable to pay depositors, were forced to close. A shortage of cash meant that less money was available for investment in industry or in farm products. In the USA drought and dust storms devastated parts of the Midwest and south-west, causing the so-called Dust Bowl.

▲ *Banks in America were forced to close during the Depression of the 1930s.*

1930s   THE DEMISE OF THE GOLD STANDARD

THE gold standard is a system under which money may be converted, on demand, into gold. It was widely adopted in the second half of the nineteenth century, principally to make international transactions easier to settle and to stabilise foreign-exchange rates and domestic money supply. Great

Britain was the first country to go on the gold standard (1816) followed by the USA (1873). Most countries abandoned it again in the 1930s in the wake of the Great Depression. This was because they believed that their exports would be boosted if they devalued their currencies in terms of foreign exchange. Once this practice had become widespread, however, no country was left with any competitive advantage. By the late 1970s gold had become more of a commodity than a standard and no major currency could be redeemed as gold.

1933   THE NEW DEAL

IN 1933 the US president, Franklin Roosevelt, inaugurated a 'New Deal' in response to the Depression that afflicted the country. Immediate measures included the provision of employment on public works, government loans to farmers at low rates of interest and restriction of agricultural output to raise prices. Other reforms included old-age and unemployment insurance, measures to prevent forced ('sweated') and child labour, protection of employees' rights to organise to protest against unfair employment practices and assistance with slum clearance. The New Deal reduced unemployment from 17 million to eight million. Interestingly, the Supreme Court in 1935–36 declared many of the provisions of the New Deal unconstitutional. A major New Deal project was the Tennessee Valley scheme, that harnessed the Tennessee River, providing cheap electricity and protection from floods.

▲ *US president Franklin D. Roosevelt.*

1944   ORGANIC FARMING

THE organic farming movement, known also as biological, regenerative or sustainable farming, was started by Lady Eve Balfour. Not only a talented jazz trombonist and pilot, Lady Balfour was an assiduous agricultural researcher and in 1944 published *The Living Soil*. Two years later the Soil Association was formed. Organic farming as much as possible excludes the use of synthetically produced fertilisers, pesticides, feed additives and growth regulators. Preferred farming methods therefore include crop rotation, the use of green and animal manures and biological pest and weed control. Organic farming methods are sometimes the only option in underdeveloped and developing areas. In developed countries organic farming is gaining ground, often as a reaction against intensive or factory farming or scares about food safety.

1945   TECHNOLOGICAL ADVANCE

THE most spectacular technological developments from 1945 onwards were in the military field, but a greater number occurred in other areas. Chemical fertilisers, insecticides, herbicides, scientifically designed animal feeds, seed selection and animal breeding changed agriculture out of all recognition. New drugs were developed, which went into production on an unprecedented scale. Television found its way into millions of homes, especially, to begin with, in Europe and North

▲ *Scientific advances in agriculture have had profound effects worldwide.*

America. Although these advances brought obvious advantages, they also tended to widen the gap between rich and poor nations. The former had the physical resources and skilled manpower to pursue research; the latter often suffered a 'brain drain'. Scientists and innovators also attained a not wholly enviable status as 'ivory-tower' boffins, remote from the rest of society.

1947   GATT AND WTO

THE General Agreement on Tariffs and Trade (GATT) was signed in Geneva in 1947 by representatives of 23 non-Communist nations. By 1988 there were 96 members. GATT created an international forum dedicated to the expansion of multilateral trade and the settlement of trade disputes. Members agreed to treat all other members equally – the most-favoured-nation policy. In theory this represented a desire to abolish all non-tariff barriers to trade. The eighth round of trade negotiations, the Uruguay Round, continued from 1986 to 1996, and the final agreements resulted in the creation of the World Trade Organisation (WTO), superseding GATT. The WTO incorporates the original principles of GATT but extends them to include trade in services, intellectual property rights and investment, and, since February 1997, the liberalisation of telecommunications trade.

1950s   THE NUCLEAR AND SPACE RACE

IN 1945 only the United States possessed atomic bombs. By 1949 Soviet scientists, working partly on information collected by spies, were able to duplicate the technology and detonated their first atomic bomb. The US government then started work on the H-bomb, a more powerful type of nuclear warhead, in which energy is derived from hydrogen fusion. The Soviets were only a few months behind; both nations exploded their first hydrogen warheads in 1953–54. The next goal was to develop rockets capable of delivering nuclear warheads,

▲ *Nuclear coding towers in the United States; the nuclear race was fought between America and the Soviet Union.*

which both had achieved by the early 1960s. Into the 1970s the armaments race demanded a very considerable part of national resources. A remarkable by-product was the exploration of space. Since rockets could carry warheads they could also launch artificial Earth satellites.

1959 THE PETROLEUM INDUSTRY

THE petroleum industry celebrated its first centenary in 1959, when world output attained around one billion tonnes for the first time. The industry began with Drake's well at Titusville, Pennsylvania, USA. The USA was the world's leading producer almost unbrokenly until the 1960s. Its feverish attempts to search for oil had included the digging of more than a million wells. Of the top 10 producers in 1989, the first four, measured in terms of years of reserves, were in the Persian Gulf area. Oil offers tremendous advantages over most other forms of energy: it is a liquid and thus easier to handle than, say, coal; it has a

▲ *Drake's Well in Pennsylvania, where oil was first struck in 1959.*

higher calorific value than coal, weight for weight; and it can be refined for different purposes.

1960s   CHANGES IN ENERGY PRODUCTION

IN the hundred years after 1860, when statistics of energy production first became available, world energy production increased about 30 times. Most of that increase occurred in the few countries that had a high level of economic development. Energy supplies may be regarded as either primary or secondary. Primary energy consists of new increments of energy, whereas secondary energy is primary energy that has been transformed, that is, rendered into a more convenient and usable form. Primary energy resources are of either the perpetual or the accumulated type. The former come from solar radiation and accordingly exist in enormous quantities, but they are difficult and expensive to harness because the energy is dissipated almost as fast as the Earth receives it. Hydroelectric, tidal and solar energy are examples. Accumulated resources consist of the fossil fuels such as coal and oil.

1960s   GREEN REVOLUTION

THE Green Revolution is the term used since about the 1960s to describe the effort to increase and diversify crop yields in developing countries. The

▲ *A modern coal mine in Wales; coal is a primary energy resource.*

American agricultural scientist Norman E. Borlaug is often considered the founder of the Green Revolution. Many countries have taken steps to implement Borlaug's programme for achieving agricultural efficiency. The programme stresses the need to: abandon local, traditional strains of plants and breeds of animals in favour of new strains and breeds; conduct research to enable new procedures to be adapted to local conditions; obtain long-term support from local government to apply and extend knowledge and achieve changes in the infrastructure in order to stabilise the numbers of people in a society and to enhance the quality of their lives.

1960s THE COMPUTER INDUSTRY

THE computer industry did not exist until the 1940s and its products were not widely used until the 1960s. This industry is now one of the fastest growing. The largest companies making machines include IBM (which has set the standard, especially for home computers), Hewlett Packard, Apple and Acorn. Other companies make the components used to build computers. Computer hardware is sometimes now made in developing countries where the labour is inexpensive.

▲ *The first computer, dating from 1944; over the next five decades, the computer industry would advance beyond recognition.*

Components such as silicon chips are still made in industrial countries such as the USA and Japan. The software–operating systems that computers use are written by computer programmers. The largest software company is Microsoft Corporation, which provides millions of computer-operating systems worldwide. Computers continue to become faster and more efficient with larger memories and more power.

1965   THE RISE OF INTERNATIONAL TRADE

INTERNATIONAL trade has grown enormously as a proportion of total economic activity in the twentieth century. This is due to increasing inter-dependence among national economies. Protectionist interests within regional trading communities, such as Mercosur (Latin America), may cause them to restrict trade with countries outside their own circle, but equally the regional groupings can serve as first steps towards reaching broader trade agreements. World trade increased by five times between 1965 and 1976 and then almost doubled again by 1985. In 1995 the total value of exports and imports throughout the world was estimated at $5 trillion. Trade growth was particularly marked in the oil-exporting developing countries between 1976 and 1982. Worldwide the trend continued strongly throughout the 1980s and the 1990s, with fluctuations caused by recession in Europe and Japan.

1979   EMS AND EMU

THE European Monetary System (EMS) aimed to aid financial co-operation and to establish monetary stability within the European Union (EU). It came into force in 1979 as a means of correcting the fluctuations in exchange rates that followed the 1974 oil crisis. The central component of the EMS was the Exchange Rate Mechanism (ERM), a voluntary system of partly fixed exchange rates, based on the European Currency Unit (ECU, the standard monetary unit, the level of which was set according to a basket of currencies of member states). Participating currencies under the ERM were allowed to fluctuate in relation to each other and to the ECU within a fixed band only. The ERM was a stepping stone to European Monetary Union (EMU), which began on 1 January 1999. Proponents of EMU claimed that a fixed exchange rate will act as an anchor against inflation. Opponents feared loss of national autonomy over monetary and exchange-rate policy.

▶ *Robots at work in a car factory.*

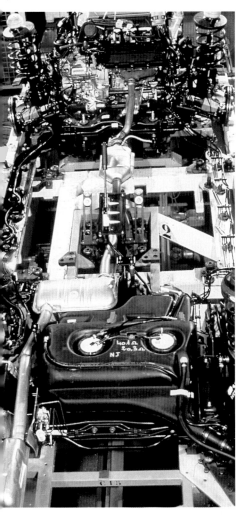

1980s ROBOTS

NOT only has the computer changed people's personal and business lives: it has also changed manufacturing. In many factories, robots can perform simple tasks faster and more accurately than people. When computers are used to design, make and assemble product parts, this is called Computer Integrated Manufacturing (CIM). Computers may control robots, which can be adapted to do new tasks very quickly, simply by changing the computer program, whereas people need to be retrained for new tasks. The use of robots makes smaller factories possible: robots take up little space and are flexible. A robot can make a small number of a particular product and then switch to making a different one. Factories can thus produce the wider range of low-cost products that customers want.

1980s GOVERNMENT SERVICE

IN economies at all stages of development the State has, historically, usually been by far the largest employer. Some developing countries in the early days of independence developed a disproportionately large civil service. This was because employment by the State was sometimes regarded as a reward to individuals for having helped the nation to achieve self-determination or prosperity. Often there was little for the new bureaucrats to do, however.

The quintessential State bureaucracy, that of imperial China, was particularly riven with favouritism and bribery. When the planned economies, especially in the then Soviet Union and eastern Europe, collapsed in the late 1980s, they took with them their inflated bureaucracies. In capitalist states, too, the need was recognised for a reduction in government's role in the economy.

▲ *Chinese youths showing support for their Communist leader Chairman Mao.*

1990 TOURISM

TOURISM has become a gigantic business in the last 30 years or so. As people become more affluent, they spend more on holidays. Many developing countries are promoting themselves as tourist destinations in order to earn foreign currency, which they can use to pay for the imports they need. The Gambia, in West Africa, is one country in which tourism has become a major sector of the economy. In 1965 it received just 20 visitors. In 1990 there were

114,000. The gains and losses in the tourism industry can be quite complex. The profits from hotels and other tourist services may go to foreign owners, although taxes paid to the host government represent a gain. Some of the goods and materials provided for tourists, such as food and drink, may be imported, at the expense of support for local agriculture and manufacture. On the other hand, the business provides jobs for local people.

1990s   INDUSTRY VS MANUFACTURING

THE word 'industry' is often used interchangeably with 'manufacturing'. Manufacturing is the making of goods by taking raw materials and applying skills and machines to them. Until the mid-twentieth century more people worked in manufacturing than in any other form of work. Now, with the advent of automation and more advanced machinery, including computer-assisted processes, no more than 30 per cent of people work in manufacturing. Industry in its widest sense includes manufacturing and the provision of services, mining, extraction and semi-processing and trade. A

▲ *Shipbuilding in northern England, an example of 'heavy industry'.*

distinction may be made between heavy and light industry. Heavy industry includes such basic industries as coal mining, shipbuilding and steel making, requiring heavy equipment. Light industry refers to the processing in smaller factories of such goods as electronics components and glass.

1990s   SUPPLY AND DEMAND

THE price of a commodity tends to depend on supply, that is, the amount available for sale, and demand, the amount that consumers want to buy. The higher the price of a commodity, the more of it suppliers will want to sell. Supply therefore generally increases as the price increases. On the other hand, rising prices discourage buyers. In a free market a balance is usually achieved between supply and demand by pitching prices at the right level. Governments are responsible for printing money. It might be supposed that if they simply print more, everyone will be richer. In fact, if the money supply increases, people are keener to buy more goods and services. The higher demand leads to higher prices (inflation).

1998   CRISIS IN THE GLOBAL ECONOMY

IN the late 1990s an economic crisis occurred in South-East Asia and spread across the world. In July and August 1998 alone, four trillion dollars were wiped off the value of shares worldwide. Commodity prices, including oil and grain prices, collapsed to their lowest level in real terms since the 1930s. The Asian 'miracle' came to grief as a result of massive speculation against fixed currencies. Singapore, for example, had pegged its dollar to the US since the early 1970s and had succeeded in attracting huge flows of inward investment. China's devaluation of its currency in 1994 was a last straw. Just as the other Asian economies were moving into a boom, their fixed link to the dollar was making exports uncompetitive. Inflation rose. One by one the countries were forced off the dollar peg, currencies plunged and stock markets crashed. Leading economists suggested exchange controls as the least damaging way out of the crisis.

▶ *Traders on the London Futures Exchange during
the economic crisis in 1998.*

1998   THE POLITICS OF SCARCITY

SURPLUS was the key feature of the world food economy in the 50 years after the Second World War. Now scarcity is dominant. The economies of Asia, from Pakistan east to Japan grew dramatically in the 1990s. China's economy grew by two-thirds between 1990 and 1995. Never before have so many people become affluent and therefore moved up the food chain so fast. With demand burgeoning, Japan, South Korea and Taiwan import more than 70 per cent of the grain they consume. Asia is becoming strong industrially but agriculturally vulnerable – particularly as it depends for nearly half its grain imports on the USA, where harvests vary widely from year to year. Intense heatwaves (for example in 1988) also shrink grain harvests.

Science and Technology

1900s ELECTRIC APPLIANCES

THE introduction of domestic electricity supplies led to an inevitable vogue for electrical 'labour-saving' devices for the home. There have been many and various appliances marketed, some of which have become ubiquitous components of the household; others have become obsolete or just didn't take off. The familiar inventions include: iron (1882); kettle (1891); toaster (1893); hairdryer and heater (1899); washing machine (1907); dishwasher (1914); mower (1916); clock (1918); blanket (1927); microwave oven (1947); watch (1957); calculator (1964); and personal organiser (1993). The fact that these devices are so often taken for granted is testament to their usefulness. They are so much a part of our lives that they become very conspicuous by their absence if they break down or if the electricity supply is cut off.

1900s GADGETS

THERE have been many useful gadgets introduced during the twentieth century, that are not technologically significant, but nonetheless are important for our daily routine in the modern environment. They include: safety razor (1901); lipstick (1915); electric razor (1931); aerosol canister (1941); ballpoint pen (1944); disposable pen (1953); quartz watch (1960); electric toothbrush (1961); tab opening drink can (1962); colour polaroid camera (1963); digital watch (1971); disposable lighter (1973); disposable

▼ *Illustration showing the first Gillette safety razor with replaceable blade.*

razor (1974); disposable camera (1986). The use-once-and-throw-away philosophy is indicative of the ethos of modern society, where new is perceived
to be good and old bad. It is generally an optimistic outlook that arose in the
1950s and 1960s and has since created a consumer-led market. It is worth
pointing out though, that the recycling of disposed materials has become an
intrinsic part of the philosophy over the latter part of the twentieth century.

1900s   MEDICAL SCANNING

MODERN technology has provided new ways for scanning the body since
the advent of X-rays at the turn
of the twentieth century. Sound
waves at frequencies inaudible to
humans are used in the ultra-
sound scanner. The sound
waves, emitted by the scanner,
penetrate the tissue and bounce
back in different ways according
to the density and depth of tissue types. The returning waves
are interpreted by the scanner in
relation to those released and an
image is assembled on a screen.
Sound waves with very high
power, called ultrasonics, can be
used to disintegrate kidney or
gall stones. The advantage of

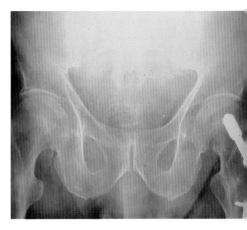

▲ *Example of a modern X-ray showing a
pin in the hip.*

using sound waves is that they are a non-invasive and safe way of scanning.
Use of X-rays has been developed in recent years to result in the CAT
(Computerised Axial Tomography) scanner. This is a machine that uses
X-rays to build up a stereoscopic image of the body by building up layer after
layer of cross-sectional images with a scintillator.

1900s SYNTHETICS

THE modern world uses many synthetic materials, which are the brain–
children of chemical scientists who have been working on them since the
turn of the twentieth century, largely thanks to the petrochemicals industry.
Synthetic materials, collectively known as plastics, because they can be
moulded or formed, have become ubiquitous and frequently used in place of
other 'natural' materials, over the past hundred years. Most are polymeric
structures, which means that they have large molecules that are made up of
many relatively simple repeated units. Plastics belong in two groups:
thermosetting and thermo-melting, the latter being recyclable by heating.
The first plastics used were celluloid and Bakelite, but by the 1930s the
polymer plastics began to be developed. They include; polyethylene
(Polythene), polypropylene, polystyrene, polyester, polyamides (nylon),
polyvinylchloride (p.v.c. or vinyl), acrylics, viscose (rayon), epoxies, acetates
and polytetrafluoroethene (PTFE). Their applications are many and various,
for example moulded components, synthetic fibres, sheeting, resins,
adhesives, hardeners, plasticisers, non-stick coatings and so on.

1903 POWERED FLIGHT

IT was John Stringfellow
(1799–1883) who first
proved that powered flight
was possible, with a large
model aeroplane powered
by a steam engine in 1848.
The first manned powered
flight came in 1903, when
Orville Wright

▶ *Postcard showing Louis Blériot,
who made the first flight across
the Channel.*

(1871–1948) took to the air in the 'Flyer', built by him and his brother Wilbur (1867–1912), and propelled by a petrol engine. By 1908, Louis Bleriot (1872–1936) had perfected his powered monoplane and established the standard layout for future aeroplanes. The Heinkel He 178, built by Hans von Ohain, was the first plane to use a turbo-jet engine in 1939, which was superseded by the gas-turbine jet engine, first fitted into the Gloster-Whittle E.28/29 in 1941, and invented by Frank Whittle (1907–96). Modified versions of the Whittle engine went on to become the standard power unit for military and commercial jet planes alike. The earliest helicopters were experimented with after 1905, but the first practical design, with the standard layout, came in 1935. The first production model was the Focke-Wulf FW61, designed by Heinrich Focke in 1936.

1905   EINSTEIN'S THEORIES OF RELATIVITY

ALBERT Einstein (1879–1955) formulated theories about the nature and structure of the universe that totally transformed human understanding of the way things behave. Isaac Newton's theories had been accepted as fact for almost two hundred years because they worked as far as most observations were concerned, but scientists, especially astronomers, were noticing anomalies, that couldn't be explained by Newtonian rules. In 1905 Einstein's *Special Theory of Relativity* was

▲ *Albert Einstein, whose theories of relativity form the basis of modern science.*

published. In it, he proposed various ideas on the subject of matter, light, space and time, not least that they are all interrelated, hence the name of the theory. He provided complex mathematical formulae to reinforce his ideas and went on to release his *General Theory of Relativity* in 1915 and

Unified Field Theory in 1953. Einstein's work led to the developments in nuclear fusion and fission, and to Arthur Stanley Eddington (1882–1944) proposing, in 1933, that the universe was expanding from a central point of origin.

1908   THE FORD MODEL T

IN 1890 the French car manufacturers, Panhard, produced the motor car that established the standard layout of most cars to come. At first, motor cars were very expensive to own, but by 1908, Henry Ford (1836–1947) had started producing his Model T. It was designed to be affordable by the lay-person and by 1927, 15 million had rolled out of his factories. In 1913 Ford had introduced the first conveyor belt assembly line and truly interchangeable parts, which revolutionised the car industry, as well as others. After 1918 the motoring era took off; inspired by Ford, other car manufacturers followed suit, such as Citroen, Peugeot, Renault, Austin, Morris, Fiat and Volkswagen. Petrol motor lorries and buses appeared in the 1890s but the diesel engine took over in the 1920s and 1930s. Felix

▲ *Car factory showing the use of conveyors, first introduced by Henry Ford in 1913.*

Wankels' (1902–88) rotary petrol engine was first used in 1967, but the four-stroke cylinder engine has remained popular.

1913   CONVEYORS

MEAT-processing factories in America had introduced conveyor cables, for moving carcasses, by the 1890s. Henry Ford (1863–1947) introduced a conveyor to his assembly line for producing the Model T in 1913. After that, conveyors became accepted as part of the route to achieving optimum efficiency in all kinds of industries. Many kinds of conveyor have been developed, for handling unit and bulk materials, according to different process requirements. They include belt, roller, chain, bucket and carousel conveyors. Other conveyors have been invented for carrying people themselves. Escalators, elevators and moving walkways are all conveying machines designed for saving the effort of walking or climbing.

1926   ROCKETS
AND MISSILES

THE first liquid-fuel rocket was fired in 1926, by Robert H. Goddard, in America. A German, Wernher von Braun, developed the principle during the 1930s and made the V2 liquid-fuel rocket used by the Nazis, between 1943–45. After the Second World War, he travelled to America, where his work led to the series of Saturn rockets which launched the Apollo missions between 1961–72. Space rockets have since been superseded by space shuttles, and there are current developments using laser technology as the propellant force. Use of both liquid and solid fuel rockets has carried on evolving in the realm of weaponry. Some very sophisticated missiles with guidance systems have become the state-of-the-art weapons in recent years.

▲ *Rocket technology greatly advanced throughout the twentieth century, leading to developments in missile weapons.*

1926   TELEVISION

THE principle that led to the invention of the television was discovered in 1873. It was found that selenium, a non-metallic element, was photoconductive. This meant that electrons fired at it would illuminate the surface and that electrical impulses could therefore by made into images by illuminating dots with varying brightness. It was John Logie Baird who first demonstrated 'black and white' or monochromatic television, in 1926. Only two years later he was able to demonstrate full colour television. In 1908, Campbell Swinton suggested the use of a cathode ray tube as a transmitter and receiver for electrical information. It had been developed for experimentation purposes in the late 1800s – Rontgen discovered X-rays while using one – and provided a clear path for electrons because it contained a vacuum. By 1934 the cathode ray tube had been perfected and was adopted as the most suitable device for production televisions. The BBC made the first public transmission of television pictures to an amazed public in 1936.

1933   ELECTROSCOPES

ALTHOUGH the optical telescope and microscope still give useful service, the twentieth century has given us electronic means for 'looking' at things in more detail. In 1932 an astronomer called Karl Jansky (1905–50) detected the presence of 'radio noise' coming from outer space. This led to the development of radio telescopes, with the realisation that radio waves, instead of light waves, could tell scientists a lot more about the universe. Radio waves have a much lower frequency than those of

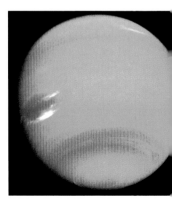

▶ *The planet Neptune, taken from* Voyager 2.

light, so a radio telescope is in the shape of a large dish, to catch enough information. The first scanning electron microscope (SEM) was developed by Max Knoll and Ernst Ruska between 1928–33, in Berlin. It works by detecting electrons that are bounced off the surface of objects being scanned, and creating a visual image on a screen. It can magnify up to 200,000 times. The scanning tunnelling microscope (STM) can achieve up to 100 million magnifications and works by allowing electrons to jump from a tungsten scanning tip on to the subject, measuring the distance each time to create an image.

1934   NUCLEAR TECHNOLOGY

HAVING come up with the form $E=mc^2$, Einstein had shown that matter is lost in the form of heat energy and radiation by nuclear reactions. Nuclear fission is the splitting apart of nuclei by neutrons in a chain reaction. It was first achieved in practice by an Italian scientist, Enrico Fermi, in 1934. Julius Robert Oppenheimer (b. 1904) led the team that developed the first fission atomic bomb, tested in New Mexico in 1945. By 1952 a new type of weapon, the Hydrogen bomb had been tested. It was a fusion atomic bomb, which joined the nuclei of hydrogen atoms to make helium atoms and emit lots of heat, thus called a thermonuclear weapon. Hydrogen bombs also create spare neutrons as part of their exhaust, which decay and give off high levels of radiation. This fact is exploited in the neutron bomb or ERW – Enhanced Radiation Weapon.

▲ *The first nuclear power stations were built in the 1940s.*

The first nuclear power-station experiments were carried out by Fermi in 1942, and the first working reactor was set up in Russia in 1954. Nuclear power has also been used to run submarines and warships since 1959.

1935   RADAR AND SONAR

RADAR, an acronym of Radio Direction and Ranging, was invented in 1935, as a way of locating enemy aircraft, by Robert Watson-Watt (1892–1973). It works by emitting radio waves at regular intervals, which bounce back if an object is within range. A receiver translated the returning radio waves into a visual location dot on a screen. Radar is a vital means for tracking the movements of commercial and domestic air traffic. Sonar is an acronym for Sound Navigation and Ranging. It works in a similar way to radar, except that it uses ultrasonic waves, because radio waves will not travel through water. Sonar serves the equivalent purpose to radar, but in a marine environment and was invented by Frenchman Paul Langevin (1872–1946) in 1914 for detecting German U-Boats.

1936   CIRCUIT BOARDS AND MICROPROCESSORS

IN 1936 an Austrian named Paul Eisler, living in England, decided that it would be a good idea to incorporate the workings of his home-made radio on to a board. Having invented the circuit board he attempted for some years to sell the idea of printed circuit boards to electronics companies. Having been passed around from place to place, necessity in warfare eventually created a need for the rapid reproduction of electronic circuits, which were used to control the proximity fuses for the anti-aircraft shells fired at Nazi V1 'Doodle-bugs' in 1944. After the war the Americans embraced the printed circuit board, which revolutionised a burgeoning electronics industry. By the 1950s America was developing miniature circuit boards using silicon as a semiconductor. These became known as silicon chips, and could comprise many thousands of components all scaled down into a microprocessor. Circuit boards for larger components are still used in conjunction with silicon chips, which are mounted onto them.

1945   MICROWAVES

MICROWAVES are beams of short wave, or high frequency, electromagnetic radiation or infrared light. They can carry a lot of energy with them and as a result, have been used in a variety of ways by technology. Uses include ovens, radar, radio broadcasting and lasers. Percy LeBaron Spencer invented the first microwave oven in 1945, which was marketed as the Radar Range by Raytheon in 1947. He discovered the potential of microwaves when they melted a chocolate bar in his pocket. Laser is an acronym for 'Light Amplification by Stimulated Emission of Radiation'. The first laser beam was produced by Theodore Maiman of California in 1960, using a ruby crystal to create the familiar red path of light. Since then, many solids, liquids and gases have been used as laser materials and lasers have found many uses.

Communication signalling, cutting, drilling and welding, satellite tracking, weaponry, medical and biological research and surgery have all benefited from laser technology. The laser used for reading information on RAMS and CDs is a blue short-wave laser developed in 1988 by Japan. IBM introduced micro-lasers for computer circuitry switching in 1989.

▶ *Early lasers used ruby crystals to create light; today many other materials are used.*

1950s   DIGITAL CODING

THE term 'digital' means to be made up of numbers, as digital information is indeed a numerical code. The numbers used are usually binary, which means just two numbers which run in sequences. 1 and 0 are used, representing 'on' and 'off' in effect. Different sequences comprise each piece of data, which is deciphered using a microprocessor within the machine using the digital information. Digital has become the prime means for the coding, storage, transmission, processing and reconstructing of information. It was adopted readily by industries concerned with computer, audio and visual information as early as the 1950s because it offered the advantage of virtually eliminating any degradation or distortion of signals, during transmission, storage and processing.

▲ *A length of DNA, showing a double helix.*

1953   DNA UNRAVELLED

AFTER Darwin and Wallace had hit on the process by which evolution occurs, it came to others to reveal the mechanism and the components within. Gregor Mendel (1822–84) performed experiments, using successive generations of pea plants, which demonstrated how particulate inheritance is controlled by dominant and recessive genes. When the value of his work was recognised in the early 1900s it encouraged scientists to tread further ground. By the 1940s it was realised that genes must be components of DNA (deoxyribonucleic acid) and the race was on to describe how DNA was structured, and therefore, how genes controlled characteristics and duplicated themselves. In 1953, James Watson (b. 1928) and Francis Crick (b. 1916) announced their discovery that DNA must be a double helix, with connecting rungs like a twisting ladder. Each rung was a base pair of cytosine-guanine or adenine-thymine, thus forming a double-binary code. A different code was thus carried by each gene comprising the DNA strand, and was used to control the production of amino acids in

▲ *James Watson*

▲ *Francis Crick*

constructing proteins. What was more, the DNA could 'unzip' itself and attract the necessary chemicals to become two identical strands.

1957   SATELLITES AND PROBES

SATELLITES have been orbiting the Earth since *Sputnik I* was launched by Russia in 1957. Thousands have been sent into orbit over the intervening years, by various countries, for a wide variety of uses. Many satellites are used to observe or scan the Earth for geological information, some are spy satellites, others track the weather, still more are there to make astronomical observations, such as the Hubble telescope, launched in 1990. Communications satellites receive and transmit information from one place to another on the Earth's surface, and are usually in geostationary orbits. The first probe was the Russian *Luna 3*, which sent back pictures of the dark side of the Moon in 1959. A number of probes have since been sent on voyages of astronomical discovery. They have supplied a great deal of valuable information about the other planets in our solar system.

1961   ROBOTICS

THE first industrial application of a robotic machine came in 1961. General Motors, in America, introduced the Unimation 1900 into their car-assembly line. By 1980, General Motors had a 'seeing' robot, which was able to select and separate components by recognition. Since then, many program-mable, computer-controlled and remote-controlled robots have been developed, and

▲ *Robots have been increasingly used in factories on assembly lines to replace human labour.*

their applications have been very varied. Most robots are used to complete tasks that they can perform more effectively than humans, usually because the job is boring or laborious, which may lead to problems with concentration. Some robots though, have proved very useful in situations that are too dangerous, or simply impossible, for humans to function in. Good examples of these are bomb-disposal robots and roving robots used on the surface of other planets. There are also nanorobots being developed and sophisticated robotic prosthetics.

1969   MEN ON THE MOON

THE first human in space was Russian cosmonaut Yuri Gagarin (1934–68), who completed a single orbit of the Earth aboard *Vostok I* in 1961. In 1969

▲ *Neil Armstrong, Buzz Aldrin and Michael Collins.*

the first person set foot on the moon. Neil Armstrong (b. 1930), accompanied by Edwin 'Buzz' Aldrin (b. 1930) and Michael Collins (b. 1930), landed on the lunar surface in the *Apollo 11* module. The first re-usable space craft was the NASA Space Shuttle *Columbia*, first launched in 1981. The first permanently manned space station was *Mir*, established by the Russians in 1986. The experiences of cosmonauts and astronauts, having lived for long periods in space stations, have been carefully researched as part of the preparation for planned missions to Mars in the twenty-first century, which will take several months travel.

1973 GENETIC MANIPULATION

AFTER it was discovered how DNA and their genes work, scientists set about trying to alter the genes of species to achieve new characteristics. Gene splicing, the insertion of bits of new DNA into an existing DNA strand, was invented in 1973 by American scientists Stanley Cohen and Herbert Boyer. This has enabled scientists to produce transgenic species, so called because they have had foreign genes introduced. Transgenic or genetically engineered species can thus possess desired characteristics that make them economically more viable through resistance to disease and pests, higher yields and so on; or they may be used to produce valuable chemicals, drugs or hormones for medical use. Genetically manipulated foods became available in 1994 and developments have continued apace. Cloning of species has also been developed so that the desired characteristics are maintained, rather than being diluted by the natural evolutionary process, although cloning does have the inherent danger of removing the survival mechanism, which is genetic variety.

1984 E-MAIL AND INTERNET

THE technical foundations for the internet and WWW (World Wide Web) were developed as a project, funded by the Advanced Research Project Agency (ARPA), to build an electrically run communications network able to withstand damage by nuclear warfare. Work began in 1984 and, with extra funding from the United States' National Science Foundation, was able to link up American universities, via five supercomputing centres. By the early 1990s the service became cheap enough for domestic use. Sending and receiving e-mail (electronic mail), searching for information on the Internet and advertising on web sites became a familiar feature of modern life by the end of the twentieth century.

1990s   **PERIPHERAL DEVICES**

THE computer processor has become a multi-functional 'nerve centre' for information and communication technology, in both the workplace and home. There are various essential accessories, known as peripheral devices,

which plug into the processor and enable the effective use of it. Peripherals include: monitors; keyboards; scanners; printers; mice; modems; microphones; videophones; speakers; floppy disc and CD-Rom units. Together with the processor, the peripherals make up the ICT (Information and Communication Technology) kit, which can be assembled according to the specific requirements of the individual user. The memory size of the processor itself, can be increased by the insertion of extra silicon chips.

▲ *Computer technology saw incredible advance during the last decade of the twentieth century.*

1990s   **NANOTECHNOLOGY**

THE invention of the scanning tunnelling microscope (STM) has led to a new technology being possible, nanotechnology. Using a process similar to that used in making microchips, the STM is used to etch or sculpt silicon into minute shapes, which are the components of tiny machines. They are so small that the STM is actually building them using single atoms or molecules. Tiny electric motors have been made that can rotate at several thousand revolutions per second, yet they are less than a tenth of a millimetre in size. The uses for such small machines and devices are potentially very varied. It has been suggested that nanomachines could be injected into the body to perform tasks such as fighting pathogens, delivering drugs or cleaning arteries. Others might be used to operate flying micro-robots for reconnaissance work, spying or hunting down crop pests.

Religions, Belief and Thought

1900s   CHRISTIANITY IN THE THIRD WORLD

CRITICISM of colonialism and the brutality of missionaries dates back to the time of Bartolome de Las Casas (1474–1566), a Spanish Dominican missionary who defended the rights of indigenous peoples in Latin America. Franz Fanon's (1925–61) book about colonialism in Algeria, *The Wretched of the Earth*, was one source of the modern Liberation Theology movement. Liberation Theology sees Christ as the friend of the poor, who lived amongst them and died for them. It stresses biblical opposition to the pursuit of wealth and biblical teachings on justice. Archbishop Oscar Romero (1917–80), who was assassinated by the El Salvador government for speaking out for the poor, is their

▲ *From the earliest days of exploration, native peoples were forced to accept the religion of the new settlers.*

leading martyr. Theologians include the Catholics Leonardo Boff (b. 1938) of Brazil, Gustavo Gutierrez (b. 1928) of Peru, Juan Luis Segundo (b. 1925) of Uruguay and Jon Sobrino (b. 1938) of El Salvador; and the Protestants José Miguez Bonino (b. 1924) of Argentina and Rubem Alves (b. 1933) of Brazil.

1900s   SYSTEMS THEORY AND THE REDISCOVERY OF HOLISM

THE mathematician, Ludwig von Bertalanffy; the ecologist, Aldo Leopold; and the statesman, Jan Smuts are three diverse sources of systems theory and ecological science. Study of complex systems, such as computer programmes, ecological systems, human communities and the human body, has led scientists to realise that it is impossible to try to understand these structures by analysing each of its components. In the absence of this detailed knowledge, it is still possible to predict the behaviour of these systems with statistical models and general principles of systems theory. Complex systems are self-organising and naturally maintain themselves unless severely disrupted. This understanding provides a basis for an approach to medicine centred upon allowing the body to heal itself, an approach to sociology based upon allowing communities to develop naturally an approach to agriculture based upon allowing nature to maximise its own productivity.

1900s   THE DISCOVERY OF THE UNCONSCIOUS: FREUD, JUNG AND ADLER

THE introduction of the concept of the unconscious mind has had a major impact upon the way that we treat mental illness and behaviour problems. Psychology has, however, come in for much criticism from philosophers, such as Popper, because most of its theories cannot be proven or found faulty and because the few testable theories have not performed well. The vagueness and lack of evidence in psychology

◄ *Sigmund Freud, the inventor of psychoanalysis.*

has also been criticised – Freud reduces all problems to sex, Adler to the will to power and Skinner to past programming – models that contradict one another.

1900s THE DISESTABLISHMENT AND ABOLITION OF CONFUCIANISM

1912 marked the overthrow of the emperor by the Chinese Republicans led by Sun Yat Sen. Confucianism, which put great emphasis upon loyalty to the emperor, was seen as a threat and was disestablished but allowed to continue. After the revolution in 1949 Confucian teachings were condemned by the Communists as elitist and reactionary, however it is significant that the concept of an authoritarian state run for the welfare of the people has had much influence upon the contemporary government of China.

1913 BEHAVIOURISM

BEHAVIOURISTS teach that psychology should only study physical behaviour – how a human or animal responds to a stimulus – and not attempt to speculate about feelings, emotions or the unconscious. Established in 1913 by J. B.

▲ *The ancient teachings of Confucius were outlawed in 1949.*

Watson, behaviourism was popularised by B. F. Skinner (1904–90). In Skinner's book *Walden II* he advocated that a better society should be created by programming people to modify their behaviour. In his *Beyond Freedom and Dignity* (1971) he denies that humans have free will or responsibility for their behaviour.

1930   THE BIRTH OF JACQUES DERRIDA

JACQUES Derrida was born in Algeria in 1930. His thought developed as a response to that of Heidegger. He felt that metaphysical philosophy was without meaning, that it had reached the end of its history and that the only true philosophy concerned the nature of being. The question he asks is 'What can we say about Being without resorting to any metaphysical assumptions?' – and he tries to answer this by deconstructing philosophical statements on this matter and showing their limitations, contradictions and false assumptions.

1932 & 1949   ALDOUS HUXLEY'S *BRAVE NEW WORLD* AND GEORGE ORWELL'S *1984*

▲ *Aldous Huxley, author of* Brave New World.

BRAVE New World (1932) and *1984* (1949) are dystopias, not visions of an ideal world but their opposite. In *1984* Orwell illustrates an authoritarian Communist world similar to Stalin's Soviet Union – a world in which everything is controlled by Big Brother and his Thought Police for the benefit of the masses. In *Brave New World*, by contrast, Aldous Huxley (1894–1963) describes a world where the arts of the salesman are used by the government, where people are genetically engineered and psychologically normalised to fit into society, where brainwashing and subliminal advertising are used to keep people consuming and to prevent them thinking. It is the possible future of the consumer society.

1934   SIR KARL POPPER'S LOGIC

THE Viennese philosopher, Karl Popper (1902–94), argued that it is never possible to have certain knowledge. In his *Logic of Scientific Discovery* (1934) he shows that no scientific hypothesis can be proved – it can only be falsified. Indeed if it could never be falsified it would not be a scientific theory.

Therefore, every good scientific theory is simply a model that has yet to be disproven. His opposition to the concept of certainty led him, in his *The Open Society and its Enemies* (1945), to criticise authoritarian models of human society, such as those proposed by Plato and Marx.

1941 THE HOLOCAUST AND THE FOUNDATION OF THE STATE OF ISRAEL

ANTI-SEMITISM, which had declined since the fifteenth century began to return to France, Germany and Eastern Europe in the late nineteenth century. From 1941 Germany embarked upon the rounding up and systematic murder of all the Jews in Europe and by the end of the war in 1945 no less than six million had died in the gas ovens. In 1948 Britain, following its victory in the Second World War, was obliged to end its mandate and offer its Palestinian territory as a homeland for the Jewish people. This return to the 'promised land', after 2,000 years of exile and closely following the horrors of the Holocaust, was a cause of great joy and determination to succeed. A millenarian sense of hope has helped them to build a modern nation in just a few decades but it has also encouraged a nationalism that has led to the oppression of the Palestinians and ongoing conflict with their Arab neighbours.

1943 JEAN-PAUL SARTRE AND EXISTENTIALISM

'EXISTENCE precedes essence' and 'man makes himself'. These phrases encapsulate the atheist existentialism of the French philosopher Jean-Paul Sartre (1905–1980). In the absence of a God who created us with a purpose, he pointed out, we arrive in the world with nothing but our own existence. This problem is explored in his *Being and Nothingness* (1943).

▲ *French writer and philosopher Jean-Paul Sartre.*

We have no choice but to decide for ourselves who we are – we must invent our own essence. The self is not an entity but a project, not something that has being but something that is forever becoming. Whoever defines themselves by their current role in life (for example 'I am a waiter') lives in 'bad faith'. It is a philosophy that gives each of us an enormous responsibility but also complete freedom.

1949 ALDO LEOPOLD: THE ECOSYSTEM

ALDO Leopold (1887–1948) worked as a conservationist for the US Forest Service. His posthumously published work *A Sand County Almanac* (1949) introduces the concept of the ecosystem as an interacting web of living organisms that has its own natural balance. To manage an ecosystem it is necessary to 'think like a mountain' and obtain an overview of the whole system. His 'Land Ethic' is based on the moral maxim that 'a thing is right when it tends to preserve the integrity, stability and beauty of the biotic community. It is wrong when it tends otherwise'.

1949 MAO ZEDONG AND COMMUNISM IN CHINA

▲ *Chinese Communist Leader Mao Zedong.*

MAO Zedong (1893–1976), Chinese Communist leader, was chairman of the Communist Party of China and the principal founder of the People's Republic of China. Mao helped found the Chinese Communist Party in Shanghai in 1921. In 1927 their then allies launched a military campaign against the Communists, who retreated to rural areas where they gained the support of the peasants. After Nationalist forces surrounded them in 1934 the Red Army retreated 6,000 miles to the north-west in the Long March. In 1949 they eventually captured most of China and declared the People's Republic. Chairman Mao promoted rural development, equality and the pursuit of economic self-reliance in the villages, but his government was extremely authoritarian and up to 100 million dissidents may have died in his labour camps.

1950s   THE DESTRUCTION AND REVIVAL OF BUDDHISM

COMMUNIST revolution in China, Vietnam, Laos and Cambodia led to the abolition of Buddhism, the destruction of nearly all the temples and the murder of most of the monks. In Cambodia only eight monks survived. In Sri Lanka, colonialism virtually destroyed the tradition. A new Buddhism concerned with peace work and community building has emerged. Dr. A. T. Ariyaratne's Sarvodaya movement in Sri Lanka involves almost every village, in Cambodia Maha Ghosananda leads massive peace walks across regions sown with land mines, in Vietnam Thich Nhat

▲ *Buddhist practices were ruthlessly suppressed in the Far East in the 1950s.*

Hanh , now exiled, founded *Tiep Hien*, the Order of Interbeing, and in Thailand Sulak Sivaraksa challenges the government's westernisation policy. Buddhism is one of the fastest growing religions in Western nations. Today severe oppression of Buddhism continues in Burma and Tibet.

1950s   THE WEST TURNS EAST

THE American 'beat' poets of the 1950s, including Allen Ginsberg, Jack Kerouac and Gary Snyder, drew upon Buddhism as a philosophy for rejecting the materialism and 'work ethic' of the Western world. Their example inspired the counter-cultural hippie movement of the 1960s. The Beatles became followers of the Maharishi and thousands of young people travelled to India or began to follow Eastern teachers – Hindu, Buddhist and Sufi. Within 10 years Eastern practices, such as meditation and yoga, became almost universally available to the public.

▲ *R. D. Laing.*

1960s   R. D. LAING AND ANTI-PSYCHIATRY

R. D. LAING (1927–89) was one of the most radical critics of psychiatric practice. In his books *The Divided Self* (1960) and *Sanity, Madness and the Family* (1964) he rejected the orthodox view that schizophrenia is simply an illness and saw it instead as normal response to an impossible social situation. He therefore favoured group therapies and attacked chemical therapies and electric-shock treatments. He also viewed madness not as a sign of mental decline, but as a phase through which the mind passed whilst healing itself. This led him to see the therapist as a companion on a journey through madness.

1971   B. F. SKINNER AND BEHAVIOURISM

BEHAVIOURISM is a school of psychology based on empirical science. Originating around 1913 by J. B. Watson, and outlined in his book *Behaviourism* (1925), behaviourists believe that the only valid form of psychology is the study of how animals and humans physically respond to stimuli. B. F. Skinner states the position in its purest form in his *Beyond Freedom and Dignity* (1971) in which he presents the mind as an automatic machine and rejects the idea of free will. He concludes, controversially, that our minds should be scientifically programmed by psychologists to ensure socially beneficial behaviour.

1973   POST-INDUSTRIALISM AND THE REDEFINITION OF WORK

SOCIOLOGIST Daniel Bell argues that the original Protestant Work Ethic underlying capitalism will collapse as a result of the massive productive capacity of modern technology. This is argued in his books, *Towards a Post Industrial Society* (1973), *The Cultural Contradictions of Capitalism* (1976), *The*

End of Ideology and The Coming of Post Industrial Society. Modern capitalism requires consumers in pursuit of leisure and so is moving us towards a world where work is no longer seen as a virtue. Professor Charles Handy points in a similar direction, predicting the end of the full-time nine-to-five job and forecasting instead that people will increasingly work part-time on a freelance basis.

1973　SMALL IS BEAUTIFUL

E. F. SCHUMACHER'S *Small is Beautiful: A Study of Economics as if People Mattered* was published in 1973. He challenged the vast institutions that were emerging in both capitalist and communist countries and called for small communities, decentralisation and technology on a human scale. Excessive size was, he believed, the cause of unemployment, poor working conditions, inequality and a decline in freedom. In particular he was keen to help poor countries develop without suffering the problems of giantism and to this end he helped develop 'Intermediate Technologies', machines that could be owned and used on a village scale – an approach that has now been widely adopted.

▲ *E. F. Schumacher encouraged the use of Intermediate Technologies that could help developing countries.*

1975　MICHEL FOUCAULT

THE French philosopher, Michel Foucault, sought to understand the origin and nature of institutional controls over how we see ourselves. In his *Discipline and Punish* (1975) and his *Madness and Civilisation* (1961) he explored the origins and development of concepts and normality by looking at the history of punishment and of asylums. State concepts of normality are internalised and determine how we see ourselves. The 'work of freedom' is to step outside these definitions and to create ourselves.

1976   GENETIC DETERMINISM

IN *The Selfish Gene* (1976), Professor Richard Dawkins argues that the process underlying life and evolution is the survival and replication of the fittest gene. Derived directly from Darwin's theory of the survival of the fittest organism, Dawkins argues that plants and animals, as well as their nests, burrows and even ideas, are merely the machines that genes use to survive. Although accused of reductionism by his opponents, his theories have taken a new twist. He argues that any basic unit that self-replicates, whether a gene, a process or an idea, is capable of evolution through natural selection. This means that not only would individual animals evolve, but so would artefacts, cultures and religions, communities and ecosystems. He argues that 'God' is merely an idea that uses a whole range of effective techniques to survive – but a potential weakness of this argument is that it could be applied to any idea, including his own.

1979   JAMES LOVELOCK AND THE GAIA HYPOTHESIS

THE Gaia hypothesis, as outlined in biochemist James Lovelock's *Gaia* (1979) is a hypothesis that the planet Earth, its soil, oceans, atmosphere and bio-sphere constitutes a self-regulating system that can be thought of as living. He has often been accused, by scientists, of arguing that the Earth is con-scious, but this view, common amongst many of his supporters, forms no part of the theory. His studies of atmospheric chemistry, which led him to discov-er the hole in the ozone layer and the wide distribution of pesticides, have also provided much evidence for the theory.

1980   THE RESURGENCE OF ISLAM

THE Islamic revival that has shaken Iran, Afghanistan, Algeria and most of the Muslim world since 1980 has several aspects that are hard to disentangle. It is both a spiritual revival, although most of the mystic sects have been subjected to harsh oppression, and a militant response to the economic and intellectual dominance of the West. The Islamic Revolution in Iran, led by Ayatollah Khomeini, marked the start of the movement, which inspired the Taliban movement in Afghanistan, the Hezbollah in Palestine and terrorist groups in many other nations. It is probably too early to tell whether the intellectuals, whose main concerns are cultural and spiritual, will gain the upper hand or whether the fundamentalists will instigate increasingly violent attacks on secular societies.

1992 SUSTAINABILITY: THE RIO DECLARATION

THE Rio Declaration on Environment and Development was signed at the largest-ever meeting of heads of governments, held in Rio de Janeiro, Brazil, in 1992. 169 nations signed the document. Whilst the agreement is important for this reason, many have pointed out that it is worded so as to avoid committing any nation to taking significant action. It has also been questioned whether its support for accelerated economic growth can be reconciled with its advocacy of 'sustainability'.

◀ *Environmental problems have become significant world issues in the closing years of the millennium, as human behaviour and progress causes irreparable damage to the environment.*

Glossary

ANARCHISM
Theory where society runs without coercive authority from government, religion, education and industry, which impose limits on individuals' freedom.

ANGLICANISM
Belief in the Christian teachings and doctrine of the Church of England as opposed to that of the Roman Catholic Church.

ANGLO-SAXON
Germanic Angle and Saxon tribes settled England from the fifth century taking advantage of Roman withdrawal to set up kingdoms.

APARTHEID
An Afrikaans word to describe the segregation of races in South Africa based on a belief in white superiority.

ARABS
First used ninth century BC for Semitic people from Arabia whose descendants settled throughout North Africa and the Middle East.

AVARS
Central Asian nomadic people who defeated the Huns in the sixth century; the Slavs and Bulgars in the seventh century.

BOERS
Seventeenth century Dutch, Flemish and Huguenot settlers in South Africa whose descendants call themselves Afrikaners and introduced racial apartheid.

BOLSHEVISM
Ideology leading to the Russian Revolution in 1917 with the aim of setting up a workers' socialist state under Lenin.

BRETONS
Celtic people and language of Brittany in France descended from those who left Britain after fifth-century Anglo-Saxon invasions.

BRONZE AGE
Describes the period after 2000 BC when people began using metal-making technology based on copper and its alloys.

BUDDHISM
Buddha's sixth-century teachings were that the destruction of mortal desires and anguish could be attained by following virtuous paths.

BYZANTIUM
An ancient Greek city at the centre of a Mediterranean empire with a distinctive architecture and orthodox religious art.

CAROLINGIAN
A Frankish royal dynasty that ruled France from the eighth to tenth centuries and became Europe's most powerful Christian Kingdom.

CATHOLICISM
A division of Christianity marked by worship of the Virgin Mary, repentance and forgiveness and the power accorded the pope.

CHRISTIANITY
World religion derived from the teachings of Christ, the Son of God, who came to earth to suffer and die.

COLD WAR
Ideological and political tensions 1945–90 between the Soviet Union and the US, involving nuclear threats, arms races, espionage, destabilising governments.

COLONIALISM
Where one country dominates another for economic gain and imposes its own language and culture to control the native people.

COMMUNISM
A classless economic system of public ownership where producing goods and food is a communal activity for the general good.

CONFEDERACY
An alliance of self-determining states such as the southern US states during the civil war of the 1860s.

CONSTITUTIONALISM
Belief maintaining that states be defined by a body of fundamental laws on government and the judiciary concerning individual freedom.

COUNTER-REFORMATION
Sixteenth-century movement initiated by the Catholic church using the Inquisition and Jesuits to counter the spread of Reformation thinking.

CRUSADES
A series of wars eleventh to thirteenth centuries ostensibly to recover Palestine, the holy city, from Muslim control but imperialist in design.

DEMOCRACY
A political system where a country is governed by the people usually through elected representatives and sometimes through referendums.

DIVINE RIGHT OF KINGS
Christian political thinking that hereditary monarchy is approved by God, the sovereign is answerable only to God so rebellion is blasphemous.

ECOLOGY
Study of organisms, their relationships and environments in ecosystems but also conservation of habitat, species and control of pollution.

EMPIRICISM
A philosophical view basing our knowledge of the world on experience gained through our senses rather than through inherent knowledge.

ENLIGHTENMENT, THE
A seventeenth-century intellectual movement where rational thought and science came to bear over the irrationality and superstition marking earlier periods.

ENVIRONMENTALISM
Theory that sees environmental influences as the primary factors in determining behaviour or activism that aims to preserve the planet.

FASCISM
Authoritarian political movements, particularly powerful in the 1930s–40s, where democracy and liberalism are opposed and nationalistic ideology followed.

FEMINISM
Intellectual and political thinking that argues women's rights to equality in education, the law and the workplace.

FEUDALISM
Social and legal system whereby peasant farmers worked a lord's land and in return would serve them in battle.

FRANKS
Germanic people who dominated France and Germany after the Romans, building a powerful Christian empire up to the ninth century.

FRISIANS
Germanic people who settled Germany and the Netherlands in prehistoric times by chasing out the Celts; conquered by Charlemagne.

GAUL
An area of Europe during Roman times covering what is now France and stretching to Northern Italy and the Netherlands.

HABSBURG EMPIRE
An imperial European dynasty from the fifteenth to twentieth centuries originating in Austria, incorporating eastern Europe, Spain and the New World.

HINDUISM
The dominant religion of India, Hinduism's complex system of customs and beliefs include numerous gods, reincarnation and a caste system.

HOLY ROMAN EMPIRE
Denotes from the thirteenth-century lands ruled by successive German kings which at its height covered much of central Europe.

HUGUENOTS
Calvinist Huguenots fought the French Wars of Religion (1562–98) against Catholics, co-existed, then fled from persecution in 1685.

HUMANITARIANISM
Thinking and actions where the interests of mankind override personal or national interests as in environmental policy and third-world aid.

HUNS
A number of nomadic Mongol tribes from 2 BC invaded China and Europe, dominating Germanic people until Atilla's death AD 453.

IMPERIALISM
The policy and practice of a state to influence or conquer others so to widen its wealth, power and influence.

NDUSTRIAL REVOLUTION
The process by which Britain and other countries were transformed during the eighteenth and nineteenth centuries into industrial powers.

INQUISITION
Operating across Spain, France, Italy and the Holy Roman Empire thirteenth to nineteenth centuries to suppress heresy for the Catholic Church.

INTERNATIONALISM
Viewing politics or economics in a global way ideally through the practice of co-operation between nation states.

IRON AGE
After 1000 BC barbarian tribes used iron rather than bronze and were contemporaries of classical Mediterranean and African civilisations.

ISLAM
Founded in the seventh century by the prophet Muhammad, messenger of Allah, Islam emphasises God's omnipotence and inscrutability.

JESUITS
Roman Catholic order founded in the sixteenth century aiming to protect the Church against the Reformation through missionary work.

JUDAISM
The religion and cultural tradition of the Jewish people, Judaism follows one God and is based on the Pentateuch.

LIBERALISM
Thinking that attaches importance to the civil and political rights of individuals and their freedoms of speech and expression.

LIBERTARIANISM
Theory upholding the rights of an individual above all else and seeking to reduce a state's power to safeguard these rights.

LOMBARDS
Germanic people who invaded Italy in the sixth century, settling in what is now Lombardy but were conquered by Charlemagne in AD 774.

MAGYARS
Ethnically mixed people who settled in Hungary in the ninth century and would raid deep into Italy, France and Northern Europe.

MAMELUKE EMPIRE
Dominating Egypt and west of the Gulf, 1250–1517, Mamelukes, descended from freed Turkish slaves, remained Egypt's ruling class until 1811.

MARXISM
Economic ideology framed by nineteenth-century thinker Karl Marx that feudalism, capitalism and socialism would be replaced by a classless society.

MEDICI
Powerful Italian dynasty from Florence, ruling the city from 1434 to 1737, overseeing the flourishing Renaissance period.

MEDIEVAL
The cultures and beliefs of the Middle Ages; after the Roman Empire's fifth-century decline to the fifteenth-century Renaissance.

MERCANTILISM
Economic theory from sixteenth to eighteenth centuries that a nation's prosperity depended on how much bullion or treasure it held.

MIDDLE AGES
European period from the fall of the Roman Empire to the fifteenth-century Renaissance marked by feudalism, Catholic dominance and religious art.

MOGULS
North Indian dynasty 1526–1858 of great artistic, architectural and commercial achievement until overthrown by the British.

MONGOLS
Nomadic tribes that conquered Central Asia and attacked Eastern Europe in the thirteenth century building an empire under Genghis Khan.

MOORS
North-west Africans Muslims of mixed Arab and Berber origin, dominated southern Spain AD 711–1492 when converted to Christianity.

NATIONALISM
Ideological movements to build national identities, reviving interests in native languages, histories and traditions, but extremes are viewed as fascism.

NAZISM
German fascism of the National Socialist Party led by Adolf Hitler who desired an empire for his 'Aryan' race.

NEOLITHIC
Final part of the Stone Age period marked by the development of agriculture and forest clearance around 8000–3000 BC.

NORMANS
Viking 'Northmen' who settled France expanded and took control of what is now Normandy then conquered England under King William.

OTTOMAN EMPIRE
Turkish Muslim empire 1300–1920, stretching to Hungary, South Russia and North Africa, but crumbled after supporting Germany during the First World War.

PACIFISM
Belief that war cannot be justified and is immoral. Those refusing to fight have been called conscientious objectors.

PALEOLITHIC
From two million years ago up to Mesolithic Stone Age period, Paleolithic times saw modern man develop from earlier types.

PREHISTORIC
From the beginning of life on earth 3.5 billion years ago to 3500 BC when humans began to keep records.

PROTESTANTISM
Takes its name from Martin Luther's 1529 protest for Roman Catholic church reform, which precipitated major splits in European Christianity.

RACISM
A belief in the superiority of one race over another often manifesting itself in social and civil discrimination or violence.

REFORMATION
Sixteenth-century European movement to reform the Catholic Church, used by Henry VIII to separate the Church of England from Rome.

RENAISSANCE
Fourteenth to seventeenth century European intellectual and artistic movement ending the Middle Ages with its emphasis on science and exploration.

REPUBLICANISM
Support for a system where heads of state are not monarchs was only once realised in England under Oliver Cromwell.

SEMITES
Peoples of ancient cultures in the Middle East, speakers of Semitic languages and founders of Islam, Judaism and Christianity.

SOCIALISM
Belief in classless society with equal access to education and employment through state intervention and ownership of major industries and utilities.

SOVIET
Countries dominated by communist Russia after 1922 i.e. Estonia, Ukraine, Uzbekistan were termed Soviets within the Union of Soviet Socialist Republics.

STONE AGE
The earliest period of human culture marked by the use of stone implements and covering Paleolithic, Mesolithic and Neolithic times.

SUFFRAGISM
Belief in the extension of suffrage, generally to women and the working classes traditionally denied the right to vote.

TAOISM
Chinese philosophical system from sixth century BC, Ying and Yang balance the universe, the 'way' stresses harmonious existence with the environment.

TARTAR
Muslim Mongol followers of Genghis Khan, their Tartar state was conquered by Russia, 1552, now the Republic of Tartarstan.

◀ *The Mongol conqueror Genghis Khan.*

VIKINGS
Medieval Scandinavian warriors, traders and settlers, Vikings travelled vast distances by sea and river often plundering from gold and land.

Author Biographies

Jeremy Black: General Editor

Jeremy Black is Professor of History at the University of Exeter. His books include *History of the British Isles, Maps and History, War and the World 1450–2000* and *Why Wars Happen.* He is a member of the Councils of the Royal Historical Society and the British Records Association.

Paul Brewer and Anthony Shaw: Exploration and Empires

Paul Brewer has contributed to several historical encyclopedias, as well as a work on the Second World War. Anthony Shaw has written over 50 books; his specialist interests include military history.

Malcolm Chandler: Power and Politics

Malcolm Chandler is a historian and author, who has written widely on all manner of historical subjects, particularly for schools.

Gerard Cheshire: Science and Technology

Gerard Cheshire is a specialist science writer, whose recent works have included articles for *BBC Wildlife Magazine* and many part-works.

Ingrid Cranfield: Trade and Industry

Ingrid Cranfield is an experienced author and editor. Her works include *The Challengers,* a survey of modern British exploration and adventure, and she contributes frequently to periodicals, encyclopedias and compilations.

Brenda Ralph Lewis: Society and Culture

Brenda Ralph Lewis has been writing on historical subjects for 35 years. She has published 85 history books, and has contributed to many others, as well as to numerous magazines and BBC programmes.

Jon Sutherland: War and Peace

Jon Sutherland is an experienced writer, whose specialist interests include military history. He has written over 50 books.

Robert Vint: Religions, Belief and Thought

Robert Vint is a lecturer and educationalist at the Religious and Environment Programme; he has contributed widely to books and magazines on all aspects of religion and belief.

Picture Credits

Bridgeman Art Library: 14.

Christie's Images: 12, 17, 21, 27 (t), 33 (b), 34 (l), 42, 70, 71, 74, 96, 99, 110, 120, 147, 158, 187, 198, 206, 335.

Foundry Arts: David Banfield 23, 24; Claire Dashwood 59, 122, 164, 225; Nick Wells 113.

Image Select: Petr Placek 34 (r), 44, Exley 60, 63, 67, 83, 101, 109, Bibliotheque Nationale, Paris 114, 129, CFCL 143, 144, 145, CFCL 147 (t), 178, 191, 235, 240, 274, 281, 320, 334.

Image Select/Ann Ronan: 54, 61, 117, 123, 138, 142, 153, 159, 173, 189, 192, 195, 201, 207, 208 (l), 262, 305, 307, 314, 317, 325, 332.

Image Select/FPG: 27 (b), 33 (t), 124, 161, 177, 232, 249, 264, 275, 288, 315.

Image Select/Giraudon: 16, 18, 25, 38, 43, 55, 65, 68, 69, 107, 118, 128, 130, 131, 156, 160, 169, 170, 193, 194, 199, 202, 214.

Mary Evans Picture Library: 13, 15, 19, 31, 35, 36, 37, 39, 45, 46, 47, 48, 49, 50, 52, 56 (b), 58, 64, 73, 75, 78, 81, 82, 84, 85 (l), 86, 87, 88, 90, 93, 94, 95, 100, 104, 106, 108, 115, 116, 119, 127, 134, 136, 137, 139, 140, 141, 149, 150, 151, 152, 154, 155, 157, 174, 175, 179, 180, 181, 182, 183, 184, 186, 188, 200, 203, 205, 208 (r), 210, 211, 212, 213, 215, 217, 218, 220 (t), 222, 223, 224, 226, 227, 228, 229, 230, 231, 233, 234, 238, 239, 241, 242, 253, 255, 258, 259, 260, 269, 270, 271, 272, 278, 283, 284, 286, 287, 290, 299, 300, 301, 302, 316, 329, 331, 333, 337.

Still Pictures: 91, 121, 303.

Topham Picturepoint: 20, 22, 28, 29, 30, 53, 56 (t), 79, 80, 89, 97, 105, 111, 112, 125, 135, 165, 166, 168, 171, 172, 176, 185, 190, 204, 216, 220 (b), 221, 243, 244, 245, 246, 247, 248, 251, 252, 256, 257, 261, 262, 265, Associated Press 267, 268, Associated Press 276, 277, 279, Associated Press 280, 289, 291, 292, 293, 294, Associated Press 295, 296, 297, 298, 304, 306, 309, 310, 311, Press Association 313, 318, 319, 321, 323, 324, 326, 327, 340, 336, 339.

Visual Arts Library: 66.

www.aldigital.co.uk/: 328.

Index